Trans-Asia as Method

Asian Cultural Studies: Transnational and Dialogic Approaches

Series Editor:

Koichi Iwabuchi, Professor of Media and Cultural Studies and Director of Monash Asia Institute, Monash University, Australia

Editorial Collective

Ien Ang (University of Western Sydney)
Chris Berry (King's College London)
John Erni (Hong Kong Baptist University)
Daniel Goh (National University of Singapore)
Ariel Heryanto (Australian National University)
Kim Hyun Mee (Yonsei University)

The series advances transnational intellectual dialogue over diverse issues that are shared in various Asian countries and cities.

Titles in the Series

Contemporary Culture and Media in Asia
Edited by Daniel Black, Olivia Khoo, and Koichi Iwabuchi

Transnational Memory and Popular Culture in East and Southeast Asia: Amnesia, Nostalgia and Heritage
Liew Kai Khiun

Multiculturalism in East Asia: A Transnational Exploration of Japan, South Korea and Taiwan
Edited by Koichi Iwabuchi, Hyun Mee Kim, and Hsiao-Chuan Hsia

Precarious Belongings: Affect and Nationalism in Asia
Edited by Chih-ming Wang and Daniel PS Goh

Islamic Modernities in Southeast Asia: Exploring Indonesian Popular and Visual Culture
Leonie Schmidt

Cultural Policy and East Asian Rivalry: The Hong Kong Gaming Industry
Anthony Y. H. Fung

Trans-Asia as Method

Theory and Practices

Edited by Jeroen de Kloet, Yiu Fai Chow,
and Gladys Pak Lei Chong

ROWMAN & LITTLEFIELD

INTERNATIONAL

London • New York

Published by Rowman & Littlefield International Ltd
6 Tinworth Street, London, SE11 5AL
www.rowmaninternational.com

Rowman & Littlefield International Ltd.is an affiliate of Rowman & Littlefield
4501 Forbes Boulevard, Suite 200, Lanham, Maryland 20706, USA
With additional offices in Boulder, New York, Toronto (Canada), and Plymouth (UK)
www.rowman.com

British Library Cataloguing in Publication Data
A catalogue record for this book is available from the British Library

ISBN: HB 978-1-78661-078-2
ISBN: PBK 978-1-5381-4810-5

Library of Congress Cataloging-in-Publication Data

Library of Congress Control Number: 2019951792

Contents

Figures

Tables

Acknowledgments

This is a book advocating an intellectual move away from Eurocentrist modes of theorizing. Yet, the birthplace of this book was the beautiful city of Prato in Italy in June 2017. This paradox underlines our own position: we may need to move away from Europe, sometimes, but let's not quite move beyond it. It is thanks to the financial and logistic support of Monash Asia Institute of Monash University that we gathered in their Prato campus. We especially want to thank Koichi Iwabuchi, the then director of the institute, not only for organizing this wonderful event, but also for his trust in us to transform this event into a book. We are also indebted to the generous support of various funding organizations, which make this edited volume truly a trans-Asia collaboration. Jeroen wants to thank the European Research Council (consolidator grant ERC-2013-CoG 616882-ChinaCreative) for their financial support. In Hong Kong, Yiu Fai and Gladys would like to express their gratitude to the Research Grants Councils RGC (RGC project number 22609415 and project number 12610118) and Hong Kong Baptist University for their support. Without them, this trans-Asia exploration would not be possible. We want to thank Natalie Linh Bolderston and Gurdeep Mattu from Rowman & Littlefield International for their support and the cheerful cooperation over the past two years. We thank the reviewers for their insights and helpful comments. We want to thank Gordon So for his speedy and accurate help in the production process. We thank all our contributors: academic work is all about thinking together, about cooperation and conviviality, and what started as a conversation under the sun in Prato has now been translated into this book. Let's make sure the trans-Asian conversations will continue, that this volume is just one moment in a much longer dialogue. Finally, however strangely, we like to thank you, the reader. Please read on! In a time of information overload, of numerous books and articles that are waiting on your desk(top) to be read, we are aware what a privilege it is that you read these words. We sincerely hope that you join our dialogue. Let's keep on talking, writing, thinking, discussing, eating—together.

Jeroen de Kloet, Yiu Fai Chow, Gladys Pak Lei Chong

Introduction

Toward Trans-Asia: Projects, Possibilities, Paradoxes

Gladys Pak Lei Chong, Yiu Fai Chow, and Jeroen de Kloet

Meteor Garden 2018, produced by the successful Hunan Television from China, also currently available on Netflix, is a remake of the 2001 Taiwanese television series *Meteor Garden*. The high school drama focuses on a girl of working-class background who enters an elite university. There she encounters, and clashes with, the popular F4, an exclusive group of four popular boys with an elite background. The Taiwanese series, in turn, was an adaptation of a Japanese manga series titled *Boys over Flowers*. This was also the name of its Korean adaptation for television, which was broadcast in 2009. Over the years, other unlicensed versions emerged in India (*Kaisi Yeh Yaariaan*) and Indonesia (*Siapa Takut Jatuh Cinta*). As Hsiu-Chuang Deppman argues in her analysis of the regional circulation of the 2001 Taiwanese version, "the show's various local audiences envision a democracy of cultural alignment that includes, on equal terms, East Asian viewers from Tokyo, Seoul, Taipei, Singapore, Jakarta, Beijing, Hanoi, and Kuala Lumpur."[1] While we may question the equality and democracy celebrated by Deppman, *Meteor Garden* does tell us a complex story of cultural flows across and, thanks to Netflix, beyond Asia. This flow consists not only of the regional circulation of one specific version, but also includes its multiple local reinterpretations and adaptations. Parallel to the alleged "rise of Asia," and also afforded by rapid technological changes like streaming technologies and the ubiquity of mobile screens, such flows have intensified over the past two decades.

This emerging field of cultural flows across Asia has generated expanding interests and attention on how "Asianness" has been utilized in transnational cultural industries. *Rogue Flows* (2004), *Feeling Asian Modernities* (2004), and *Routledge Handbook of East Asian Popular Culture* (2016) are examples of works that examine "trans-Asian" cultural flows. These cross-border connections among the (East) Asian countries have coincided as well as emerged along the political and network building efforts embodied by *Inter-Asia Cultural Studies* and *Traces* since the 1990s.

"Trans-Asia as method," as a concept, was coined and explored by Koichi Iwabuchi in 2004.[2] Frequently used, it however often conflates with two related conceptual frameworks: Asia as method and inter-Asia referencing. What, then, is the added value of using the idea of trans-Asia? How does it differ from inter-Asia; and when we add the notion of "as method" to it, what difference does it make from Asia as method? And, above all, what are the empirical implications when we make such a conceptual move? These are the thorny questions, both conceptually and empirically, that this volume aims to unpack.

This edited volume is founded on a small-scale, discussion-oriented workshop in which participants (most of whom are contributors) vigorously discussed and exchanged over trans-Asia approaches.[3] Thus, this volume does not only build on these earlier collaborative efforts; more importantly, it aims to advance this "trans-Asia" project into a method that combines conceptual discussion (theory) with empirical studies (practices). This introduction addresses three sets of fundamental questions: first, what kind of *project* is trans-Asia as a method? Second, what necessitates trans-Asia as method, what are its *possibilities*, when Asia as method and inter-Asia cultural studies seem to have carried out similar tasks? In other words, how do these approaches and trans-Asia as method diverge and converge, and what does it add methodologically and theoretically? What are its strengths, challenges, and limitations? Third, what are the *paradoxes* we encounter when making such a conceptual move, what do we gain, and what do we lose? When we critically unpack what "trans-Asia" signifies by questioning what "trans-" and "Asia" mean respectively—not taking them as descriptive words but as time- and place-specific discursive geopolitical constructs—we are inspired to question and debate their meanings, potentials, challenges, and limitations.

AS PROJECTS: FROM ASIA AS METHOD TO *TRANS*-ASIA AS METHOD

Over the last hundred years, intellectuals across Asia have been exploring the potential of an integrated Asia as a way to gain autonomy from the influential West. Koichi Iwabuchi's "Trans-Asia as Method" (2004) and Chen Kuan-Hsing's *Asia as Method* (2010)[4] both build on earlier formulations by Takeuchi Yoshimi's 1960 lecture and Mizoguchi Yuzo.[5] For Iwabuchi, as he expresses in this volume, "The project of 'trans-Asia as method' is to envision and actualize Asia as a dialogic communicative space in which people across borders collaborate to connect diverse voices, concerns, and problems in various, unevenly intersecting public sites in which the national is still a major site but does not exclusively take over public interests." This resonates intimately with the objectives of the inter-Asia cultural studies movement. Iwabuchi's focus on public interests connects with Chen's attempt to bring in a politicized form of cultural studies in Asia.[6] What both Iwabuchi and Chen propose is not so much an ideological critique of the West, as scholars such as Naoki Sakai and Dipesh Chakrabarty have done. And Iwabuchi's and Chen's approaches are not identical. Before explaining our preference to add the prefix *trans* in this volume, it is important to first engage in more detail with Chen's *Asia as Method*.

In *Asia as Method*, recognizing Sakai's and Chakrabarty's good intentions and important discussions, Chen argues that these efforts also strengthen the great divide between the West and the rest.[7] Asia as method is not about going native either (e.g., "searching the roots"), or being nationalistic—both have been popular means of ex-colonies to counter the colonial influences. Chen warns against this counter-colonialization effort as it easily leads to ultranationalism, chauvinism, and racism.[8] Asia as method is a theoretical and political project, a practice, an intervention, and an epistemological strategy with implications for subjectivity transformation. Seeing knowledge production as one of the key sites in which the West exercises its domination, Chen proposes this method as an alternative epistemological paradigm. The idea of Asia, as "a product of history" and "an active participant in historical process,"[9] can function as "an imaginary anchoring point"[10] and "an emotional signifier"[11] to unite the region in solidarity.

What empowers this method, Chen believes, is the common destinies that seal the past, present, and future of Asians as a collective entity. These "common destinies" refer to the impact, subjugations, and resistance brought by imperialism, colonialism, and the Cold War. In an essay in which he revisits Takeuchi Yoshimi's 1960 "Asia as Method" lecture,[12] Chen passionately aligns himself with the frustration and agony that motivated Takeuchi to develop this inter-Asia methodology. In the post-war era, when Takeuchi tried to understand why Japan had developed this imperialistic aggression against its neighboring countries and the world, he found it unproductive and inadequate to turn to Euro-America for answers. According to Takeuchi, intelligentsias in Asia were so caught up with the modernization agenda and the desire to be like their "superior" Euro-American counterparts that they showed hardly any interest in, or avoided looking at, their neighbors for inspiration and sharing.[13] Takeuchi reflected on this psychological complex: "If one went to Europe or the United States, there would be a sense that people there are superior to or better than oneself."[14] Takeuchi pinpointed that Euro-American counterparts were not the right "interlocutors who share the same structural anxiety."[15]

The temporal gap brought by different stages of modernization has produced a hierarchical relationship between the West and Asia; Asians are caught in this endless loop of "catching up" with the advanced West. Chen is convinced that "the back and forth dialogic process" between "them" and "us" cannot provide answers to "our" problems.[16] This non-sharedness is key to this methodology:

> Only through inter-referencing places, which are closer to each other or share similar historical experiences, can we leave the mistake of the "catch up" type of normative mode of knowledge, and to produce more grounded knowledge and understanding that come closer to historical reality.[17]

Thus, this method is grounded on the idea that Asian societies share a similar temporality of "forced modernization"[18] and are less hierarchical when compared to the West–Asia relationship. Asia as method, as in its call for inter-Asia referencing, is to open up a discursive realm that enables research to be placed in its specific historical context without the epistemological and ontological burden of catching up with the West.

This method or approach urges intellectuals to shift and multiply their referencing points to their Asian neighbors and counterparts, to draw actively on the diverse historical experiences and social practices of their neighboring societies.[19] By multiplying frames of reference within Asia,[20] the West's domination and significance will be diluted and diffused. This process of relativizing enables subjects to critically engage with and reflect upon the historical environment and social conditions that configure their very own desires and subjectivity. Societies in Asia would then acquire alternative perspectives to deal with problems similar to their own, "and thus overcome unproductive anxieties and develop new paths of engagement."[21] This Asia inter-referencing is as much an academic methodology as a communitarian project that fosters "people's mundane practice of encountering Asian neighbors and making reference to other Asian modernities."[22]

Nonetheless, Asia as method is premised on a rather Asia-centric idea. Who is included and who not? As Yiu Fai Chow and Jeroen de Kloet observe elsewhere, "we cannot help but wonder: who is included in this 'our,' and who is excluded, and based on what premises: locality, ethnicity, nationality, blood? Indeed, to insist on the multiplicity of either Europe or Asia runs the danger of ignoring the power structures that render some Asian (or European, or Western) voices more vocal than others."[23] In this ever-more interconnected world, is it feasible, or even a welcoming idea, to selectively focus on a specific region, and deliberately avoid looking at the presence of the others? How to avoid academic parochialism? And methodologically, how and where does one draw the boundary that defines Asia? Is the Asian diaspora included or not? And why then, actually, do "Western" publishers like Routledge, Duke University Press, and Rowman & Littlefield remain as key platforms for knowledge dissemination?

As this volume also attests, this critique of parochialism and Anglocentrism continues to haunt academic work. Where does Asia end? We prefer an inclusive approach, in which Asia is also part of, for example, Europe, Africa, or the Americas. In this volume, Ien Ang offers a reminder that Asia is a mental construct, rather than a geographical reality. Nevertheless, such a deconstructive move will not avoid biases. In this book, East Asia once again predominates, at the expense of Southeast, South, Central, and West Asia, not to mention the presence of Asia in other parts of the world. In the meantime, as we will argue later, the prefix *trans* should and does open up such a de-parochializing move. We will revert to this discussion in the coda.

While we are ideally committed to a much more inclusive reading of the idea of "Asia" in practice, we continue to be biased—sometimes for reasons of feasibility, sometimes due to disciplinary networks clustered around specific areas. Given the publisher and the language of this volume, it cannot help but being implicated in a global linguistic and publishing hierarchy. Just scanning through the literature list of each respective chapter attests to the limits of inter-Asia referencing, and to the predominance of English-language sources. Our choices here are not dictated by principle, but pragmatic, tactical, and perhaps even lame. We urge to continue the struggle against these biases, in a belief that slowly pushing at the boundaries may in the end help move the mountain.

Indeed, and rather unfortunately, one may say, with the economic strength of the East Asian countries and above all, China's rising politico-economic influence, Asia is often reduced to a quasi-exclusionary focus on East Asia (with the "curious" addition of Singapore). Chen's call for a united "Asia" can easily help strengthen various strings of essentialized yet powerful discourses of a rising Asia and a rising China,[24] such as Lee Kuan Yew's Asian values, Tu Wei-ming's "Cultural China," or even the Chinese Communist Party (CCP)-sanctioned discourses about China-versus-the West and its distinctive Chineseness, not to mention the One Belt One Road initiative.

Various Asian theorists have warned that the dichotomy of the West and Asia/China can easily be mobilized by Asiacentrics/Sinocentrics, as the discourse of wounding reveals, to justify the violence they do upon the minorities or the relatively powerless members within the group, just as the Japanese imperialists in the early twentieth century to the other Asian countries as the Han-centrics to the Tibetans and Uighurs.[25] Asia as method thus runs the danger of reproducing an epistemological domination within "Asia" as Chen proposes to counter.[26] Much of what Chen has critiqued on the uneven global power structure remains, unfortunately, the case; it seems troubling to resist this dominance by a reductive categorization that sees the West as a collective and the point of opposition for the Asians (or the rest). This dualistic mode of operation makes it hard to break away from the East–West binary structure Chen has proposed.[27]

With the rise of neoliberalism across the globe, producing a culture of what the late Mark Fisher has dubbed *Capitalist Realism*,[28] things, events, and experiences that were once localized have increasingly become shared phenomena. For instance, "affordable home" and youth's downward social mobility, as discussed in Chong's chapter in this volume, are no longer problems faced by specific localities. Similarly, societies in Asia are also divided in terms of developmental progress; with the emergence of alleged superpowers such as China and India, can the idea of Asia still succeed in calling for and forth "regional integration and solidarity"?[29] In other words, does this Asianism not run the danger of covering up the injustice and violence within the region? How do we do justice to those in the margin and bottom both outside and within a nation-state?

This volume shares Chen Kuan-Hsing's political and epistemological concerns about the domination of the West, but we diverge in our practices and conceptual framework. To substantiate such a divergence, we take our inspiration from Iwabuchi's use of the prefix *trans*. Trans-Asia as method recognizes the importance of "Asia" as an affective and imagined framework, but it resists in drawing fixed boundaries that blocks exchanges, and therefore limits epistemological potentials. Revisiting Iwabuchi's initiative in tracking this trans-Asia movement, the prefix "trans-" not only suggests movement, flow, traffic, connection; but also how this mobility directs some forms of border-crossing that bring changes, as in trans-gression, trans-cedence, and above all, trans-formation.[30]

The cultural flows with which we open this chapter, those of *Meteor Garden*, can serve as an example of the potential of trans-Asia as a project. It does not only allow us to probe into the flows within Asia, but also opens up possible studies to its global flow, its reception in, for example, Portugal, or to pursue a comparative study with likeminded high-school dramas from the United States. Such flows are not even or unregulated; on the contrary, cultural intermediaries, including national and transnational institutions, affect the global traffic of culture and knowledge and often reify rather than challenge global cultural and intellectual hierarchies. Nevertheless, the "trans" in trans-Asia allows for a more promiscuous dealing of this fuzzy thing called "Asia," at times cheerfully embracing an approach driven by Western theorists like Foucault or Deleuze, at other times forging alliances with thinkers like Chen Kuan-Hsing or Rey Chow, and most likely making use of a productive combination of both. Whereas a deliberate circumventing of the West may be strategic politically, it is in our view untenable intellectually. Hence, the call for trans-Asia as method.

This should not, of course, stop us from zooming in on specific inter-Asia cultural flows. Take, for example, the Travel Frog hype that took over China early 2018. Travel Frog (Tabikaeru) is a mobile game developed by Hit-Point in Japan. Its interface is simple; one has to feed a frog, which lives a life on its own. The frog often travels, during which he sends pictures of his trip back to the user. There is no social interaction, except for the interaction with the frog. When one gives the frog better presents, his journeys will become more impressive. Save that, there is no way to influence the behavior of the frog; he lives a life on his own. Whereas the game did not become very popular in Japan, it took over China like a storm. In a BBC report, users, mostly from the generation born in the 1990s, explain why they like it so much. "It really suits the post-90s generation, because we are overwhelmed with work," says Shen. And "I check my frog almost every 10 minutes at work, because my job is boring. I marvel at the photos that it sends to me from its adventures," explains Xian.[31] The frog has also been compared to Chinese businessmen, who do what they like and are always on the move, regardless of the home situation. Others engage with discussions over differences between Japan and China, as one user remarks on Weibo, "How comfortable it must be to be a husband in Japan, where you don't have to do anything around the house, your wife serves you, and then you just take off with the things your wife prepared for you, and go out and seek an extramarital affair." This, in turn, is challenged by another user, stating, "Whatever, the island nation turns it into a husband, we turn it into a child." To which another Weibo user adds: "What's the difference—husbands nowadays are like babies anyway."[32] Both *Meteor Garden* as well as Travel Frog require a trans-Asian framework of analysis, given that they traverse cultures, and in each movement, trans-formations, trans-gressions, and trans-lations take place. They already alert us to the *possibilities* of trans-Asia as method.

AS POSSIBILITIES: OPENING UP

Unfortunately, despite Asian intellectuals' persistent effort, the long-standing imbalance of power between the Europe and the United States and the others have rendered Asianness a fictive and distant voice. Naoki Sakai recalled that it was a lack of likeness of any inter- and cross-disciplinary practices among the Asian studies communities that gave rise to the Inter-Asia Cultural Studies movement in the late 1990s: Not only were researchers divided into fields of specialization, they were also divided by languages, nationalities, and ethnicities. His critique of a Western-defined area studies brought him to emphasize a "trans-"national studies:

> Transnational Studies does not observe the regime of separation sanctioned by nationality, ethnicity, gender, social class or civilization. It is not a science for identity-seekers. It rather seeks to interrupt the practices of separation, but never allows itself to overlook the workings of bordering (Mazzadra and Neilson 2008), of nationality, ethnicity, gender, social class and civilization in the relation of separation.[33]

Although Sakai's "trans-"national studies does not focus on "Asia" per se, his emphasis of "trans" stresses the importance of intersectionality while simultaneously pointing to the dangers of identity politics. It tries to go against the grain of a still pervasive methodological nationalism. In the past decades, the prefix "trans" as in transnationalism has been productively employed in various conceptual milieus. Trans-Asia as method converges with Lionnert and Shih's "minor transnationalism" in recognizing and challenging the persistence of colonial power relations and global capital, as Ferrari also engages with this concept in her exploration of Asian theatricalities across the transpacific in this volume. However, "trans-Asia" is not a regional variant of this concept because trans-Asia as a method does not assume a "minority" position or perspective that still takes the "Western-based world" as point of departure and more importantly—the *only* point of reference—and second, trans-Asia as method seeks to engage with *and beyond* Asia's historical past, present, and future.

A case in point, we believe, is the film project *Ten Years*. First released in Hong Kong, by the end of 2015, *Ten Years* was an anthology of five short films surrounding a poignantly simple and complex question: How would the city fare a decade later? The five young directors who participated in the project created five gloomy, threatening scenarios, mostly delving into pressing political issues (human rights, freedoms, democracy), one environmentally concerned. In "Dialect," for instance, we see the story of a middle-aged Cantonese-speaking taxi driver in a Hong Kong of 2025 when he and his colleagues are required to pass for a Putonghua (the national language) test if they want to run their business as profitably as usual. We see him struggling, not only with his mode of making a living, but more fundamentally, his sense of living. The film is a swan song of the local language, and at the same time, an alarming call against nationalistic encroachment and hegemony. This paradox of something disappearing, and, in Abbas' formulation, something dis-appearing—a dislocated, disrupted appearance[34]—lynchpins the entire Hong Kong release, including an intriguing eco-narrative "Season of the

End" where a young couple is trying to preserve the passing as specimens, in an old apartment in an old neighborhood of Hong Kong.

First shown in an art-house cinema, *Ten Years* immediately drew media and public attention and connection with the massive popular demonstration and occupation of the city known as the Umbrella Movement, which ended just a year before the film release.[35] This low-budget, independent production became a cult hit, partly, and ironically, because of the high-profile disapproval from the Beijing government.[36] Following its cinema distribution, the film continued its screening life on university campuses and in community venues. It was subsequently named the best film at the 35th Hong Kong Film Awards. For its award-winning status and topical sensitivity, the film was also a modest success as cultural export. Following its overseas debut in the Osaka Asia Film Festival in March 2016, it was shown in Europe, North America, and Asia, mostly as film festival entry. At this point, the film demonstrated a trajectory not unlike other art-house Hong Kong productions of a similar scale. While the trans-Asia potentialities of such a trajectory—in the manner of what we discussed in the previous section—are yet to be examined, our focus here is different. It falls on the *possibilities* opened up by the Hong Kong's *Ten Years* project when its original producer Andrew Choi and the Ten Years Studio announced their plan to develop the film concept outside Hong Kong. In a press statement, Choi explained: "When *Ten Years* was screened at festivals around the world, audience members responded with much emotion and introspection; their enthusiasm sparked the team's interest in producing international versions."[37]

This internationalizing exercise has, so far, taken the form of a "pan-Asian franchise."[38] By the end of 2018, three years after the release of the Hong Kong "original," three *Ten Years* films based on the same idea and format have gone into production: set in Thailand, Taiwan, and Japan. Glancing through the reports of these films-to-be, we can indeed opt to tease out a "pan-Asian" perspective or imaginary, from the *Ten Years* series. If we follow the epithet "pan" as used by the reporter of the cited article, we may observe, to put it bluntly, a generally shared, rather dystopian Asia a decade later.[39] The Thai version sketches a future under junta dictatorship, where freedom of speech and creative expression are seriously under threat. The Japanese version, similarly bleak, imagines a future where senior citizens are ushered toward euthanasia, children are receiving automated education, memories are digitized, residents are driven to subterranean living because of radiation pollution, and militarism is celebrating its revival. The Taiwanese version portrays a society troubled by nuclear waste disposal, migrant labor abuse, urban–rural divide, familial decay, and insomnia. Looking this way, we may well conclude that these Asian localities seem to exude a common sense of anxiety, almost hopeless and intensely helpless, when they contemplate their decade ahead: a pan-Asian future.

On the other hand, we can also trace otherwise; instead of what they share, we can trace their departures, incongruities, and variations, as we follow the possibilities occasioned by this trans-Asian trajectory. The Taiwan project, for instance, positions itself clearly as distinct from the Hong Kong predecessor. In response to a frequently asked question—why the Taiwanese *Ten Years* does not have any reference to the local Sunflower movement, a student mobilization exercise reminiscent of the Umbrella Movement in Hong Kong—James Liu, its producer, says they do not want to copy the heavily politicized Hong Kong version.[40] Instead, one of their starting points is the population makeup of Taiwan: the directors contributing to the film have aboriginal, Filipino, Malaysian, and "local" Taiwanese backgrounds. Such diversity is to be found in the Hong Kong society, but its absence as a directorial paradigm may in turn serve as a critical lens to revisit the Hong Kong film project. Fundamentally, it foregrounds the specific contexts where the Asian projects are embedded in. The Thai context—stringent military regime and censorship practices—lends itself to more subtle ways of critique against the government, more subtle than the Hong Kong version, for instance. "The original Hong Kong one is sort of a warning of too much interference from China, so it's very concrete. But when we translate it and do it in Thailand," one of the directors Aditya Assarat explains, "we can't be that direct, we have to use metaphors to try to talk about issues in a disguised way."[41] In addition to specific filmic language, the Thai context also generates other tactics so that the film will eventually hit the local cinemas, one of which is the contracting of internationally renowned Thai director Apichatpong Weerasethakul to contribute.[42] To state the obvious, there must be more to be examined. Suffice it, for the purpose of this introduction, to note, for now, the very possibilities as opened up along the trans-Asian axis, the possibilities that do not take the West always already as its reference point, and that seek to engage with Asian specificities, instead.

AS PARADOXES: MESSINESS, DANGERS, AND CHALLENGES

When visitors from China find that they have to use cash here, they ask: "How can Singapore be so backward?"

—Lee Hsien Long, Prime Minister of Singapore,
National Day Rally 2017[43]

I want to encourage Singaporeans to learn from China's experience. If they can do it, so can we.

—Lee Hsien Long, Prime Minister of Singapore[44]

While academics are busy engaging with the debates on epistemological strategies in researching Asia, Chua Beng Huat[45] insightfully argues that inter-Asia referencing has long been actually practiced on many levels and in several areas, ranging from political governance to commercial practices. These include (1) the export-oriented industrialization, led by Japan then followed by South Korea, Taiwan, Hong Kong, and Singapore and other Southeast Asian countries[46]; (2) urban and regional planning that involves several Asian cities referencing and appropriating from each other, such as Bangalore from Singapore, Singapore from Hong Kong, Hyderabad from Shanghai; and (3) the regionalization of the media and popular culture that involves production professionals and audience from different Asian locations, in which Chua and Iwabuchi have been field pioneers. With these empirical cases, Chua pinpoints that inter-Asia referencing should be understood as a grounded practice driven by pragmatic concerns, needs, and desires in the regional contexts. We argue that it nevertheless remains important and urgent to reflect on and question the limitations of and challenges in inter-referencing. Any inter-Asian referencing is bound to be(come) a messy affair, as referencing involves translation and appropriation, and in their slipstream bifurcations and slippages in meaning are bound to happen. It is important to engage with this messiness, rather than sweeping it under a neat and tidy conceptual blanket, and to acknowledge that in the end, the prefixes "inter" and "trans" converge and diverge, overlap and differ. It is this kind of paradoxes of sameness and difference that we like to engage with in this section.

The recent hype surrounding mobile payment technology within Asia and across the world provides a possible point of entry into the messy debates about inter- and trans-Asia. Accelerating development in ICBM (Internet of Things, Cloud, Big Data, and mobile platforms) technology and AI (Artificial Intelligence) has turned technology into a buzzword for growth. Asian countries are multiplying their references within and across the region. The eye-catching development of Chinese tech giants, such as Alibaba, Tencent, Baidu, Xiaomi, and Huawei, has attracted a wide interest. Of these all, the success of mobile payment platforms—Ant Financial's Alipay and Tencent's WeChat—is said to have revolutionized monetary transactions in the modern economy. From faked (*shanzhai*, counterfeit consumer goods) in China to its recent governmental initiative of "Made in China 2025," China has positioned itself as the leader and has also recently been looked upon by Asian states as an important point of reference. News reports, for instance, have headlines like "Why China's mobile payments revolution matters for U.S. bankers,"[47] and "From Supermarkets to super apps, Southeast Asian tech start-ups are looking to China not Silicon Valley."[48]

With its Smart Nation initiative (2014), the Singaporean government aims to transform the lion city through technology. According to Prime Minister Lee Hsien Long, this initiative is "to create new jobs, new business opportunities, to make our economy more productive, to make our lives more convenient, and to make this an outstanding city in which to live, work and play."[49] Even though the city-state has envisioned the importance of information technology for its future before China's Internet Plus (2015), officials and citizens were aware of its stagnant development, especially with reference to China in mobile payments. Singapore has numerous mobile payment solutions—via connected bank account/credit/debit cards; via mobile wallet and mobile application—but, unlike today's China, it has yet to reach its desired goal of a truly cashless Singapore.

Its prime minister and other officials have in various occasions made references to China's recent success in mobile payment development and technology startups, apparently to embarrass and discipline its commercial sectors and citizens, asking them to learn from their failure. This failure, unsurprisingly, is built on the enduring modernity rhetoric with its clear-cut binary oppositioning of advanced/modern versus backward/lagging-behind. In other words, he subtly implied "how could a modern and rich Singapore fall behind China?" A significant feature of China's mobile payment systems—Alipay and WeChat Pay—is the use of QR (Quick Response) code[50] in ensuring speedy, convenient, and secured monetary transactions. Inter-referencing China's mobile payment method, local mobile payment applications have now included QR code features and tested them in hawker centers, with plans to roll out the systems in public transport by 2020.

Often (self-)regarded as Singapore's rival, Hong Kong has established itself as a financial center in East Asia and to the world. The city pioneered the Octopus smart card technology in 1997, which was once globally recognized as the most advanced and innovative contactless payment technology. It has subsequently inspired other cities to adopt the technology. London's Oyster card, Singapore's EZ-link card, and Sydney's Opal card are some of the examples. When inter-referenced with China's rapid mobile payment technology, Octopus has been repeatedly described as something of the past that keeps the territory from leaping forward in developing innovative technology. Today, mobile payment technology has come to represent the city's growth potential and its political prospects, which strikes an uncanny discursive resonance with Hong Kong's fading competitiveness and its position as an advanced financial center. The current situation reminds one of the moral tale of the rabbit and the turtle.

In 2017, when Carrie Lam became the territory's fourth chief executive, her government prioritized the development of fintech (financial technology). It urges Hong Kong to learn from neighboring areas, such as Mainland China and Singapore. Parallel to this governmental call, Cheung Kong-Hutchison (owned by the tycoon Li Ka Shing) partnered with Ant Financial to expand the Alipay mobile payment service to the city. In the same year, WeChat Pay also established its Hong Kong subsidiary—WeChat Pay HK. Building on their existing promotion experiences in the mainland, both payment applications have rolled out aggressive campaigns to lure locals to subscribe to their payment platforms.

Like Singapore, local banks, such as HSBC (Hong Kong and Shanghai Banking Corporation Limited), have included QR code features in their latest mobile payment applications, for instance, HSBC PayMe. Other public services and events, such as the yearly music and art festival Clockenflap and mass transit railway (MTR) system, have followed suit. In response to the call for fintech innovation, the city's MTR public transport system has recently added a new payment solution (in addition to the existing Octopus). AlipayHK has won the bid to be the exclusive provider of this additional payment solution till 2021. In the name of offering payment alternatives, these seemingly strategic commercial decisions are mingled with politics. Their penetration in the practices of everyday life would accentuate and normalize the dependence (and their stickiness) of these made-in-China payment platforms. Their omnipresence can erode the discursive differences between Hong Kong and China; above all, they would cleanse the territory's long-standing prejudice that sees China as the backward counterpart. Besides, mobile payment platforms amass an ocean of big data about who the consumers are and what they do.[51] Given that these tech giants' existence in China is dependent on their compliance to the state, the data collected could very well enable the government to follow the money to learn and monitor citizens' behavior.

Thus, inter-referencing practices have produced a governmental discourse of lagging behind in both Singapore and Hong Kong, so as to impose self-disciplinary measures to further the state and corporate interests. If inter-referencing, as Aihwa Ong elucidates, refers to "practices of citation, allusion, aspiration, comparison and competition,"[52] then this recent development should warn one about its disciplinary function that promotes hierarchal competition. In the case of Singapore, inter-referencing becomes a governmental tactic that borrows the troubling idea of a Darwinian "survival of the fittest" to encourage competition so as to further advance Singapore's Smart Nation initiative. In Hong Kong, this horizontal comparison between Mainland China and Hong Kong may marginalize and subject Hong Kong and its citizens to further economic subordination, in the name of national integration. These examples of inter-referencing seem to betray the original communitarian effort proposed by the inter-Asia cultural studies movement. But "betray" may be too strong a word here; what we like to point at is that however promising the move to inter-Asia referencing may be, we need to be aware of its pitfalls, dangers, and paradoxes. And the same goes for trans-Asia as method.

When "inter-" converges with "trans-" in referring to "between" and "among" Asia, trans-Asia as a method runs similar dangers as mentioned in the above case studies. In the postscript of *Rogue Flows*, Meaghan Morris gave a broad definition of trans-Asia as "what happens across a geographical space that you decide to demarcate in a certain way."[53] Being an "outsider," an Australian female academic not specializing in China studies but teaching in a Hong Kong university, she was skeptical of this spatial delineation and categorization. She wittily recalled a personal encounter—that related to Australia's awkward geopolitical position of being in Asia but often not (self-) identified as Asia—in troubling this boundary and critically reflecting what "trans-Asia" means and what its limitations are. She flagged the danger of what lurks behind the seemingly celebratory concept of "trans-Asia," which could in practice become "intra-Asia," in her words, "once a space is in some way bounded as 'Asia,' then intra-Asian *traffic* can simply be defined as traffic taking place between various elements in that space as contrasted with whatever other relations those elements might maintain with places outside the borders that you have defined."[54]

The conceptual framework of trans-Asia, as a communitarian effort, is woven together by a recognition of sameness and likeness. Morris continued, "Likeness is not identity; the magical power of 'likeness' resides in all the space it allows for invention and deviation. Similarly, relationships based on unlikeness can have their productive power; unlikeness can also give rise to closeness or proximity."[55] This spatio-temporal "likeness" has empowered generations of intellectuals, not only Chinese or Japanese intellects but also others, such as Indian thinker Taraknath Das discussed in Wang's chapter 4 in this volume, to unite Asia to achieve de-imperialization and de-colonization.

However, when this likeness is built on the rhetoric of "if they can do that so do we," intra-Asian referencing is becoming more competitive and violent. In other instances, it deserves scrutiny when this likeness is constructed to serve the interests of expansion, control, and domination. Ant Financial (that owns Alipay) has taken over Lazada Group (a Southeast Asian e-commerce company) and its payment platform of online retail service, helloPay, has been rebranded under Alipay in Indonesia, Malaysia, Singapore, Thailand, and the Philippines. This takeover has accelerated the growth of Alipay in the region. One of the regular marketing statements builds on this rhetoric of sameness and similarities, that is, China's shared demographic compositions and experiences with its Southeast Asian counterparts—Ant Financial is experienced in getting a large population of unbanked consumers, who have no or little exposure of traditional banking, to use its platform.[56] Ant Financial has regularly positioned itself as sharing and understanding their needs by engaging with the developmental discourses on #techforgood and #inclusive-finance, #remittance service to garner, as stated in its Twitter posts, the "large underserved populations in Asia and beyond."[57]

If inter-Asia has unintentionally tilted heavily on the ideas of "likeness," trans-Asia, in its ideas of going beyond and crossing boundaries, introduces difference and trans-formation. The differences in nationality, ethnicity, gender, social class, and culture are not only productive but also necessary when addressing the harms and danger that lie in claiming too much sameness and likeness. Returning to the discussion above, the current expansion of technology in everyday life would require us to look beyond Asia on issues related to privacy law and regulations. Inter-referencing with the West is not only a suggestion but a much-needed practice to explore possibilities to curtail the power of techno-commercial giants. Similarly, differences in socioeconomic and cultural practices between Mainland China and Hong Kong have posed challenges for Alipay and WeChat to garner supports from the local Hong Kong population—they would rather use WhatsApp and are avid avoiders of WeChat and prefer to pay with Apple Pay or PayMe. Such frictions and tensions are important to study if we are using trans-Asia as a method.

THIS BOOK

Chapter 1, by Koichi Iwabuchi, discusses the potentials of a trans-Asian approach through an autobiographical account of an intellectual journey and research since mid-1990s. Iwabuchi draws on his research projects of dialogic mediation and multiculturalism from below in East Asia and migrant diplomacy to demonstrate the empowering potentials presented by trans-Asia comparison, referencing, and reciprocal learning as well as the enhancement of collaboration across various divides and borders. With the growing East Asian rivalry and antagonism, Iwabuchi articulates the urgency of transferring these academic approaches to our daily practices to open up cross-border dialogue. In chapter 2, Yiu Fai Chow and Jeroen de Kloet—recalling their recent encounter of Bruno Latour's public lecture in Beijing—start by critically interrogating the West's epistemological domination and exclusion of the Oriental others to foreground the necessity and potentials of these trans-Asia aspirations. Drawing their attention on the prefixes *de-*, *inter-*, and *trans-* intrinsically linked to "trans-" studies, they compel readers to think about what "trans-" signifies, pointing to, first, the dangers of methodological nationalism (as to denationalize); second, the importance of grounded and lived experiences (as to incorporate inter-sectional perspectives); and, third, the call for dialogic conversation and reciprocal learning (as to transgress and to trans-formation).

Ien Ang's chapter 3 interrogates the meanings of yet another prefix, *pan-*, in comparison with *inter-*, and teases out the logical tensions and connections between notions of *pan-* and *trans-*. She points out the danger of falling back to a unified "Pan-Asia" project through a comparison between notions of "trans-Asia" and "trans-Europe." With the establishment of the supranational, territorially bounded entity of the European Union, this actually existing "Pan-Europe" project has dissolved internal national borders but imposed an external circumference that demarcates the European "us" within from the non-European "them" outside, limiting the freedoms associated with "trans-Europe" to those who are defined as "us." Political tensions generated by the European refugee crisis exemplify the difficulties, challenges, and risks involved in this trans-Europe project, providing useful lessons for our thinking about the complexities of trans-Asia. Chih-Ming Wang revisits Das's transpacific and inter-Asian trajectories from the 1910s to the 1950s, demonstrating in chapter 4 that the discourse of pan-Asianism is not merely an "Asian" discourse but "an affective frame of mind" and "a figure of the greater desire for decolonization that continues to have impact in Asia and North America where white supremacy and discrimination against people of color remain critical problems" (Wang, this volume). Wang not only reclaims an earlier model of inter-Asia critique but also demonstrates the importance to attend to the regional divergences to make possible a trans-Asian solidarity. Soyoung Kim's visual essay in chapter 5 draws on her documentary practice, titled *Exile trilogy,* to explore a turbulent trajectory of Korean diaspora in Russia and Central Asia. Her engagement with trans-Asia project is rooted in this still unresolved post-Cold War situation where she has viscerally felt captive since childhood. This trilogy looks at the issues of translation, intermediality, art practice of diaspora, writing history, and collective trauma. It encourages one to understand trans-Asia as mediatic-historical-affective events.

In chapter 6, Rossella Ferrari takes an expansive approach to trans-Asia to explore the potential of what she designates as trans-Asian theatricalities to comprise intercultural contacts taking place both within and outside the confines of geopolitical Asia. She investigates the nexus of the trans-Asian and the transpacific along the Sino-Hispanophone geolinguistic axis through an analysis of the first production of a contemporary Chinese play in Latin America. The chapter presents a relational study of the Chinese and Peruvian performances of *The Crowd*, a dramatization of the Chongqing armed fights of 1967/68 written by Shanghai-based author Nick Rongjun Yu and premiered at the Hong Kong Arts Festival in 2015 in the aftermath of the Umbrella Movement. Ferrari's assessment of the transculturation of narratives and imageries of the Chinese Cultural Revolution takes into account both the realm of theatrical production and the performative reproduction of political behavior in the appropriation of Maoist ideology in Peru. Stevie Suan explores in chapter 7 the production network of anime that has spread throughout the Asia-Pacific, to re-examine anime production and distribution history from a transnational perspective, focusing on the trans-Asian production network (including the non-Japanese in Japan). In light of recent, openly transnational anime—some produced entirely outside of Japan then dubbed into Japanese—their contextualization from this perspective shows that they are not exceptional cases: most anime productions are transnational, but become "Japanese."

In chapter 8, Jiyu Zhang embarks on a Sino-American co-production documentary—*Out of Place. Transgender Stories from Asia*—so as to negotiate a diverse array of transgender subjects across borders in Asia. For Zhang, trans-Asia as a theoretical framework, on the one hand, allows for an intersectional analysis of transgenderism, which crisscrosses both tangible and intangible boundaries, such as those of geography, culture, body, and psyche. On the other hand, trans-Asia as method alerts to an abusive conception of mobility in current formulation of identity politics, which presumes an unconditional mobility irrespective of people's differentiated situations and uneven access to social resources. Chapter 9, by Gladys Pak Lei Chong, explores the merits and pitfalls or challenges of Asia as method. By inter-referencing young people's physical dwellings in Beijing and Hong Kong, this chapter focuses on the spatial organization and the material objects so as to trace how young people's desires for the good life are generated, disciplined, regulated, and governed spatially in these two Chinese cities of different historical, politico-, socio-cultural contexts. Chong demonstrates the limitations and dangers of a quasi-exclusionary retreat to the local and the regional, as in Asia as method. Finally, in the coda, we ask ourselves: what is the future of trans-Asia as method?

NOTES

1. Hsiu-Chuang Deppman, "Made in Taiwan: An Analysis of Meteor Garden as an East Asian Idol Drama," in *TV China*, eds. Ying Zhu and Chris Berry (Bloomington, IN: Indiana University Press, 2009), 91. Deppman's list gestures to the importance of the city as a site of identification, rather than, or parallel to, the nation-state.

2. Koichi Iwabuchi, ed., "Houhou to shite no toransu ajia" (Trans-Asia as a Method) (in Japanese), in *Koeru bunka kousaku suru kyoukai* (Transgressing Cultures and Intersecting Boundaries) (Tokyo: Yamakawa Shuppan, 2004), 3–24.

3. Monash Asia Institute, "Trans-Asia as Method: Exploring New Potentials of 'Trans-Asian' Approaches," International Conference, Monash University, Prato Centre, Italy, June 12–13, 2017.

4. Iwabuchi, "Houhou to shite no toransu ajia"; Chen Kuan-Hsing, *Asia as Method: Towards Deimperialization* (Durham, NC: Duke University Press, 2010).

5. Mizoguchi Yuzo, *China as Method*, trans. Li Suping, Gong Ying and Xu Tao (Beijing: China Renmin University Press, 1996).

6. Mark Harrison, "How to Speak about Oneself: Theory and Identity in Taiwan," in *Cultural Studies and Cultural Industries in Northeast Asia: What a Difference a Region Makes*, eds. Chris Berry, Nicola Liscutin and Jonathan D. Mackintosh (Hong Kong: Hong Kong University Press, 2009), 51.

7. See Angel M.Y. Lin, "Towards Transformation of Knowledge and Subjectivity in Curriculum Inquiry: Insights from Chen Kuan-Hsing's 'Asia as Method,'" *Curriculum Inquiry* 42, no. 1 (2012): 167.

8. Ibid., 160.

9. Chen, *Asia as Method*, 215.

10. Ibid., 212.

11. Ibid., 213.

12. Chen, "Takeuchi Yoshimi's 1960 'Asia as Method' Lecture," *Inter-Asia Cultural Studies* 13, no. 2 (2012): 317–324.

13. Ibid., 320.

14. Takeuchi Yoshimi, "Asia as Method," in *What Is Modernity? Writings of Takeuchi Yoshimi*, ed. Richard F. Calichman (New York: Columbia University Press, 2005), 150.

15. Ibid.

16. Chen, "Takeuchi Yoshimi's," 320.

17. Ibid., 323.

18. Koichi Iwabuchi, "De-Westernization, Inter-Asian Referencing and Beyond," *European Journal of Cultural Studies* 17, no. 1 (2013): 47.

19. Chen, *Asia as Method*, 216.

20. Ibid., 254.

21. Ibid., 212.

22. Iwabuchi, "De-Westernization," 47.

23. Yiu Fai Chow and Jeroen de Kloet, "The Spectre of Europe: Knowledge, Cultural Studies and the 'Rise of Asia,'" *European Journal of Cultural Studies* 17, no. 1 (2014): 9.

24. See, for instance, Ien Ang, "Can One Say No to Chineseness? Pushing the Limits of the Diasporic Paradigm," *Boundary 2* 25, no. 3 (1998): 223–242; Rey Chow, "Can One Say No to China?" *New Literary History* 28, no. 1 (1997): 147–151.

25. See Shu-Mei Shih, "Theory, Asia and the Sinophone," *Postcolonial Studies* 13, no. 4 (2010): 465–484; and Naoki Sakai, "From area studies toward transnational studies." *Inter-Asia Cultural Studies* 11, no. 2 (2010): 265–274.

26. An alternative paradigm in the realm of "Chinese" cultures is proposed by Shu-mei Shih with her notion of the Sinophone. She claims, "Sinophone studies—conceived as the study of Sinitic-language cultures on the margins of geopolitical

nation-states and their hegemonic productions—locates its objects of attention at the conjuncture of China's internal colonialism and Sinophone communities everywhere immigrants from China have settled" (Shih 2011, 710). Her attempt to decenter the mainland from discourses of Chineseness runs the danger of completely sidetracking the mainland as a possible object of study. As Lim (2011) writes, "Shih's critique of the diasporic model is trenchant but her attempt to replace it with the Sinophone does not so much decentre the China-centrism that she challenges; rather, it replaces one form of essentialism with another. . . . [T]he Sinophone model proposed by Shih is not the solution as it does not sufficiently address either the complexity of the diasporas or the reality of translingual film-making" (38). A Sino-centrism is replaced in this model by a still problematic lingua-centrism.

27. Chen, *Asia as Method*, 216.

28. Mark Fisher, *Capitalist Realism: Is There No Alternative?* (London: Zone Books, 2009). The term refers to "the widespread sense that not only is capitalism the only viable political and economic system, but also that it is now impossible even to imagine a coherent alternative to it" (2).

29. Chen, *Asia as Method*, 213.

30. See chapter 3 for Yiu Fai Chow and Jeroen de Kloet's take on "trans."

31. Wei Zhou, "Travel Frog: The Cute Japanese Game That Has China Hooked," *BBC News*, Febraury 1, 2018, https://www.bbc.com/news/world-asia-china-42871181.

32. Manya Koetse, "Chinese Media Ascribe 'Traveling Frog' Game Hype to China's Low Birth Rates," *What's on Weibo*, February 7, 2018.

33. Sakai, "From Area Studies," 273. See our further discussion in connection with area studies in the coda.

34. Ackbar Abbas, *Hong Kong: Culture and the Politics of Disappearance* (Minneapolis, MI: University of Minnesota Press, 1997).

35. Elaine Yau, "Ten Years: Hong Kong Film that Beat Star Wars at the Box Office, and the Directors behind It," *South China Morning Post*, December 29, 2015, https://www.scmp.com/lifestyle/film-tv/article/1895992/ten-years-hong-kong-film-beat-star-wars-box-office-and-directors. For an analytical account of the Umbrella Movement, see Veg (2015). It should also be noted that the conceiver of the film project Ng Ka-leung claimed that the "ten years" idea predated the Umbrella Movement and was inspired by persistent problems confronting Hong Kong.

36. "社评：《十年》吓唬香港社会，内地管不了" (*Ten Years* Terrorizes Hong Kong Society, It Is not the Mainland [Government's] Business), *Huanqiu.com*, January 22, 2016, http://opinion.huanqiu.com/editorial/2016-01/8425632.html.

37. Edmund Lee, "Controversial Hong Kong film Ten Years to Spawn International Versions in Thailand, Taiwan and Japan," *South China Morning Post*, August 16, 2017, https://www.scmp.com/culture/film-tv/article/2107012/controversial-hong-kong-film-ten-years-spawn-international-versions.

38. "Bleak Hong Kong Film to Become Pan-Asia," *Agence France-Presse*, October 18, 2017, http://www.thestandard.com.hk/sections-news_print.php?id=188549.

39. For Ien Ang's critical discussion on the prefix "pan," see chapter 4.

40. Ching Ha Ip, "《十年台灣》多元思維 刻劃在地生活" (*Ten Years Taiwan*, Diversified Thinking Describing Everyday Life), *Ming Pao Weekly*,

November 22, 2018, https://www.mpweekly.com/culture/%E6%96%87%E5%8C%96/20181122-87179

41. Clarence Tsui, "How Ten Years Thailand, Inspired by Controversial Hong Kong Film, Reflects on History and Politics," *South China Morning Post*, May 14, 2018, https://www.scmp.com/culture/film-tv/article/2146040/how-ten-years-thailand-inspired-controversial-hong-kong-film.

42. Apichatpong Weerasethakul has received numerous awards; his *Uncle Boonmee Who Can Recall His Past Lives*, for instance, won the prestigious 2010 Cannes Film Festival Palme d'Or prize and *Tropical Malady* won a jury prize at the 2004 Cannes Film Festival. His participation in the Thai *Ten Years* is believed to reduce the likelihood of the military government to step in and cause international outcry.

43. Joanna Seow, "National Day Rally 2017: When Lim Swee Say Felt 'Suaku' in Smart City Shanghai." *The Strait Times*, August 20, 2017. https://www.straitstimes.com/singapore/national-day-rally-2017-when-swee-say-felt-suaku-in-smart-city-shanghai.

44. "Learning from Chinese on How to Go Cashless, S'poreans Urged," *TODAY*, September 18, 2017, https://www.todayonline.com/singapore/singapore-should-learn-chinas-advanced-e-payment-systems-pm-lee.

45. Chua Beng Huat, "Inter-Asia Referencing and Shifting Frames of Comparison," in *The Social Sciences in the Asian Century*, eds. Carol Johnson, Vera Mackie, and Tessa Morris-Suzuki (Canberra: The Australian National University, 2015), 67–81.

46. Terutomo Ozawa, *Institutions, Industrial Upgrading, and Economic Performance in Japan: The 'Flying-Geese' Paradigm of Catch-up Growth* (Northampton, MA: Edward Elgar, 2005).

47. John Engen, "There Is No Disputing that China Is Ahead of the Rest of the World in Mobile Payments. What Insight Does It Offer U.S. Bankers?" *American Banker*, accessed December 5, 2018, https://www.americanbanker.com/news/why-chinas-mobile-payments-revolution-matters-for-us-bankers.

48. Zen Soo, "From Supermarkets to Super Apps, Southeast Asian Tech Start-ups Are Looking to China Not Silicon Valley," *South China Morning Post*, October 26, 2018, https://www.scmp.com/print/tech/apps-social/article/2170181/supermarkets-super-apps-southeast-asian-tech-start-ups-are-looking.

49. Judith Tan, "PM: Singapore Can Do More as a Smart Nation." *The Business Times*, August 20, 2017. https://www.businesstimes.com.sg/government-economy/pm-singapore-can-do-more-as-a-smart-nation.

50. QR code was first invented by Denso Wave, a Japanese company, in 1994.

51. Gladys Pak Lei Chong, "Cashless China: Securitization of Everyday Life through Alipay's Social Credit System—Sesame Credit," *Chinese Journal of Communication* (2019): 1–18.

52. Aihwa Ong, "World Cities, or the Art of Being Global," in *Worlding Cities: Asia Experiments and the Art of Being Global*, eds. Ananya Roy and Aihwa Ong (Chichester: Wiley-Blackwell, 2011), 17.

53. Meaghan Morris, "Participating from a Distance," in *Rogue Flows*, eds. Koichi Iwabuchi, Stephen Muecke, and Mandy Thomas (Hong Kong: Hong Kong University Press, 2004), 249. We will reflect on Morris's "outsider" position in the coda.

54. Ibid.

55. Ibid., 257.

56. Bien Perez, "Alipay Expansion Gathers Speed with Move into Southeast Asia," *South China Morning Post*, April 20, 2017, https://www.scmp.com/tech/china-tech/article/2089267/alipay-expansion-gathers-speed-move-southeast-asia.

57. Ant Financial (@AntFinancial), "'This is a new starting point and significant step forward in accelerating #techforgood. We hope to work with local wallet partners to bring #inclusivefinance to large underserved populations in Asia and beyond.' @AntFinancial Executive Chairman and CEO Eric Jing #GCashXAlipayHK," tweet, June 25, 2018, https://twitter.com/AntFinancial/status/1011202902755381248/photo/1.

BIBLIOGRAPHY

Abbas, Ackbar. *Hong Kong: Culture and the Politics of Disappearance*. Minneapolis, MI: University of Minnesota Press, 1997.

Ang, Ien. "Can One Say No to Chineseness? Pushing the Limits of the Diasporic Paradigm." *Boundary 2* 25, no. 3 (1998): 223–242.

———. *On Not Speaking Chinese: Living Between Asia and the West*. London: Routledge, 2001.

"Bleak Hong Kong Film to Become Pan-Asia." Agence France-Presse, October 18, 2017. http://www.thestandard.com.hk/sections-news_print.php?id=188549.

Chen, Kuan-Hsing. *Asia as Method: Towards Deimperialization*. Durham, NC: Duke University Press, 2010.

———. "Takeuchi Yoshimi's 1960 'Asia as Method' Lecture." *Inter-Asia Cultural Studies* 13, no. 2 (2012): 317–324.

Chong, Gladys Pak Lei. "Cashless China: Securitization of Everyday Life through Alipay's Social Credit System—Sesame Credit." *Chinese Journal of Communication* (2019).

Chow, Rey. *Primitive Passions: Visuality, Sexuality, Ethnography and Contemporary Chinese Cinema. Film and Culture*. New York: Columbia University Press, 1995.

———. "Can One Say No to China?" *New Literary History* 28, no. 1 (1997): 147–151.

Chow, Yiu Fai, and Jeroen de Kloet. "The Spectre of Europe: Knowledge, Cultural Studies and the 'Rise of Asia.'" *European Journal of Cultural Studies* 17, no. 1 (2014): 3–15.

Chua, Beng Huat. "Conceptualizing an East Asian Popular Culture." *Inter-Asia Cultural Studies* 5, no. 2 (2004): 200–221.

———. "Inter-Asia Referencing and Shifting Frames of Comparison." In *The Social Sciences in the Asian Century*, edited by Carol Johnson, Vera Mackie, and Tessa Morris-Suzuki, 67–81. Canberra: The Australian National University, 2015.

Deppman, Hsiu-Chuang. "Made in Taiwan: An Analysis of Meteor Garden as an East Asian Idol Drama." In *TV China*, edited by Ying Zhu and Chris Berry, 90–110. Bloomington, IN: Indiana University Press, 2009.

Engen, John. "There Is No Disputing That China Is Ahead of the Rest of the World in Mobile Payments. What Insight Does It Offer U.S. Bankers?" *American Banker*, accessed December 5, 2018. https://www.americanbanker.com/news/why-chinas-mobile-payments-revolution-matters-for-us-bankers.

Fisher, Mark. *Capitalist Realism: Is There No Alternative?* London: Zone Books, 2009.

Foucault, Michel. "Governmentality." In *The Foucault Effect: Studies in Governmentality*, edited by Graham Burchell, Colin Gordon, and Peter Miller, 87–104. Chicago, IL: University of Chicago Press, 1991.

Harrison, Mark. "How to Speak about Oneself: Theory and Identity in Taiwan." In *Cultural Studies and Cultural Industries in Northeast Asia: What a Difference a Region Makes*, edited by Chris Berry, Nicola Liscutin, and Jonathan D. Mackintosh, 51–70. Hong Kong: Hong Kong University Press, 2009.

Hillenbrand, Margaret. "Communitarianism, or, How to Build East Asian Theory." *Postcolonial Studies* 13, no. 4 (2010): 317–334.

Ip, Ching Ha. "《十年台灣》多元思維　刻劃在地生活" (*Ten Years Taiwan*, diversified thinking describing everyday life). *Ming Pao Weekly*, November 22, 2018. https://www.mpweekly.com/culture/%E6%96%87%E5%8C%96/20181122-87179.

Iwabuchi, Koichi. *Recentering Globalization: Popular Culture and Japanese Transnationalism*. Durham, NC: Duke University Press, 2002.

———, ed. "Houhou to shite no toransu ajia" (Trans-Asia as a Method) (in Japanese). In *Koeru bunka kousaku suru kyoukai* (Transgressing Cultures and Intersecting Boundaries), 3–24. Tokyo: Yamakawa Shuppan, 2004.

———. "De-Westernization, Inter-Asian Referencing and Beyond." *European Journal of Cultural Studies* 17, no. 1 (2013): 44–57.

de Kloet, Jeroen. "Europe as Façade." *European Journal of Cultural Studies* 17, no. 1 (2013): 58–74.

Koetse, Manya. "Chinese Media Ascribe 'Traveling Frog' Game Hype to China's Low Birth Rates." *What's on Weibo*, February 7, 2018.

"Learning from Chinese on How to go Cashless, S'poreans Urged." *Today*, September 18, 2017. https://www.todayonline.com/singapore/singapore-should-learn-chinas-advanced-e-payment-systems-pm-lee.

Lee, Edmund. "Controversial Hong Kong film Ten Years to Spawn International Versions in Thailand, Taiwan and Japan." *South China Morning Post*, August 16, 2017. https://www.scmp.com/culture/film-tv/article/2107012/controversial-hong-kong-film-ten-years-spawn-international-versions.

Lim, Song Hwee. "Six Chinese Cinemas in Search of a Historiography." In *The Chinese Cinema Book*, edited by Song Hwee Lim and Daniel Ward, 35–43. London: British Film Institute, 2017.

Lin, Angel M. Y. "Towards Transformation of Knowledge and Subjectivity in Curriculum Inquiry: Insights from Chen Kuan-Hsing's 'Asia as Method.'" *Curriculum Inquiry* 42, no. 1 (2012): 153–178.

Lo, Kwai-Cheung. "Rethinking Asianism and Method." *European Journal of Cultural Studies* 17, no. 1 (2013): 31–43.

Mizoguchi, Yuzo. *China as Method*. Translated by Li Suping, Gong Ying, and Xu Tao. Beijing: China Renmin University Press, 1996.

Morris, Meaghan. "Participating from a Distance." In *Rogue Flows*, edited by Koichi Iwabuchi, Stephen Muecke, and Mandy Thomas, 249–262. Hong Kong: Hong Kong University Press, 2004.

———. "Inter-Asian Banality and Education." *Inter-Asia Cultural Studies* 11, no. 2 (2010): 157–164.

Ong, Aihwa. "World Cities, or the Art of Being Global." In *Worlding Cities: Asia Experiments and the Art of Being Global*, edited by Ananya Roy and Aihwa Ong, 1–26. Chichester: Wiley-Blackwell, 2011.

Ozawa, Terutomo. *Institutions, Industrial Upgrading, and Economic Performance in Japan: The 'Flying-Geese' Paradigm of Catch-up Growth*. Northampton, MA: Edward Elgar, 2005.

Perez, Bien. "Alipay Expansion Gathers Speed with Move into Southeast Asia." *South China Morning Post*, April 20, 2017. https://www.scmp.com/tech/china-tech/article/2089267/alipay-expansion-gathers-speed-move-southeast-asia.

Sakai, Naoki. "From Area Studies toward Transnational Studies." *Inter-Asia Cultural Studies* 11, no. 2 (2010): 265–274.

Seow, Joanna. "National Day Rally 2017: When Lim Swee Say Felt 'Suaku' in Smart City Shanghai." *The Strait Times*, August 20, 2017. https://www.straitstimes.com/singapore/national-day-rally-2017-when-swee-say-felt-suaku-in-smart-city-shanghai.

Shih, Shu-Mei. "Theory, Asia and the Sinophone." *Postcolonial Studies* 13, no. 4 (2010): 465–484.

———. "The Concept of the Sinophone." *PMLA* 126, no. 3 (May 2011): 709–718.

Soo, Zen. "From Supermarkets to Super Apps, Southeast Asian Tech Start-ups Are Looking to China Not Silicon Valley." *South China Morning Post*, October 26, 2018. https://www.scmp.com/print/tech/apps-social/article/2170181/supermarkets-super-apps-southeast-asian-tech-start-ups-are-looking.

Takeuchi, Yoshimi. "Asia as Method." In *What Is Modernity? Writings of Takeuchi Yoshimi*, edited by Richard F. Calichman, 149–166. New York: Columbia University Press, 2005.

Tan, Judith. "PM: Singapore Can Do More as a Smart Nation." *The Business Times*, August 20, 2017. https://www.businesstimes.com.sg/government-economy/pm-singapore-can-do-more-as-a-smart-nation.

Tsui, Clarence. "How Ten Years Thailand, Inspired by Controversial Hong Kong Film, Reflects on History and Politics." *South China Morning Post*, May 14, 2018. https://www.scmp.com/culture/film-tv/article/2146040/how-ten-years-thailand-inspired-controversial-hong-kong-film.

Veg, Sebastian. "Legalistic and Utopian: Hong Kong's Umbrella Movement." *New Left Review* 92 (March-April 2015).

Yau, Elaine. "Ten Years: Hong Kong Film that Beat Star Wars at the Box Office, and the Directors behind It." *South China Morning Post*, December 29, 2015. https://www.scmp.com/lifestyle/film-tv/article/1895992/ten-years-hong-kong-film-beat-star-wars-box-office-and-directors.

Zhou, Wei. "Travel Frog: The Cute Japanese Game That Has China Hooked." *BBC News*, February 1, 2018. https://www.bbc.com/news/world-asia-china-42871181.

"社评：《十年》吓唬香港社会，内地管不了" (*Ten Years* Terrorizes Hong Kong Society, It Is not the Mainland [Government's] Business). *Huanqiu.com*, January 22, 2016. http://opinion.huanqiu.com/editorial/2016-01/8425632.html.

Chapter 1

Trans-Asia as Method:
A Collaborative and Dialogic
Project in a Globalized World

Koichi Iwabuchi

With the intensifying globalization processes, transnational connections engendered by human mobilities, media culture flows, and people's solidarity across Asian region have been much developed and we are required to understand how transnationally shared issues are specifically and inter-relatedly articulated in a particular country or society. This chapter will address the potential of "trans-Asia as method" approaches to further advance such intellectual engagement and collaborative practice. Referring to research projects that I have been conducting, it will discuss some ways to engage and tackle the issues that Asian societies share through tactical progression of trans-Asia comparison, mutual referencing, and reciprocated learning as well as the enhancement of collaboration and dialogue across various divides and borders.

RISE OF TRANS-ASIA AND INTER-ASIA APPROACHES

In the last twenty years, we have observed the rise of inter-Asia and trans-Asia approaches to the study of socio-cultural issues in Asian regions. It testifies the growing concern to engage with the promotion of cross-regional critical dialogue. In this respect, Inter-Asia Cultural Studies has been organizing highly successful academic activities in terms of journal publication, bi-annual conference, consortium, and postgraduate students camp since 2000, aiming to "build a platform for an 'inter-Asia' intellectual community by creating links between and across local circles." More specifically, it sets out to: "(1) generate and circulate critical work and out of Asia and beyond; (2) slowly link and facilitate dialogues between the disconnected critical circles within Asia and beyond; and (3) provide a platform on which academic and movement intellectual work can intersect." While not being exclusive to researchers located outside Asian regions and being "conscious that there is no unity to the imaginary entity called 'Asia,' hence the term 'Inter-Asia,'" it still has some emphasis on the promotion of hitherto unrealized conversation and alliance among "local" academics and their works (in local languages). As Chen argues, it is a project of Asia as method that generates de-imperialization of knowledge production: "using Asia as an imaginary anchoring point can allow societies in Asia to become one another's reference points, so that the understanding of the self can be transformed, and subjectivity rebuilt" and this will lead to the construction of "an alternative horizon, perspective, or method for posing a different set of questions about world history."[1] As Chua paraphrases Chen's point as the co-leader of IACS project, hitherto underexplored, inter-Asian comparison or referencing is considered meaningful for understanding modern trajectories of Asian countries in a new critical light, as it is based on shared experiences of "forced" modernization and less hierarchical relationships than a prevailing West Asia comparison that is based on the assumed temporal distance between them.[2]

While also engaging de-Westernization of knowledge production, trans-Asia studies more specifically aim to investigate the advancement of globalization process that engenders cross-border flows and connections of capital, people, and media culture and renders many issues transnationally linked. For example, Social Science Research Council in the United States has developed Inter-Asia programs since 2008. It aims to "reconceptualize Asia as a dynamic and interconnected formation" and "move beyond the territorial fixities of area-studies research." It also encourages junior scholars via a grant program and the organization of inter-Asia connections conference series. Some new journals also focus on inter-Asia or trans-Asia approaches such as *Transnational Asia: an online interdisciplinary journal* (Rice University) and *TRaNS: Trans-Regional and -National Studies of Southeast Asia*. They aim to "challenge traditional understandings of Asia, moving beyond the confines of area studies and nation-state focus," as it "posits that these boundaries are unnecessarily limiting, and attempt to examine issues on the supra-national level." National University of Singapore has launched a new PhD program of Comparative Asian Studies (CAS) that "attuned to Asia's interconnectedness and its deepening integration at the local level" and "One of the programme's distinctive feature is its attention to inter-Asian connections across regional boundaries and cultural zones." University of Wisconsin, Madison, has also been organizing annual Trans-Asia Graduate Student Conference to reflect the emerging significance and interests in trans-Asia approaches. These developments clearly reflect on the escalation of cross-border flows and connections that makes many issues transnational.

"TRANS-ASIA AS METHOD" PROJECTS

In my academic trajectory of cultural and media studies, I have been taking trans-Asia approach since mid-1990s, even before these trends occurred. I have been engaging with the examination of trans-Asia culture flows, exchanges, and connections and developing an approach of what I call "trans-Asia as method." It has three key features, which overlap but not identical with the abovementioned approaches of inter-Asia and trans-Asia studies. One is concerned with issues and phenomena for academic investigation and socio-historical context of globalization in which they have become significant. Trans-Asia as method, unlike inter-Asia approaches, particularly concerns how the intensification of cross-border cultural flows and human mobilities have been newly engendering trans-local dialogues, connections, association, rivalry, and antagonism in Asian (mostly East Asia for my recent investigation) contexts. I have been considering whether and how they are implicated in historically constituted unevenness and gives rise to cross-border dialogue over transnationally shared issues. Also relevant is the consideration of how many issues have been transnationally shared and cannot be well dealt with by the existing framework of nation-state or Asia–West binary, while we have observed a new kind of global or internationalized governance that tends to re-highlight the national borders.[3] Second, such study of trans-Asia flows and connections of capital, people, and media culture in Asia aims to advance the de-Westernized knowledge production. It enables us to have a new perspective and understanding of the issues regarding cultural globalization processes from similar and different Asian experiences and facilitates localized (re-) conceptualization and theorization through comparison and mutual referencing of (post)modern experiences in Asia. My approach also examines how mutual referencing has been developing as mundane practices among people who consume cultures from other parts of Asia and whether and how they have been generating cross-border dialogue. This is related to the third feature of "trans-Asia as method" approach, which is not confined to the production of knowledge per se. "Trans-Asia as method" is a collaborative project to not just go beyond the compartmentalized conception of "Asia" and region/ nation, and produce de-Westernized knowledge from Asian experiences but also take seriously academic's role as public coordinator in a globalized world to engage with the question of how to facilitate cross-border dialogue over and mutual engagement with transnationally shared issues by promoting collaboration with diverse social actors across borders.

That is to say, trans-Asia as method takes perspectives and approaches that "trans" implies seriously—critical engagement with transnational circulation of capital, people, and culture and uneven connections it engenders ("across/

through"); going beyond a mutually exclusively demarcated understanding of region and nation ("beyond"); and striving to conceptualize *and* materialize an open and dialogic social relation ("into another state of things"). The project of "trans-Asia as method" is to envision and actualize Asia as a dialogic communicative space in which people across borders collaborate to connect diverse voices, concerns, and problems in various, unevenly intersecting public sites in which the national is still a major site but does not exclusively take over public interests. In this respect, the "method" in "trans-Asia as method" suggests less a pure academic methodology, parallel to Chen's point that "'Asia as method' ceases to look at Asia as object of analysis."⁴ It is a tactic by which to engender alternative modes of knowledge production and dialogic collaboration that enable people to tackle and transform the existing unequal composition of society and the world. What is required for researcher is, then, to conjointly advance two kinds of engagement with trans-Asian connection—the production of critical knowledge accessible and relevant to wider publics *and* the coordinating role in the promotion of people's mediated dialogue—to enhance a sense of together-ness and dialogic relationship among various social subjects and across various borders.

One would be inclined to ask if such approaches as trans-Asia or inter-Asia tend to be parochial and exclusive to non-Asia regions and researchers. Other related questions might be how Asia can be defined and which Asia is included and excluded. These are very important reminders of the danger of implicit reproduction of uneven power relations and cultural exceptionalism. Aiming to advance the innovative production of knowledge through reciprocal learning from other Asian experiences, trans-Asia as method, and inter-Asia approaches too, is a self-critical tactical invitation to activate dialogue among hitherto internationally unattended scholarly work of Asian regions—through still mostly limited to English language works, which is an imperative issue beyond the scope of this paper. But it is neither a closed-minded regionalism nor to elucidate Asian modern experiences in an essentialist term in contrast to and/or separate from Western and other non-Western experiences. By "re-embracing" deep-seated Western inflections on Asian experiences, an inspired Asian comparison and referencing aims to refreshingly elucidate and theorize specific processes in which the experiences of Asian modernizations have been formulated, whereby the production of knowledge derived from Asian experiences leads to the articulation of visions and values trans-locally relevant for transmuting not just Asian societies but also European societies and the world as a whole. As such trans-Asia or inter-Asia approach must be differentiated from parochial regionalism for it does not discount researchers working in and on the contexts outside Asia nor underestimate the significance of transnational collaboration including other parts of the world either.

It should also be noted that trans-Asia as method is more of a tactical approach (hence "method") rather than aiming to be set up as a comprehensive academic methodology of a particular discipline and it does not aim to be all inclusive of "Asia" and regional connections. The definition of Asia is rather difficult and eventually impossible to make apart from that of "non-West." I would contend that it is indeed imperative to give more attentions to hitherto neglected (sub)regions, connections and people. "Trans-Asia as method" is not a magical approach to solve these issues. The following discussion of my projects are just a few instances of trans-Asia as method approaches, and the activation of various trans-Asia approaches to cover diverse regions and issues would be required to topple regional and subregional exclusion and hierarchy. While the exclusion and uneven power relation should be always kept in mind whenever we use such a regional term, however, it would not be productive either if we try to be all inclusive of Asian regions and connections within. The question of which Asia to be analyzed by "trans-Asia as method" depends on aims, key questions, objects, and the scope of places/regions of investigation and uneven power relations and the reproduction of hierarchical relationship within the region is always part of the issue to be analyzed. Trans-Asia, as method in my research projects, is specifically concerned with the investigation of regional flows and connections of people and media culture and associated issues of diversity and multicultural inclusion in East Asian contexts. This is not to discount the significance and necessity of attending to Southeast Asia or South Asia in such investigation, but the focus on East Asia, and particular locales, people, and cultures within and across it is relevant and productive to consider specific issues, with which my projects are dealing with. At the same time, through thematic investigation of globalization process, trans-Asia as method would open up an alternative idea, scope, and cultural geography of "Asia" and its "regional" connections. Dealing with ethno-cultural cross-border flows, connections, and dialogues, trans-Asia as method expands the definition of "Asia" in terms of experience and practice of migrants and diaspora dwelling in other regions and countries and the circulation of media culture outside the conventionally understood geography of Asia such as Australia or the United States.

MUTUAL REFERENCING AND CROSS-BORDER DIALOGUE AS MUNDANE PRACTICE

The project of trans-Asia as method has been developed through my own academic works and experience of relocation. Moving back and forth between Japan and Australia and frequent contacts with other East Asian cities and researchers have much to do with the shaping of my own trans-Asia approach. Being concerned with the rise of East and Southeast Asian media culture

flows and connections with some focus on Japan, my PhD research was concerned with trans-Asian flows and connections though I tended to use "intra-
regional" at that time. Located in Australia, I could have a kind of bird's-eye
view of such cultural dynamic while conducting field research in various
parts of East and Southeast Asia. After completing a PhD, I have worked
in Tokyo for more than twelve years. The first part of the period coincided
with the rise of inter-Asia cultural studies and a growing academic interest in
trans-Asia media culture flows and connections. Since the middle of 1990s,
production capacity of media cultures such as TV drams, films, and popular
music has considerably developed in East Asia. Furthermore, inter-Asian
promotion and co-production of media cultures have become commonplace
by the partnerships among media and cultural industries. There has emerged
a loose cultural geography as most of East Asian media cultures except some
cultures are capitalized, circulating and consumed predominantly, if not
exclusively, in East Asia (including those migrants and diasporas from the
region living outside it). Examining socio-historically contextualized experiences that intersect East Asia as region, many researchers have been seriously
examining cultural dynamics of production, circulation, and consumption
that have been engendered under the globalization processes. I eventually
met many cultural studies scholars in East and Southeast countries as well
as in Australia and Euro-American countries who were conducting similar
researches. Collaborating with them, I further developed my PhD project by
extending the scope especially to other East Asian culture especially that of
South Korea, Taiwan, and Hong Kong.

It was in this context that I developed an idea of "trans-Asia as method."
I first used the term in the Japanese publication in 2004.[5] While I was
involved if indirectly in inter-Asia cultural studies project, I preferred a term
"trans-Asia" to "inter-Asia" not least because of my interest is mostly analyzing the growing occurrences of transnational cultural flows and connections
in Asia. I also use "as method," being inspired by Takeuchi Yoshimi's notion
of "Asia as method" like Chen and many others to suggest that comparison
and Asian modern experience and the construction of modern subjectivity
under Western domination might induce a new perspective and knowledge
while it would be impossible and unproductive to define "Asia" in a clearly
demarcated way. At that time, I was fascinated with a possibility that trans-
Asia approaches critically and innovatively reconsider the politics of cultural
transgression in the Asian contexts through the examination of the flows and
connections by media, capital, and people across and through Asian regions
under globalization processes, which problematizes the clearly and exclusively demarcated boundaries of the nation and the region. It aimed to analyze
the dynamic process in which transnational circulation and intersection of
various flows of capital, media culture, and people interconnect Asia both

spatially and temporally, materially and imaginatively, and dialogically and antagonistically to highlight historically constituted relationship and regionally and globally shared emergent issues. I have conducted field research in East Asia, organized international conference and seminars and published papers, monographs, and edited volume regarding trans-Asian media and cultural flows and connections.

In my investigation of trans-Asia media culture flows and connections, mutual referencing of Asian experiences has been a key notion in two senses. One is the advancement of de-Westernized knowledge production. Conceptualization and theorization about globally shared matters from Asian contexts is essential to de-Westernized knowledge production and mutual referencing and comparison of Asian common and different experiences productively enables us to develop a new perspective and conceptualization, which cannot be obtained by comparison between the experiences of Western and East Asian societies and cultures. One example is the notion of *mukokuseki* (literally meaning non-nationality and also implying the erasure of ethnic and racialized images of a particular nation). I conceptualized it in my research on the popularity of Japanese media culture overseas in association with other notion of "cultural odor" to consider whether and how Japanese manga, animation, and game, which are internationally well received, represent tangible images of Japanese culture to be consumed as such. The notion has been further developed by Jung's referencing to it in her work on the international popularity of South Korean media culture.[6] Using a Korean equivalent term, Jung makes conceptualization of "*mugukjeok*" in the South Korean context by referring to the notion of "*mukokuseki*" in a way to refine and expand it.[7] Referencing to other Asian experience adopted by Jung's work makes the notion of "*mukokuseki*" transnationally applicable and valid to other media culture such as popular music. The case demonstrates how a close attention to similar and different experiences in East Asia produces a new understanding of transculturation process, which can be conceptually relevant outside Asian contexts.

The examination of cultural mixing and adaptation of media culture in East Asia would also contribute to de-Westernized knowledge production. Many studies have discussed how East Asian countries have actively hybridized American media cultures in terms of production techniques, representational genres, and textual formats,[8] but a comprehensive examination of how similar and different experience of negotiation with American media culture in Hong Kong, Japan, and South Korea for example has not yet been conducted. Such comparative analysis would show the continuum of cultural mixing and adaptation in East Asia, ranging from creative translation that produces something new, selective appropriation and reformulation of local cultures, eventual replication based on global mass culture formats, and the nationalist discourse of indigenization.[9] Furthermore, cultural mixing and adaptation has also been active among East Asian media cultures, especially in terms of the influences of Hong Kong, Japanese, and, more recently, South Korean media cultures. And this trend has become even more conspicuous with the development of trans-Asia media culture connections. Remaking of popular TV dramas and films of other parts of East Asia are frequently made and Japanese comic series are often adapted for TV dramas and films outside Japan.[10] The analysis of the dynamic processes of inter-textual reworking and inter-Asian cultural adaptation as well as East Asian negotiation with American media culture will intriguingly generate a new perspective to the notion of mixing, localization, and hybridization.

Mutual study and learning from other Asian experiences are not just beneficial to the production of knowledge but has also become an integral part of people's mundane practices in East Asia via the consumption of media cultures such as TV dramas, pop music and films. As media cultures of various places regularly cross the national boundaries in East Asia, a sense of cultural resonance among people in the region has been generated. Mediated encounters with other Asian modernities make many people in East Asia mutually appreciate how common experiences of modernization, urbanization, Westernization, and globalization are similarly and differently experienced in other East Asian contexts and realize that they now inhabit the same developmental time zone with other parts of East Asia. Accordingly, people have much wider repertoire for self-reflexivity rethinking their own lives, socio-political issues and self-other perception.[11] Inter-Asian media culture connections thus work as a great opportunity for many people to critically review the state of their own culture, society, and historical relationship with other parts of Asia. It can be argued that mutual referencing via East Asian media cultures has significantly brought about cross-border dialogue in the sense that it encourages people to critically and self-reflexively reconsider one's own life, society, and culture as well as socio-historically constituted relations and perceptions with others. This emerging landscape of people's mundane experiences of mutual referencing is resonant with Takeuchi Yoshimi's eye-opening surprise that he perceived when he first visited China. Takeuchi was then very impressed by his observation that people's thinking, feeling, and experiences in China looked very familiar (and different) to those in Japan as both shared a catch-up positioning and mentality of developmental temporality vis-à-vis Western counterparts. This experience made him realize that he had only compared Japanese experiences with Euro-American counterparts and urged him to explore the idea of "Asia as method." I would suggest that a similar sense of excitement has also driven academic research on media culture connections in East Asia, but researchers, including myself, have also realized, and avidly documented and interpreted, how mutual referencing of other Asian experiences is a historic opportunity of engendering people's cross-border dialogue as mundane practices.

As power configurations of cultural globalization are constantly shifting, on-going collaborative examination of how uneven globalization processes interfere with media culture connections in East Asia is essential. Although critical studies have dealt with media representations and expressions of queer culture, race, ethnicity, region, class, migrants, and diaspora in a national context, the study of media culture connections has not sufficiently attended to whether and how these hitherto marginalized voices have been crossing borders. Researchers of trans-East-Asian media culture are required to critically examine whether and how transnationally circulating media cultures represent cultural differences, inequality, and marginalization of each nation, and how, if any, they are received in other parts of East Asia. Furthermore, recently we are witnessing the growing trends that suppress or discourage dialogic potentials of cross-border media and culture flows and connections such as pragmatic uses of media culture for narrowly defined national interest as is shown by soft power and nation branding that work to discourage the fostering of diversity in society and the promotion of cross-border dialogue.[12] Also has become conspicuous a vicious circle of jingoism and nationalism in East Asia.[13] In this context, researchers also need to examine what kinds of mutual understanding and exchange are mainly promoted if any and whose voices and which issues are not well attended to in the newly developed mediated connectivity across East Asia.

PROMOTION OF CROSS-BORDER COLLABORATION: TRANS-EAST-ASIA MULTICULTURALISM

Since my relocation back to Australia in 2012 as director of Monash Asia Institute, the research-centered position has enabled me to even more actively facilitating trans-Asia approaches together with researchers within and outside university. I have been organizing a regular seminar series of "Trans-Asia as method" with an aim to facilitate mutual referencing on globally shared socio-cultural issues. I have also been organizing international conferences and publishing edited volumes based on them.[14] At the same time, I have also become more devoted to the promotion of cross-border dialogue and collaboration by involving diverse non-academic social actors as well as researchers. It is based on my conviction that if we take seriously the potential of trans-Asia connections to facilitate cross-border dialogue, researchers themselves need to take up the role of activating and coordinating the dialogue and collaboration across divides and borders, which is also an important objective of trans-Asia as method projects as mentioned earlier. One such collaborative project is "Trans-East-Asia Multiculturalism" (TEAM), which concerns trans-Asia human mobility and accompanying multicultural situations and cultural diversity in East Asian societies such as Japan, South Korea, Taiwan and Hong Kong.[15]

The first decade of the twenty-first century has witnessed the profusion of multicultural policies and discourses in East Asian countries, which have historically identified themselves as more "ethnically homogenous" than most other countries in the world. While these societies have not yet developed a comprehensive, consistent policy on migration and multiculturalism, the increasing number of migrants they have accepted and the intensifying cultural diversity that accompanies this transition has already become important socio-cultural issues they are faced with. In addition to a problematic legacy of the Japanese imperial project, Japan, South Korea, and Taiwan share an experience of inter-Asian migration in the process of ethno-cultural globalization since the late 1980s. In these three countries—in addition to their own indigenous or long-term racial and ethnic minorities—the number of foreign national residents, migrants, and people of mixed heritage has risen notably in the last two to three decades. Although none of the governments welcomed migrants with open arms, the influx of laborers and international marriage migrants has been observed, primarily from China and Southeast Asia. More recently, due to the sharply declining birth rate and the rapidly aging population, with a strong push from domestic industrial sectors, governments in Japan, South Korea, and Taiwan have begun to discuss under what conditions migrants should be accepted and what policies should be implemented.[16] While Hong Kong as an ex-colony of the Britain has a different historical trajectory, four societies share the advancement of multiculturalism from below in the absence of a well-established policy of multiculturalism and social cohesion with growing multicultural interactions and the impacts of cultural diversity on the fabric of societies.

One aim of TEAM is to add relevant voices from the experiences of South Korea, Japan, Taiwan, and Hong Kong to our understanding of multiculturalism as a set of policies, discourses, and mundane practices that manage, negotiate with, and embrace growing human mobility and the accompanying cultural diversity—a field that has developed primarily in Euro-American and Australian contexts. Researchers collaboratively examine the growing multicultural encounters, the accompanying policy discussions and racialized discourses on cultural diversity, as well as the processes of political and cultural negotiation that the marginalized newcomers and old-comers are drawn into. Organizing seminars and collaborative projects, researchers have learned much from common and different experiences in East Asia. As was the case with trans-Asian media culture connections, East Asian mutual referencing on trans-Asia human mobility and accompanying cultural diversity gives a new light in which the situation of the local can be reviewed and a new vision and aspiration for collaboration beyond the constraint of national governance. Taking a trans-East-Asian comparative and collaborative approach to examining emergent multicultural situations in Japan, South Korea, Taiwan, and Hong Kong, researchers have been consciously making reference to and compare domestic situations with other East Asian cases as well as to situate their cases in a wider, transnational context. TEAM project also aims to denationalize the discussion of multiculturalism as a policy and discourse for managing cultural diversity within the nation-state from trans-Asia perspective and engagement. A trans-East-Asia perspective is significant as it elucidates the shared-ness and the "similarity-in-difference" when examining multicultural issues in Japan, South Korea, Taiwan, and Hong Kong as it endows us with fresh insights into the multicultural issues in a more transnationally informed sense. Denationalized exploration of multicultural issues engenders a better understanding of both the possibilities and limitations of multicultural policies, discourses, and practices as they have been addressed by national policymakers, local communities, nongovernmental organizations (NGOs), nonprofit organizations (NPOs), civic organizations, and the migrant subjects themselves in East Asian societies.

Furthermore, TEAM project will also aim to facilitate cross-border collaboration and dialogue in order to empower migrant and ethnic minority youth and supporting NGOs/NPOs and citizens' groups, which have been playing a significant role in advancing multicultural questions by promoting cultural and artistic expressions of migrants' stories. With an aim to get various social actors learn from each other and collaborate to mutually develop their activities, we have been organizing an annual event called "EthniCities: Embracing Cultural Diversity in East Asia" since 2016 by inviting migrant/ethnic minority filmmakers, singers, and performers, and the NGOs and NPOs that support their activities and organize film festivals in each society. In this event, researchers self-consciously play a role of coordinator to facilitate dialogue and collaboration between diverse social actors. Many participants were excited to know similar but different experiences in other East Asian societies as it encouraged them to have a refreshing perspective on multicultural activities they have been engaged in and inspired them to do something meaningful together with other East Asian fellows. While there are many issues to be resolved such as funding, how to make collaboration sustainable, and how to get wider publics involved, TEAM project creates precious occasions in which various social actors exchange experiences and ideas about how grassroots action in local space can effectively challenge exclusionary politics of the nation-state, new partnership, and cross-border collaborative projects are created, and researchers learn by action how they can play a coordinating role in facilitating dialogues across borders and divides.

Chapter 1

SITUATING AUSTRALIA IN TRANS-ASIA MOBILITIES AND CONNECTIONS

As mentioned earlier, trans-Asia as method projects also complicate existing regional boundaries. Being currently located in Australia, I have been engaging with the projects of de-compartmentalizing an Australian–Asia binary and reimagining Australia as part of trans-Asia ethno-cultural mobilities and connections. The study of Asian regions in Australia like other Western countries has tended to be compartmentalized as a study of "over there," which is apt to be dissociated from the local context of Australia and have no substantial dialogue with general theoretical and conceptual issues of various disciplines whose research is domestic-oriented. In a globalized world, many issues are shared, though diversely articulated according to local contexts, and required to be transnationally and collaboratively tackled. Thus, the study of Asian socio-cultural issues would much benefit for the consideration of Australian counterparts. This point is especially pertinent to the study of Asia in Australia since Australia is geographically part of a wider Asian region and trans-Asian human mobilities, and cultural connections are even more seriously constitutive of Australian society than other Euro-American societies.

In Australia, the necessity to cultivate "Asia literacy and capability" has been long discussed but has attracted renewed attention since late 2012, when the then government published the "Australia in the Asian Century" white paper. It emphasized the significance of enhancing "Asia literacy" to "seize the opportunities that will flow from the Asian century" and proposed to implement the cross-curriculum priority of "Asia and Australia's engagement with Asia" as well as Asian languages educated at Australian schools. An apparent problem with the notion of Asia literacy is an underlying assumption that dichotomizes Asia and Australia. Asia literacy represents a lingering Orientalist desire to know and control the Asian other, which has been historically constituted in Australia. The hitherto dominant conception of Australia's relationship to Asia can be explicated in terms of "in but not of" in double senses as is the case with Japan.[17] Australia is regarded as geographically located in the periphery of the Asian (and Pacific) region, which gives Australia advantage as well as the sense of threat. However, the social and cultural legacy of the UK and the durable identification with the West daunts the development of the sense of belonging to the region and Asia has been perceived as clearly demarcated other. The government's pursuit of Australia's engagement with Asia has accompanied a reminder that "Australia is not, and can never be, an Asian nation" (a statement made by then prime minister, Paul Keating in 1993) and "Australia does not need to choose between its history [and culture] and its geography" (1997 Foreign Policy White Paper when John Howard was prime minister). Currently the overt rise of economic power of many Asian countries has put an instrumentalist rationale more in foreground to exploit the given opportunity of the Asian century to the maximum for Australia is, unlike other Western countries, luckily located adjacent to Asia.

The conception of "Australia being in but not of Asia" works in tandem with that of "Asia being in but not of Australia." Apart from economic partnership, cultural influences of Asian countries and the noticeable presence of migrants and diaspora from the region actually comprise significant parts of the Australian society. However, such "Asian" presence is not generally conceived as part of Australian society. The interplay of the two "in but not of" imaginations is requisite for the construction of an Asia–Australia binary but it has been becoming more noticeable that a clearly demarcated dichotomy of Australia and Asia does not match the material realities and mundane experiences in contemporary Australian society where "Asia" has been inseparably composing everyday life through intensifying cross-border mobility and interconnections. If we are to take "Asia literacy and capability" positively and seriously, "Australia" needs to be reimagined as part of Asia networks and commons so as to generate cross-regional conversation over globally shared issues.

Toward this objective, I have been undertaking projects that situate Australia in trans-Asian human mobilities and cultural flows and connections to reconceptualize "Australia" in terms of its relation to Asia's presence of linkage as constitutive of Australian society. One collaborative project examines media culture flows connections in terms of co-production and consumption.[18] It is a kind of advancement of my previous study of East Asian media culture connections. We have been interviewing with media producers and consumers in Australia to explore what kinds of Asia–Australia connections have been forged, how the relationship between Asia and Australia has been conceived, and whether and how any perception of Australia as part of Asia or Asia as part of Australia has been held by them. Another project I have been engaged with is "migrant diplomacy," which promotes exchange and dialogue between Immigration Museum in Melbourne and related museums, organizations, and artists in Japan. This project aims to facilitate Australia–Japan mutual learning on a significant role of museum in fostering diversity and inclusion through cultural and artistic projects in the age of hypermobility. The project organizes exchange and builds up collaborative relations between Immigration Museum in Melbourne and Immigration Museum Tokyo (pilot project), whose establishment was inspired by the former and other related people and institutions, Tokyo Metropolitan Art Museum, and the city of Hamamatsu and Nagoya, which are major multicultural cities in Japan. While various kinds of Australia–Japan bilateral relationship have been developed, this project innovatively enhances it in terms of the presence and experience of embracing migration and fostering diversity in both countries. It will contribute to increased awareness and dialogue of two countries facing the same issue of growing human mobilities and diversity inclusion, though to different extents, and the significance of mutual collaborative engagement in the embracing of them in society. It will contribute to enhancing our understanding of Australia and Japan on common ground of trans-Asian human mobilities rather than highlighting the difference between the two, hence complicating the existing conception of Australia–Japan relations. It also offers a new insight into the notion of public diplomacy, which tends to promote exchange between people and culture in the mainstream. Highlighting the exchange between migrants and ethnically marginalized people, "migrant diplomacy" makes their presence and experience in society as representative of the country and the engagement with the shared issue of diversity inclusion as the key agenda of international exchange. It, like TEAM project, also denationalizes the issue of fostering diversity, creates an opportunity that various social subjects collaborate across borders, and advances researchers' role to facilitate cross-border dialogue and collaboration.

TOWARD THE PROMOTION OF CROSS-BORDER DIALOGUE AND COLLABORATION

My project of trans-Asia as method can be defined by four "de-" terms— "de-" not as negation but productive and innovative advancement of the existing situations by critically interrogating them: de-Westernization via mutual referencing of Asian experiences; de-compartmentalizing "Asia" beyond West–Asia binary and beyond clearly separated national-cultural entities; denationalized perspective, exchange, engagement; and de-academicized role of researchers to promote exchange and collaboration. Combining them together, trans-Asia as method projects would facilitate the innovative knowledge production and cross-border dialogue to actualize a vital meaning of "trans," that is "advancing to alternative state of things."

Toward this objective, researchers are required to engage with a reciprocal and collaborative engagement with the issues concerned with an aim to enhance scholarly exchange among researchers working on diverse locations and grasp the issues as transnationally shared ones to be tackled together. What is also required for researchers is making more attentive exploration of the already existing critical thoughts and practices at the grassroots. Researchers need to work hard to communicate with people inside and outside of academia to convey in intelligible words the relevance of the advancement of imagination, connection, and dialogue, which transgress existing borders and divides to people's lives. Closely related to this, researchers are required to pursue the active role in creating public spaces and opportunities in order to activate the dialogues of and mutual learning among diverse social actors across various divides, which include governments, the mass media, NGOs/NPOs, citizen activists, and individuals concerned. As translators of critical knowledge, researchers can serve an important function in the instituting of a dialogic learning process in society in which diverse citizens personally and collectively transform themselves and foster alternative views of the self-other, the nation, and the world.

Trans-East-Asia as method project transnationally extends our commitment to the local by taking East Asian connection as a tactical focal point. As such, with a cosmopolitan scope and relevance, it collaboratively seeks after the enhancement of a sense of shared-ness and togetherness across borders. In the world of intense digitalized communication and interconnection, so many issues and diverse voices are "sharable but not necessarily or inevitably shared."[19] To tackle globally shared issues such as the impact of intensifying transnational ethno-cultural flows and growing cultural diversity, and the rise of jingoism and racism, learning from the experiences of other cultures and societies, and conversing over transnationally common issues is required more than ever. Trans-Asia as method is a tactical call to all researchers of/on Asian regions to pursue radical potentials of cross-border dialogue and cooperative practice by working with nonacademic social actors for it will be meaningfully achieved only by forming transnational collaborations across borders.

NOTES

1. Chen Kuan-Hsing, *Asia as Method: Toward Deimperialization* (Durham, NC: Duke University Press, 2010), xv.

2. Chua Beng Huat, "Conceptualization and Inter-Referencing," paper presented at ELLAK (English Language and Literature Association of Korea) International Conference, Onyang, Korea, December 18, 2011.

3. Koichi Iwabuchi, *Resilient Borders and Cultural Diversity: Internationalism, Brand Nationalism and Multiculturalism in Japan* (Lanham, MD: Lexington Books, 2015).

4. Chen, "'Asia' as Method," *Taiwan: A Radical Quarterly in Social Studies* 57 (2005): 141.

5. Iwabuchi, ed., "Houhou to shite no toransu ajia" (Trans-Asia as a Method) (in Japanese), in *Koeru bunka, kousaku suru kyoukai* (Transgressing Cultures and Intersecting Boundaries) (Tokyo: Yamakawa Shuppan, 2004), 3–24.

6. Sun Jung, *Korean Masculinities and Transcultural Consumption* (Hong Kong: Hong Kong University Press, 2011).

7. Chua, "Conceptualization and Inter-Referencing."

8. For example, Paul S. N. Lee, "The Absorption and Indigenization of Foreign Media Cultures. A Study on a Cultural Meeting Point of the East and West: Hong Kong," *Asian Journal of Communication* 1, no. 2 (1991): 52–72; Iwabuchi, *Recentering Globalization: Popular Culture and Japanese Transnationalism* (Durham, NC: Duke University press, 2002); Doobo Shim, "Hybridity and the Rise of Korean Popular Culture in Asia," *Media, Culture & Society* 28, no. 1 (2006): 25–44.

9. Iwabuchi, *Recentering Globalization*; Younghan Cho, "Desperately Seeking East Asia Amidst the Popularity of South Korean Pop Culture in Asia," *Cultural Studies* 25, no. 3 (2011): 383–404.

10. A prominent example is *Meteor Garden* (*Liuxing Huayuan*), a Taiwanese TV drama series that adopts Japanese comic series.

11. For example, Chua and Iwabuchi eds., *East Asian Pop Culture: Approaching the Korean Wave* (Hong Kong: Hong Kong University Press, 2008); Iwabuchi, *Recentering Globalization*; Iwabuchi, "Houhou to shite no toransu ajia"; Youna Kim, ed., *Media Consumption and Everyday Life in Asia* (New York: Routledge, 2008).

12. Iwabuchi, *Resilient Borders*.

13. See Iwabuchi, "Introverted Jingoism in a Post-Imagined-Community Digital Era: The Upswing of Hate Speech Demonstration in Japan," in *Precarious Belongings: Affect and Nationalism in Asia*, eds. Chih-Ming Wang and Daniel P. S. Goh (London: Rowman & Littlefield International, 2017), 39–55; Chih-Ming Wang and Daniel P. S. Goh, eds., *Precarious Belongings: Affect and Nationalism in Asia* (London: Rowman & Littlefield International, 2017).

14. For example, Iwabuchi, Kim Hyun Mee, and Hsiao-Chuan Hsia, eds., *Multiculturalism in East Asia: A Transnational Exploration of Japan, South Korea and Taiwan* (London: Rowman & Littlefield International, 2016); Dan Black, Olivia Khoo and Iwabuchi, eds., *Contemporary Culture and Media in Asia* (London: Rowman & Littlefield International, 2016); Wang and Goh, *Precarious Belongings*.

15. Key collaborators are Kim Hyun Mee, Hsiao-Chuan Hsia, Yuko Kawai, and John Erni.

16. See Iwabuchi, Kim, and Hsia, *Multiculturalism*.

17. Iwabuchi, *Recentering Globalization*.

18. Other investigators are Olivia Khoo, Fran Martin and Audrey Yue.

19. Roger Silverstone, "Media and Communication in a Globalized World," in *A Demanding World*, eds. Clive Barnette, Jennifer Robinson and Gillian Rose (Milton Keynes, UK: The Open University, 2006), 91.

BIBLIOGRAPHY

Black, Dan, Olivia Khoo, and Koichi Iwabuchi, eds. *Contemporary Culture and Media in Asia*. London: Rowman & Littlefield International, 2016.

Chen, Kuan-Hsing. "'Asia' as Method." *Taiwan: A Radical Quarterly in Social Studies* 57 (2005): 139–218 (in Chinese with English abstract).

———. *Asia as Method: Toward Deimperialization*. Durham, NC: Duke University Press, 2010.

Cho, Younghan. "Desperately Seeking East Asia amidst the Popularity of South Korean Pop Culture in Asia." *Cultural Studies* 25, no. 3 (2011): 383–404.

Chua, Beng Huat. "Conceptualizing and Inter-Referencing." Paper presented at ELLAK (English Language and Literature Association of Korea) International Conference, Onyang, Korea. December 18, 2011.

Chua, Beng Huat, and Koichi Iwabuchi, eds. *East Asian Pop Culture: Approaching the Korean Wave*. Hong Kong: Hong Kong University Press, 2008.

Iwabuchi, Koichi. *Recentering Globalization: Popular Culture and Japanese Transnationalism*. Durham, NC: Duke University Press, 2002.

———, ed. "Houhou to shite no toransu ajia" (Trans-Asia as a Method) (in Japanese). In *Koeru bunka kousaku suru kyoukai* (Transgressing Cultures and Intersecting Boundaries), 3–24. Tokyo: Yamakawa Shuppan, 2004.

———, ed. *Feeling Asian Modernities: Transnational Consumption of Japanese TV Dramas*. Hong Kong: Hong Kong University Press, 2004.

———. *Resilient Borders and Cultural Diversity: Internationalism, Brand Nationalism and Multiculturalism in Japan*. Lanham, MD: Lexington Books, 2015.

———. "Introverted Jingoism in a Post-Imagined-Community Digital Era: The Upswing of Hate Speech Demonstration in Japan." In *Precarious Belongings: Affect and Nationalism in Asia*, edited by Chih-Ming Wang and Daniel PS Goh, 39–55. London: Rowman & Littlefield International, 2017.

Iwabuchi, Koichi, Kim Hyun Mee, and Hsiao-Chuan Hsia, eds. *Multiculturalism in East Asia: A Transnational Exploration of Japan, South Korea and Taiwan*. London: Rowman & Littlefield International, 2016.

Jung, Sun. *Korean Masculinities and Transcultural Consumption*. Hong Kong: Hong Kong University Press, 2011.

Kim, Youna, ed. *Media Consumption and Everyday Life in Asia*. New York: Routledge, 2008.

Lee, Paul S. N. "The Absorption and Indigenization of Foreign Media Cultures. A Study on a Cultural Meeting Point of the East and West: Hong Kong." *Asian Journal of Communication* 1, no. 2 (1991): 52–72.

Shim, Doobo. "Hybridity and the Rise of Korean Popular Culture in Asia." *Media, Culture & Society* 28, no. 1 (2006): 25–44.

Silverstone, Roger. "Media and Communication in a Globalized World." In *A Demanding World*, edited by Clive Barnette, Jennifer Robinson, and Gillian Rose, 55–103. Milton Keynes: The Open University, 2006.

Takeuchi, Yoshimi. "Asia as Method." In *What Is Modernity? Writings of Takeuchi Yoshimi*, edited and translated by Richard F. Calichman, 149–166. New York: Columbia University Press, 2005.

Wang, Chih-Ming, and Daniel P.S. Goh, eds. *Precarious Belongings: Affect and Nationalism in Asia*. London: Rowman & Littlefield International, 2017.

Chapter 2

What is the "Trans" in Trans-Asia?

Yiu Fai Chow and Jeroen de Kloet

INTRODUCTION

When we were making the first draft of this chapter, we were in Beijing. Allow us to cite an incident which, we hope, will serve as a preamble of what to follow. To us, it is a reminder not only of the urgency of any project that seeks to unsettle the dominant mechanism of knowledge production; it is also a call to re-enter such projects for passion, politics and—prefixes. This we understand as pre-fixing, that is, not as an attempt to fix, define, mark boundaries, but as an occasion to loosen up, to thrust forward. We do it by way of the trans-Asia project.

First, Beijing, spring 2017. We were advised to come early, as the room should be quickly full. Indeed, shortly after we arrived, all seats were taken, mostly by young Chinese students waiting to hear Bruno Latour speak. In his lecture, he tracked his intellectual development from the 1970s onwards, in a style that also characterises his writing: witty, erudite and full of anecdotes. Toward the end of his talk, that was regularly interrupted by failing technology, Latour explained the reasons for his current tour around different places in the world: he wants to compare how different nations reacted differently to the concept of modernity. His aim, judging from the title of his talk in Shanghai a few days before Beijing, is "Resetting Modernity in Different Countries: An Exercise in Philosophical Diplomacy, Europe x China." It was at this point that we started to feel alienated by his words. Europe, he claimed, is in a crisis, especially now that the U.S. has gone astray with Trump, so what we need is a different version of a modernizing country, like China, with its completely different history and cosmology. This may help to reset modernity. As Latour writes in the notes[1] preceding the Shanghai event:

> It is clear that since every nation is faced with the contradiction between modernisation and the state of the planet, all of them are also interested in a resetting of its modernizing project. Therefore the possibility exists of comparing how different nations cope with a similar situation. The comparison is even more interesting since historically, every country has reacted differently to the concept of modernity. In spite of its apparent universality, there is nothing more historically contingent than the complex and varied cultural entanglements with what is now called "globalisation." In a way, nothing is less "global" than globalisation.

China, he claims, is a logical choice to explore the possibilities for such a resetting of modernity.

> Starting with China was an obvious choice. More than any other country, China is simultaneously the most deeply engaged in rapid modernisation, while also being the most explicitly aware of the contradiction between this project and its material and physical basis. While in other countries this contradiction can still be ignored or denied, it is official policy in China to recognise such an incongruence and to tackle it head on.

Interestingly, the word "diplomatic" was used to refer to this cross-cultural encounter:

> The way we wish to proceed similarly twins diplomatic encounters: two parties explore each other's interests and intentions, while remaining partially in the dark about their counterpart's customs and manners . . . Our goal is . . . to trigger enough interest amongst the fictitious Chinese delegation that they begin to build their own version of a project to reset modernity, with their own procedures and documentation. Given the completely different histories of modernisation in Europe and China, it would be absurd to expect any similarity in the conclusions.

But who sets the terms for this diplomatic encounter? Who speaks, and who listens, and who is forced to listen? As philosopher Gunnar Skirbekk rightly remarks, "the idea that one discipline—the Latourian version of anthropology—could be able to provide the (one and only) adequate conceptual overview of the whole of the modern world, with its plurality of values, activities and institutions, and of all the other disciplines with their various perspectives and insights, is both naive and arrogant."[2]

While cultural studies commits itself to challenging any cultural adjective, steering away from the state sanctioned ideas about the alleged uniqueness and singularity of that thing called "Chinese culture," in Latour's talk, a cultural exceptionalism returned full force, one that is mapped firmly on the nation-state, leaving us behind both astonished as well as angered. The "white man" returns to the East, this time not to extract and capitalize on its natural resources, but rather asking for spiritual input as to enable a resetting of modernity in the Anthropocene—a term featuring quite prominently in his current work, yet a term conspicuously absent from the Chinese debates.[3] His words bewildered us, in their essentializing implications, once again the West is the West, and the East the East, and never the twain shall meet. Even more problematic, his words resonate with the Party line, in which a Chinese exceptionalism is mobilized to justify a vigilant nationalism, not to mention ideas surrounding human rights and democracy. When Jeroen de Kloet posted his doubts about this position on Facebook, China scholar Ralph Litzinger responded, "this idea that China is somehow outside of European modernity, or has its own unique form of modernity rooted in centuries of tradition is hogwash, ahistorical, and plays right into the hands of a kind of Chinese nationalist script of an inscrutable 'Chinese' difference."

It is this retreat or revival of cultural essentialism conflated with methodological nationalism and yet ensconced in the grand narrative of modernities in the plural, that triggers our move toward examining trans-Asia as a potentially transnational and transgressive approach. That we attended Latour's talk in Beijing underwrites our research concern and investigation sites in Asia at large; that we were disturbed by Latour's diplomatic take guides us to seek paths not taken toward that version of conversation. Our starting point is that a transnational, or better: trans-Asian, approach as discussed in this book, holds the potential to think beyond the confines of the nation-state, an aim that resonates with the general zeal of the inter-Asia cultural studies movement. But what does this *trans* signify? In what way is it (not) different from the *inter*? What boundaries does it ask us to cross, and which boundaries are rendered less significant, or assumed crossed? And do we aspire diplomatic transnational encounters, or something more daring, something less polite?

In this chapter, we will first re-enter the trans-Asia approach with the prefixes *de*, *inter*, and *trans*, and we do so along discussions from transnational, transdisciplinary and transgender and gender studies. We draw on two of our ethnographic research projects: female migrants in China entering the city of Shanghai; and Hong Kong creative workers relocated to Beijing and Shanghai. They inspire our reflection on three different prefixes: the prefix *de*, which resonates with trans, and that we hope to also locate *within* the boundaries of the nation-state, the prefix *inter*, that we want to disentangle from either discipline or nation and instead align to intersectional feminism, and, finally, the notion of *trans*, that we read primarily in terms of transformation. As a final disquieting note, we conclude, via a detour to Europe, with a quite recent (not exclusively) trans-Asian project: the One Belt One Road (*yidai yilu*) programme initiated by China.

PREFIXING ASIA

Informed, or perhaps intrigued, by our encounter with Latour's project of diplomatic encounter, we alert ourselves to the seduction of critical sophistication and the reduction of empirical simplicity. We alert ourselves to how incredible and easy to move from one end to the other. It is with this reminder that we revisit the trans-Asia project. We do so by way of the prefixes. To repeat, our intention is not to fix what this Trans-Asia is but to pre-fix.[4]

De:Nation

The first is "de." When Chen Kuan-Hsing reconceptualizes Asia as method, his project is towards deimperialisation, which is the subtitle of his influential book. He contextualizes and explicates the project in conjunction with the processes of de-cold-war and decolonization. In the chapter devoted specifically to this problematic of "deimperialisation," Chen critically investigates the case of Club 51 whereby a group of Taiwanese intellectuals and entrepreneurs instigated action to promote Taiwan to become the 51st state of the United States. There, Chen warns of the danger of "old anticolonial nationalist and nativist positions" and "globalist positions"[5]—understood as the danger of Taiwan's dependency on the United States and American imperialism—and the approach he proposes toward deimperialization is by mobilizing experiences of different nations, or, for our discussion here, transnationally or trans-Asianly, which functions as a conceptual and methodological tool for denationalization at the same time. Trans is de. As he writes, "One effect of neoliberal globalization, however, has been regionalization, and I believe that regionalization may afford a means to move beyond earlier failed attempts to counter real strength."[6]

In the call for papers to form a conference which laid the groundwork for this anthology, one of the four intertwining patterns of trans-Asian approaches listed is "transnational & de-nationalised approaches." Here, we cite from the extended CFP:

> In a globalised world, so many issues have been shared among Asian countries (and beyond). The conference will explore transnational and de-nationalised perspectives through which we can better understand and engage with globally shared issues, which are commonly and differently articulated in a particular place. We will also consider the lessons, relevance and implications of Asian experiences to other parts of the world and vice versa.[7]

This text is underwritten by a similar logic of using trans as de. We understand the approaches that foreground experiences among various Asian nations and beyond in order to interrogate and relegate "nationhood" hopefully to a location less prone to exclusion, oppression and violence. We understand and stand by such politics and practices. At the same time, we also want to flag the inherent danger of parochialism, a danger that haunts both the inter-Asia cultural studies movement as well as the Asia as Method paradigm, a danger that is now transported from the nation towards the region.[8]

What we want to do is to add: to add the nationalizing potentials of projects that do not comfortably sit within the transnational or trans-Asian framework. From our empirical experiences—we are thinking particularly on projects that are squarely within national boundaries and yet potentially denationalizing—there is a need to loosen up the kind of methodological nationalism lynchpinning what we relayed earlier in connection with Latour's diplomatic encounter project. Yiu Fai Chow has done empirical work on creative class mobility, whereby he studies creative workers who moved from Hong Kong to Shanghai or Beijing.[9] While these three cities are "technically" of the same nation of China, the creative workers in this inquiry recount their stories vividly in the cultural differences they experienced in the transition. Largely functioning as diaspora, or living on the margins, of Cultural China, these Hong Kong subjectivities embody and evince the question of center, and thus questioning the center. These personal stories destabilize the grand national narrative precisely by their intra-national locations.[10]

Another project, supervised by Jeroen de Kloet, studies female migrant workers in the city of Shanghai. The researcher, Penn Tsz Ting Ip, includes people working in beauty salons, working as *ayi*—that is, domestic helpers—and she visits their homes, walks with them, asking for their dreams of the future.[11] Taken as a whole, their stories lay bare a city which is very different from the urban, cosmopolitan Shanghai not only in dominant imagination stirred by the nexus of state and capital, but also in everyday life experiences by many people living in Shanghai itself. The urbanites tend to glide past the migrant workers. In this project, it is not even China as a nation that is subject to duress, but Shanghai the city that threatens to fracture into various experiential worlds.[12] Again, this is a study about people who have not crossed any national borders, and yet are nationalizing.

In short, the desire to move beyond the confines of the nation-state seems to support a research agenda that validates comparative, trans-Asian research projects. Not only do such projects run the danger of remaining grounded in a methodological nationalism in tandem with a regional parochialism,[13] they also tend to sidetrack the potentials of denational approaches that are quite firmly positioned within the nation-state. To paraphrase Prajensit Duara,[14] there is a need to rescue inter-Asian cultural studies from the nation *as well as* the region, so as to allow for multiple narratives and methodologies, and to steer away from the overcoding machineries of area studies.[15] Our first pre-fixing appeal is to constantly interrogate the tendency if not practice of trans-Asia research projects and approaches to align themselves nationally or regionally and thus reify the nation and the region; we propose to rally under the rubrics of trans-Asia more and more diverse attempts that defy frontier-making of the nation and the region, unsettle such nationalism and regionalism, and examine trans-Asia problematics precisely from another, non-geopolitical optic. The following section proposes one of them.

Inter:Section

These two projects we just cited bring us to another prefix: inter. While this prefix dominates in notions revolving around intensification of academic cooperation between disciplines—the interdisciplinary approach, as well in connection to geopolitics—an international approach, we want to draw in particular insights from intersectional perspectives from feminist studies. As summarised by Leslie McCall, "Interest in intersectionality arose out of a critique of gender-based and race-based research for failing to account for lived experience at neglected points of intersection—ones that tended to reflect multiple subordinate locations as opposed to dominant or mixed locations."[16] The thrust of McCall's formulation is to "uncover the differences and complexities of experience embodied in that location [that intersects multiple categories]."[17] It is this anxiety of missing out the differences and complexities of experiences that configures some of the transnational feminist scholarship. Hence, staying sensitive to intersectional experiences and issues is the imperative raised by scholars in transnational feminist studies who, among others, see the danger of nation-to-nation studies with their accent on "nationhood" eliding feminist concerns.[18] We take this up to reiterate the anxiety of reducing complexities, and raise the appeal to situate inquiries in multiple subordinate locations, that is intersectionally.[19] When transnational approaches seek to think beyond the confinement of nation-state or a region, say, Asia, geopolitics easily takes the front seat. In this drive, we believe we need not only to think beyond the geopolitical but also to intersect it with other loci of power. From the two projects cited for this chapter, we want to flag gender and class.

In Chow's investigation of creative class mobility, the starting point was the workers' movements across cultural contexts and boundaries, but politically within the nation. Premised on this national framing, if you like, the investigation recuperates experiences from these creative workers that must be understood from their professional selves and gendered selves. It is quite beyond the scope and the aim of this chapter to discuss in length what was actually going on with their lives in Shanghai and Beijing.[20] Suffice it to note that the precarity they reported and the tactics they developed lead to deliberations of class interests and struggles; in this case, the creative class or precariat, a neologism to foreground the precarity as experienced by a certain "working" class and the possibility of class consciousness emerging from such precaritisation.[21] On the other hand, especially female participants of the investigation articulated choices, difficulties and problems, whether at work or in terms of personal and love life, that are gender-specific and align with the politics of feminist and gender studies, such as glass ceiling, sexual harassment and motherhood.[22] In similar veins, Penn Ip's research on migrant women working in Shanghai is embedded not only in the crossings of the urban and the rural, but also in the intersections with gender and class. They put into relief the lives of certain populations in China who do not only live as Chinese but also as woman and as woman coming from disenfranchised backgrounds. Again, they necessitate another, different, set of intersectional lenses in the optic of the trans. In short, we are asking not to lose sight of the categories, practices and politics that transnational or trans-Asian approaches may render invisible, such as gender and class.

Trans:Formation

In his book on the central theme of cooperation, Richard Sennett[23] takes issue with what philosopher Bernard Williams calls "fetish of assertions."[24] We all want to assert, rather than listen. That is the problem of our time. While generally endorsing the need to listen carefully, Sennett distinguishes two kinds of conversations. First, the dialectic kind, where exchanges are made with the primary aim to arrive at some sort of common ground. Second, the dialogic kind, where a discussion does not resolve itself to any common ground; rather the trick is follow "irrelevant directions," and the goal is "to drive a conversation forward."[25] Sometimes, a dialogic conversation may be killed by speaking partners who are "too eager to respond, going wherever their subjects lead; [who] do not argue, [who] want to show that they are responsive, that they care."[26]

It is this dialogic conversation we want to gesture to, as a reply, first of all, to the diplomatic encounter as practiced by Latour, as partners conversing, rather than one learning from another. Secondly, while Sennett also favours this kind of conversation for another exercise of deliberation, we are attracted to the politics and practices of dialogic conversation fundamentally for one thing: its transformative potentials. When we look at the other kind of conversation, the dialectic kind, the two partners reach a common agreement. Indeed, they move, they transport, they transgress their respective original positions. "[Trans] connotes movement."[27] This is what the "trans" in transnational and trans-Asian studies or projects can and should do, to transgress.

Again, we do not disagree. Nonetheless, we are attracted to the dialogic conversation, for its emphasis on openness, curiosity, and unpredictability. As long as the conversations continue to develop, the speaking partners will do the same, to transform.

Extrapolating this line of thinking to the transnational and trans-Asian approaches we have been discussing, we want to add the transformative to the critical potentials of "trans" as far as such approaches take the form of dialogic conversation. It is here that our take on trans-Asian approaches distinguishes from other similar calls for dialogue, for instance, inter-Asian referencing. In his critique of the "continuing hegemony of Euro-American knowledge production," Koichi Iwabuchi takes issues with scholars working in Euro-American contexts as well as those in other contexts, holding them responsible for reproducing what Iwabuchi calls the "politics of not-listening."[28] While Iwabuchi's overarching intellectual pursuit has been of a trans-Asian kind, he elaborates in this article especially on inter-Asian referencing. In his words, inter-Asian referencing is not only about researchers inside and outside of the region to communicate with each other; it is also about "people's mundane practices of encountering Asian neighbours and making references to other Asian modernities."[29] Its primary concern is to take border-crossing dialogue and reciprocal listening seriously for the project of de-westernizing knowledge production. In so far as the project of inter-Asian referencing is an appeal for another alliance, another formation, its accent on the *formative* may be related to, but conceptually and politically more confined and specific than, what we consider the most thrilling of the trans-Asian approaches: the *transformative*.

We are surely not the first to thrust forward the transformative of the prefix "trans." A decade ago, for instance, feminist and sociologist Sabine Hark, when deliberating on "inter- and transdisciplinarity," notes that they "figure as prominent emblems of knowledge *formations* that understand themselves as critical, transformative, and transgressive of modern science, knowledge, and the order of academic disciplines"[30] (Hark 2007, emphasis added). A decade later, feminist and literary scholar Jessica Berman juxtaposes the transnational and the transgender, Jessica Berman argues, "[t]he transnational shares the oppositional valence of the prefix in such words as 'transgress' and 'transform.'"[31] It remains all the more surprising that the transgressive, the movement dimension, not the transformative, has become the key word or concept or politics that feeds to transnational approaches. Berman herself says later in her article, that "the 'trans' in 'transnational,' as I conceive it, serves to decentre the 'national tradition' as an object of inquiry."[32] But, decentring is more transgressing, crossing borders, all spatially oriented, not exactly the same as transforming, which is about time.

In her article, Hark traces the trajectory of inter- and transdisciplinarity in the field of knowledge production; she cautions that they have operated as buzzwords, or in her formulation, "magical sign" for "neoliberal market- and management-oriented reforms of Higher Education."[33] But Hark also reminds us of their "radical and transformative potentials." We are not yet ready to articulate what these potentials are. We start by distinguishing two paths. First, we take Iwabuchi's treatise on the film *Lost in Translation* where Iwabuchi draws readers' and viewers' attention to Tokyo's transformations in "transnational flows and connections."[34] Citing Robins, he calls them "disorienting transformations" as they imbricate on issues of migration, transnationalization, and multiculturalism, that "cannot be made sense of within the national mentality."[35] Hence, the first path we propose is for transnational and trans-Asian approaches to place such transformations under their analytic framework. Put differently, to listen, to understand what has been going on in time, in Asia, what has been under transformation, may be one of the goals of the transnational or trans-Asia project.

And we do not only listen, we converse. We do not only want to understand what has been under transformation, we also want to transform. That is to say, if transformation can be the subject of study, then the object of study can also be transformation. The second path, we gather, is reverting to the transformative, not only the transgressive, of the transnational. As shown by the two research projects—Chow's study on creative class mobility and Ip's study on migrant women workers—we have mobilized throughout this chapter, the transformations in China manifest themselves in issues concerning the nation, gender, and class, and we hasten to add, all writ small in our neoliberal time. Going back to the prefix, if we take transformation, figuratively or not, as trans-formation, our question becomes: what formations do we want to transform by the transnational: nation, Asia, gender, class, neoliberalism . . .? In so far as any formation is intricately connected with knowledge and power, any trans-formation is needed. There is no reason for us to prioritize or to map out a research agenda for trans-Asian projects that may become hegemonic and elide other politics. That said, given the accent on the geopolitics of trans-Asian approaches, we want to be persuaded by the two (and more related) studies, that issues stemming not so much from the geopolitical, but from the global—the neoliberal structure of our life—deserve to be foregrounded in research projects anchoring in Asian experiences, especially in this so-called Asian Century. Whichever nomenclature we adhere to—the precariat, cruel optimism, or state of insecurity[36]—perhaps one urgency in trans-Asian projects is to find out how a geopolitical project may inform global politics, what neoliberal formation should be transformed and how.

CONCLUSION

While the conference we cited and joined on trans-Asia is convened in Italy, and we have backgrounds in Amsterdam, it is all too tempting—and probably transformative in its own right—to conclude by making a geographical move Westwards. Kraftwerk's 1977 song "Trans Europe Express" celebrates the transnational utopian dream as materialized in a fast European railway system.[37] They sing, "Trans Europe Express, from station to station, back to Düsseldorf city, meet Iggy Pop and David Bowie." The illustrious people we might meet on our way are not the Brexit champion Theresa May or the Dutch anti-immigration politician Thierry Baudet, but rather, and more hopeful, David Bowie and Iggy Pop. But is that really the case? In Europe, the transnational is neither new nor achieved, the recent backlash as underlined by the Brexit gestures to its frailty. If we are to recuperate the transnational from a global rising xenophobia, a constant reiteration of assumed cultural, national and religious differences, we need to insist not so much on the transnational implications of the term, but rather on its transformative, if not utopian, appeal. And as testified by Europe, such dreams are all too often undermined by ideological undercurrents we wish to ignore. In short, we need to decouple the trans from the national.

A more recent example of yet another trans-utopian longing is the "One Belt One Road" initiative of China. The meeting in May 2017 turned the infamous Beijing sky once again blue; roads were decorated with slogans like "peace and cooperation and openness and inclusiveness mutual learning and mutual benefit." If we allow ourselves some more cynicism, we might even say that these words would somewhat match the agenda of cultural studies. We happened to drive by the conference place, located two hours north of Beijing, and made a stop. As is to be expected, security and surveillance dominated this new trans-Asia initiative; we were not allowed to enter the premises, nor to take any picture. Leaders from predominantly Asian countries were to discuss how to revive an Asian cooperation, as to prepare the world for the upcoming Asian century. Here, the transformation aspired for is a hegemonic project in its formation, one in which China clearly takes the center stage, as to secure its continuous economic growth, or, if you like, neoliberalism with Chinese characteristics. It aims to export its technologies, assets, and manpower, so as to build a new silk route. This route is not to be explored by Marco Polo, but should rather be travelled inversely, from the East to the West, transforming China into a new colonizer. Indeed, this trans-Asian initiative is still miles away from the project of decolonization and deimperialization; instead, it warns us for the dangers of transnational aspirations.

NOTES

1. Bruno Latour, "Resetting Modernity in Different Countries: An Exercise in Philosophical Diplomacy, Europe x China," keynote speech, workshop series "Reset Modernity! Shanghai Perspective" on May 4–7, 2017 at Shanghai Himalayas Museum, China, http://www.bruno-latour.fr/sites/default/files/downloads/P-17 9-CATALOGUE-SHANGAI-RM!.pdf.

2. Gunnar Skirbekk, "Bruno Latour's anthropology of the moderns: A reply to Maniglier," *Radical Philosophy* 189 (Jan/Feb 2015): 47. This leads Skirbekk to conclude: "Finally, we should respond to the decisive statement, made at the end of the book: 'If this test fails, if my readers do not feel better equipped to become sensitive to the experiences assembled here, if their attention is not directed toward the beings whose specifications differ in each case, then the affair is over' (Latour 2013, 477). On its own terms, the Latourian game is, for me, over. The case is closed."

3. By "white man," we do not only refer to a corporeal category of whiteness and maleness; we refer also to colonized subjects—be they black or yellow, men or women—having internalized certain Western-centric frame of mind, and donning, in Fanon's term, white masks (Fanon 1952/2008).

4. Here we deliberately circumvent detailed discussions on the common uses of the terms inter and trans, but the following summary of Manea et al. (2014, 138) is helpful here:

> Summing up, the following lexical sequences (i.e. prefixes and combining forms) define the overall picture of today's integrative and specialized system of human scientific knowledge and action:
>
> - inter- (a prefix meaning "between" or "among", as in international; or "together", "mutually", or "reciprocally", as in interdependent; interchange; so, such associations intersect or connect);
> - trans- (a prefix meaning: (1) "across", "beyond", "crossing", "on the other side", as in transoceanic, trans-Siberian, transatlantic; (2) "transcending", as in transubstantiation; (3) "transversely", as in transect; (4) "changing thoroughly", as in transliterate; so, such associations sum up or integrate);
> - multi (combining form meaning (1) "many" or "much", as in multiflorous, multimillion; (2) "more than one", as in multiparous; multistorey; so, such associations aggregate, combine all the perspectives, changing quality);
> - cross- (combining form meaning "action from one individual, group, etc., to another", as in cross-cultural, cross-fertilize, cross-reference; so, such associations generalize or translate).

5. Chen Kuan-Hsing, *Asia as Method: Toward Deimperialization* (Durham: Duke University Press, 2010), 165

6. Ibid., 209.

7. Koichi Iwabuchi, "Trans-Asia as method: Exploring new potentials of 'trans-Asian' approaches," call for papers, international conference on June 12–13, 2017 at Monash Asia Institute, Monash University, Prato Centre, Italy, July 28, 2016, http://artsonline.monash.edu.au/mai/trans-asia-as-method-exploring-new-potentials-of-trans-asian-approaches/.

8. And as also remarked by others (Tae 2014), within this Inter-Asian regionalism, power imbalances continue to thrive, some places, most notably East Asia and Singapore, are rendered more visible than others. In the words of Tae (2014, 498): "Looking over 13 volumes of Inter-Asia Cultural Studies, the particular histories and cultures of Taiwan, Korea, China, Japan, Hong Kong, and Okinawa are frequently examined. However, Indonesia, Turkey, Myanmar, Sri Lanka, Nepal, Mongolia, and Thailand rarely appear." Both Budianta (2010) and Chen (2010b) have also observed the urgency to engage with the less powerful countries.

9. Intrigued by a controversial commentary alleging alarmingly an exodus of talents from the culture circles of Hong Kong, Chow's project aims at recuperating subjective accounts of these creative migrants in the context of changing Sino-Hong Kong relationship and the so-called Rise of China. The primary remit of his project is to supplement existing scholarship on creative work and creative class mobility (RGC GRF project 259913).

10. Yiu Fai Chow, "Exploring creative class mobility: Hong Kong creative workers in Shanghai and Beijing," *Eurasian Geography and Economics* 58, no. 4 (2017): 361–385; "Hong Kong creative workers in mainland China: The aspirational, the precarious, and the ethical." *China Information* 31, no. 1 (2017): 1–20.

11. Tsz Ting Ip, "Female Migrant Workers Navigating the Service Economy in Shanghai: Home, Beauty, and the Stigma of Singlehood," PhD Diss., University of Amsterdam, 2018. Ip's project directs itself to rural migrant women working in Shanghai, drawing on their experiences as "low-end" service providers to explore their practices of home-making, their career aspirations and their general sense of being part of the modern world—all in connection with their solo living in the city. Ip's collection of case studies is part of a larger research project designed around the central concern of female singlehood in Shanghai and Delhi (HERA SINGLE project number 586, 2013–2016).

12. In this juncture, we would also like to note two supplementary disclaimers to our mobilization of Ip's project on Shanghai. First, we do not want to presume that the experience as reported and analyzed is or must be indicative of other urban experiences in contemporary China. Second, we are also aware that such experience of fragmentation and disjuncture is or can be a constituent of the imaginary of contemporary China itself, thus running the danger we precisely want to 014, 4–57.Cultural Studies. 17Asian referencing and beyond. European ds somewhat trans-Asian approaches: the transformative.t t ward off, namely nationalizing. Having noted that, we want to reiterate the primary goal of using Penn's project, to illustrate the potential of a city-based project to interrogate the nation.

13. See also Song Hwee Lim, "Is the trans- in transnational the trans- in transgender?" *New Cinemas: Journal of Contemporary Film* 5, no. 1 (2007): 39–52.

14. Prasenjit Duara, *Rescuing History from the Nation: Questioning Narratives of Modern China* (Chicago: University of Chicago Press, 1996).

15. While we agree with Chen that "Martin Heidegger was actually doing European studies, as were Michel Foucault, Piere Bourdieu and Jürgen Habermas" (2010a, 3), as European experiences were there system of reference, we also witness a privileging of geopolitics here, above other possible factors, among which gender, class and sexuality. While we support his subsequent call for humbleness, we are less sure about his disavowal of universalist assertions of theory as such. Being confronted time and

again with the question "but can you really use Foucault for China?" (a question driven by cultural exceptionalism, rather than Chen's deimperialism project), there remains a critical and above all productive edge to humble universalist theorizations.

16. Leslie McCall, "The Complexity of Intersectionality," *Signs: Journal of Women in Culture and Society* 30, no. 3 (2005): 1780.

17. Ibid., 1782.

18. H. J. Kim-Puri. "Conceptualizing Gender-Sexuality-State-Nation: An Introduction," *Gender and Society* 19, no. 2 (2005): 137–59.

19. See also above.

20. See Chow, "Exploring" and "Hong Kong."

21. Guy Standing, *The Precariat: The New Dangerous Class* (New York: Bloomsbury Academic, 2011).

22. Chow, "Hong Kong."

23. Richard Sennett. *Together: The Rituals, Pleasures and Politics of Cooperation* (New Haven: Yale University Press, 2012).

24. Bernard Williams, *Truth and Truthfulness: An Essay in Genealogy* (Princeton, NJ: Princeton University Press, 2002), 100.

25. Sennett, *Together*, 19–20.

26. Ibid., 20.

27. Pamela Caughie, "The Temporality of Modernist Life Writing in the Era of Transsexualism: Virginia Woolf's Orlando and Einar Wegener's Man Into Woman," *Modern Fiction Studies* 59, no. 3 (2013): 508.

28. Iwabuchi, "De-westernisation, inter-Asian referencing and beyond," *European Journal of Cultural Studies* 17, no. 1 (2014): 46.

29. Ibid., 47.

30. Sabine Hark, "Magical Sign. On the Politics of Inter- and Transdisciplinarity." *Graduate Journal of Social Science* 4, no. 2 (2007): 12–13. Emphasis added.

31. Jessica Berman, "Is the Trans in Transnational the Trans in Transgender?" *Modernism/modernity* 24, no. 2 (2017): 220.

32. Ibid.

33. Hark, "Magical Sign," 13.

34. Iwabuchi, "Lost in TransNation: Tokyo and the urban imaginary in the era of globalization." *Inter-Asia Cultural Studies* 9, no. 4 (2008): 554.

35. Kevin Robins, "To London: the city beyond the nation," in *British Cultural Studies: Geography, Nationality, and Identity*, eds. David Morley and Kevin Robins (Oxford: Oxford University Press, 2000), 486.

36. To cite but three of the treatises on the precaritization of our time, respectively, by Guy Standing (2011), Lauren Berlant (2011) and Isabell Lorey (2015).

37. See Ien Ang's reflection on trans-European flows in chapter 4.

BIBLIOGRAPHY

Berlant, Lauren. *Cruel Optimism.* Durham: Duke University Press, 2011.

Berman, Jessica. "Is the Trans in Transnational the Trans in Transgender?" *Modernism/modernity* 24, no. 2 (2017): 217–44.

Budianta, Melani. "Shifting the Geographies of Knowledge: The Unfinished Project of Inter-Asia Cultural Studies." *Inter-Asia Cultural Studies* 11, no. 2 (2010): 174–177.

Chen, Kuan-Hsing. *Asia as Method: Toward Deimperialization*. Durham: Duke University Press, 2010a.

———. "Living with Tensions: Notes on the Inter-Asia Movement." *Inter-Asia Cultural Studies* 11, no. 2 (2010b): 311–318.

Chow, Yiu Fai. "Hong Kong creative workers in mainland China: The aspirational, the precarious, and the ethical." *China Information* 31, no. 1 (2016): 1–20. DOI: 10.1177/0920203X16679063

———. "Exploring creative class mobility: Hong Kong creative workers in Shanghai and Beijing." *Eurasian Geography and Economics* 58, no. 4 (2017): 361–385.

Duara, Prasenjit. *Rescuing History from the Nation: Questioning Narratives of Modern China*. Chicago: University of Chicago Press, 1996.

Fanon, Frantz. *Black Skin, White Masks*. London: Pluto Press, 2008.

Hark, Sabine. "Magical Sign. On the Politics of Inter- and Transdisciplinarity." *Graduate Journal of Social Science* 4, no. 2 (2007): 11–33.

Ip, Tsz Ting. "Female Migrant Workers Navigating the Service Economy in Shanghai: Home, Beauty, and the Stigma of Singlehood." PhD Diss., University of Amsterdam, 2018.

Iwabuchi, Koichi. "Lost in TransNation: Tokyo and the urban imaginary in the era of globalization." *Inter-Asia Cultural Studies* 9, no. 4 (2008): 543–56.

———. "De-westernernization, inter-Asian referencing and beyond." *European Journal of Cultural Studies* 17, no. 1 (2014): 44–57.

———. "Trans-Asia as method: Exploring new potentials of 'trans-Asian' approaches." Call for papers. International conference on June 12–13, 2017 at Monash Asia Institute, Monash University, Prato Centre, Italy. July 28, 2016. http://artsonline. monash.edu.au/mai/trans-asia-as-method-exploring-new-potentials-of-trans-asian-approaches/.

Kim-Puri, H. J. "Conceptualizing Gender-Sexuality-State-Nation: An Introduction." *Gender and Society* 19, no. 2 (2005): 137–59.

Latour, Bruno. *An Inquiry into Modes of Existence: An Anthropology of the Moderns*. Translated by Catherine Porter. Cambridge MA: Harvard University Press, 2013.

———. "Resetting Modernity in Different Countries: An Exercise in Philosophical Diplomacy, Europe x China." Keynote speech. Workshop series "Reset Modernity! Shanghai Perspective" on May 4–7, 2017 at Shanghai Himalayas Museum, China. http://www.bruno-latour.fr/sites/default/files/downloads/P-17 9-CATALOGUE-SHANGAI-RM!.pdf.

Lim, Song Hwee. "Is the trans- in transnational the trans- in transgender?" *New Cinemas: Journal of Contemporary Film* 5, no. 1 (2007): 39–52.

Lorey, Isabell. *State of Insecurity: Government of the Precarious*. London: Verso, 2015.

Manea, Constantin, Gheorghe Săvoiu, Ion Iorga Siman, and Marian Țaicu. "Inter-, Trans- and Multidisciplinarity, and Some Ideas or Remarks on Cultural Tourism." *The Yearbook of the "Gh. Zane" Institute of Economic Researches* 23, no. 2 (2014): 133–142.

McCall, Leslie. "The Complexity of Intersectionality." *Signs: Journal of Women in Culture and Society* 30, no. 3 (2005): 1771–1800.

Robins, Kevin. "To London: the city beyond the nation." In *British Cultural Studies: Geography, Nationality, and Identity*, edited by David Morley and Kevin Robins, 473–493. Oxford: Oxford University Press, 2000.

Sennett, Richard. *Together: The Rituals, Pleasures and Politics of Cooperation*. New Haven: Yale University Press, 2012.

Skirbekk, Gunnar. "Bruno Latour's anthropology of the moderns: A reply to Maniglier." *Radical Philosophy* 189 (Jan/Feb 2015): 45–47.

Standing, Guy. *The Precariat: The New Dangerous Class*. New York: Bloomsbury Academic, 2011.

Tae, Heasook. "From inter-Asia studies toward tricontinental studies." *Inter-Asia Cultural Studies* 15, no. 4 (2014): 498–512.

Williams, Bernard. *Truth and Truthfulness: An Essay in Genealogy*. Princeton, NJ: Princeton University Press, 2002.

Chapter 3

Transcending Trans-Asia?
Lessons from Trans-Europe

Ien Ang

In invoking the idea of trans-Asia as a method, this book aims to promote a bundle of approaches or perspectives designed to generate innovative knowledge through "intellectual dialogue beyond country, region and discipline."[1] This is an ambitious aim and, I would argue, a more complex one than it seems. Following on from the two previous chapters by Iwabuchi and by Chow and de Kloet, this chapter will continue the task of conceptual ground clearing by exploring some of the difficulties and ambiguities related to the notion of trans-Asia or trans-Asian, so that we can develop a clearer idea of what is at stake—conceptually and politically—in our search for effective "trans-Asian" approaches. These difficulties and ambiguities pertain to both components of the idea of trans-Asia, namely, "trans" and "Asia" (or "Asian"). In relation to the prefix "trans," the conceptual and political issues are, as I will show, best highlighted by juxtaposing it with the competing prefix "pan"—as in "pan-Asia" or "pan-Asian." In relation to the idea of "Asia" (or "Asian") itself, I will discuss the complexities and contradictions of deploying it through a detour to an equivalent, but arguably much more developed idea, both discursively and existentially, namely that of "Europe." Thus, my aim here is to examine what we can learn from the context of Europe—and more specifically, "trans-Europe"—in our efforts to advance trans-Asian approaches to the study of Asia. In other words, what can the project of trans-Asia learn from trans-Europe?

In proposing this detour through Europe, I do not wish to suggest that the European situation can simply be transferred to Asia, or that, by posing trans-Europe as the model, trans-Asia is placed in a position of "catch up" to Europe. It is not my aim here to reproduce the old, colonial epistemological hierarchy, which is rightly abhorred by postcolonially minded Asian cultural studies scholars. As Chua Beng Huat has pointed out, the rise of Asia in the global capitalist era has been associated with a shift to inter-Asia (or intra-Asia) referencing in Asian studies, displacing the intellectual domination of the West by emphasizing the "uniqueness" of local Asian complexities, for the understanding of which European or Western realities are deemed irrelevant.[2] However, Chua argues that overemphasizing the uniqueness of Asia is also problematic, as it would ironically condemn knowledge of Asia to the fate of being "interesting" but ultimately irrelevant to locations outside Asia. He argues against the "provincialization of knowledge," stating instead that "the universalization of concepts is necessary if knowledge is to be communicated across spatial and cultural boundaries."[3] In other words, we should favor a cosmopolitan approach to knowledge, which adopts a global horizon in analyzing local or regional particularities.

In this regard, I argue that juxtaposing "Europe" and "Asia" (and their potential attachments to the prefixes of "trans," "pan," and "inter") can be potentially productive, even if we should avoid an uncritical application of European realities to Asian ones. Instead, I aim to bring trans-Europe and trans-Asia into conversation with one another as two equivalent but very different regional projects, both with enormous significance for the contemporary globalized world. At the same time, some issues we can identify in relation to the "trans" in the idea of trans-Europe point to universal processes and concepts, which are useful for us in understanding the difficulties and ambiguities related to the idea of trans-Asia.

WHAT'S IN A REGION?

In speaking about "Europe" or "Asia," we need to begin by problematizing the seemingly obvious: namely that Europe and Asia are both world regions. While some may understand this statement as a mere reflection of geographical fact, the very compartmentalization of the globe into distinct regions or continents—which conventionally include not just Europe and Asia, but also Africa, the Americas, and Oceania—is a discursive construct with significant impact in the politics and governance of global affairs and international relations in the modern world. For example, such a division of the world into regional (and underneath it, subregional) groupings is deployed in the United Nations geoscheme, developed by the United Nations Statistics Division, whereby countries are grouped together into geographical regions to facilitate the organization of statistical data in publications and databases.[4] However, the creators of this geoscheme expressly note that the assignment of countries to specific groupings "is for statistical convenience" only and "does not imply any assumption regarding political or other affiliation of countries."[5] This is an interesting proviso that points to a certain arbitrariness in the territorial demarcation of world regions. For example, a country such as Israel is grouped in the region of Asia in this scheme (and in the subregion of "west Asia"), but it has a complicated relationship to this regional assignment. With its problematic origin as a modern state established in the aftermath of the European Holocaust in the Second World War, Israel has much stronger ties with Europe than with the countries of Asia. On the other side of the globe, Australia is generally not categorized as an Asian country (but is counted as part of Oceania), but since the late twentieth century there has been a strong discourse in the country to talk up the perception that it is "part of Asia," motivated by economic as well as strategic considerations.[6] These examples demonstrate that what constitutes a region is not a given: its boundaries are not fixed, they can shift and are subject to contestation.

Although we speak about Europe and Asia as if they were natural territorial entities, then, they are labels that refer to global spatial zones with fuzzy, uncertain borders. Moreover, no region is a unitary, homogeneous space: inside a region (however demarcated) there are multiple differences and divisions, which can be more or less strictly upheld, and around which borders are variously maintained or eroded. We tend to think of regions as consisting of groupings of countries or nation-states (although there are many other territorial units within regions such as provinces or cities), which themselves are bounded by more or less secure borders. In other words, the issue of borders is crucial in our thinking about regions: both the borders around regions as wholes, and the multiple borders within regions. These borders are not simply lines on a map that serve to symbolically distinguish social forms and circumscribe cultural differences. Borders, according to Etienne Balibar, have a "world-configuring function," performing the demarcation "between distinct social exchanges and flows, between distinct rights, and so forth."[7] As Mezzadra and Neilson observe, in the contemporary globalized world borders are "finely tuned instruments for managing, calibrating, and governing global passages of people, money, and things."[8] At the same time, however, they also point to "the radically equivocal character of borders and their growing inability to trace a firm line between the inside and outside of territorial states."[9] It is by focusing on this instability and porosity of borders, I argue, that we can articulate an understanding of the epistemological affordances of the notion of trans-Asia, in juxtaposition with that of trans-Europe.

FROM "INTER-ASIA" TO "TRANS-ASIA"

This discussion of the constitutive role of borders in the configuration of regions enables us to distinguish between conceptions of "inter-Asia" and "trans-Asia," which have tended to be used interchangeably in recent scholarship. Although the ideas of "inter-Asia" and "trans-Asia" are certainly interrelated, however, from a methodological point of view there are subtle differences between the two. To be sure, both these conceptions assume "Asia" to be plural, made up of multiple territorial entities within its borders, usually (but not always and not unproblematically) equated with nation-states. Implicit in the idea of "inter-Asia," as in "inter-Asia referencing,"[10] is the consideration of different localities in Asia within a singular regional frame ("Asia"). Here, as Chua noted, "one location in Asia [uses] another as a reference point for its own ongoing social, economic and political governance."[11] Some examples provided by Chua are how Singapore is studying the public transport system of Hong Kong; Hyderabad is studying the infrastructure development of Shanghai; and Bangalore (or Bengaluru) is becoming a reference point for other cities aspiring to attract investment in high-tech industries. What is significant in this idea of inter-Asia frame of comparison is not just that Asia as a region (however one wants to demarcate its boundaries) consists of many different places (localities, cities, entire nation-states), but that each of these places—Singapore, Hong Kong, Shanghai, or India, China, Japan—are considered in their distinctiveness, each occupying their own separate territorial positioning within the region. Here, borders and boundaries (between places) remain unquestioned; in fact, they figure as the enabling markers that make comparison between places, and the illumination of similarities and differences between them, possible. In other words, what is important for inter-Asia is that there are many Asias; while linkages between them ("inter") are made through mutual referencing, each remains fixed in place.

The idea of trans-Asia, by contrast, is centrally predicated on the notion of border-crossing, transcending the fixity of different locations. According to the dictionary, the prefix "trans" is used to convey the meanings "across," "beyond," "through" or "traverse." In other words, it intrinsically signifies movement, travel, going from place to place. It is therefore not surprising that, when I googled the term "trans-Asia" (with or without dash), the few references that emerged were all to transport companies. In the 1990s, an airline in Kazakhstan (in West Asia) was called Trans-Asia Air, while in Taiwan (in East Asia) Transasia Airways operated until 2006, on both domestic and international routes, focused mainly on Southeast and Northeast Asia and cross-strait flights to Mainland China. In the world of shipping, Trans Asia Line, based in Cochin, India, provides shipping services between ports in South Asia and the Middle East.[12] At the same time, another shipping company with a slightly different name, Trans-Asia Shipping Lines, is based in the Philippines, which has existed since 1974.[13]

According to its website, Trans-Asia Shipping Lines has played a key role in the development of trade between several Filipino cities by providing the means of transportation between them. It has also developed several ports in the archipelago, which are now centers of economic activity. Thus, what the company most prides itself of is "route development," that is, the establishment of linkages between places, which form the basis for economic growth and prosperity. As it says: "We sail to different destinations to improve island economies through excellent sea transport." The company transports both cargo and passengers.[14]

Here, the name "Trans-Asia" evokes the productive impact of mobility and moving "across": it resonates with the common fact that the development of transport infrastructure—which links disparate places hitherto separate from each other—has been central for economic development throughout the history of capitalist modernity in the West. For example, the development of rail transport using the steam locomotive in nineteenth-century England was crucial for the Industrial Revolution there (and would have contributed to the expansionist drive of British imperialism), and the enormous building boom of railroads in that same century to connect new territories of the United States was essentially driven by capitalist entrepreneurs.[15] Importantly, transport systems have also been fundamental vehicles in the enactment of European colonial expansion, whether it was through seafaring or, later, through the building of railroads.[16]

What is important to stress here is that in spatial terms, "trans" involves the dynamic transcendence of specific places in favor of their interconnection; in this sense, the concept of "trans" is fundamentally associated with border-crossing and border-eroding mobility.[17] It overhauls a static notion of place or space, and instead underlines the routes and trajectories flowing and circulating through space or territory, transcending borders and boundaries along the way. Consequently, the space of "trans-Asia" can be characterized as what Manuel Castells has called a "space of flows." As Castells put it: "the space of flows . . . links up distant locales around shared functions and meanings on the basis of electronic circuits and fast transportation corridors, while isolating and subduing the logic of experience in the space of places."[18]

However, it is equally important to stress that while the space of flows transcends the space of places, it cannot be separated from it. The website of the Filipino Trans-Asia Shipping Lines provides us with a map of all the ports serviced and linked by the company's ships (see figure 3.1).

As we can see from this map, the sea routes of this company link specific, named places, which are all places (port cities) in the Philippines. As a country the Philippines is an archipelago, a bundle of islands, which can only become a cohesive territory through inter-island transport (by sea or air). The role played by the shipping company is thus not only that of connecting places through the development of viable routes, but—in a literal, physical way—of nation building: that is, of producing the territorial space of the

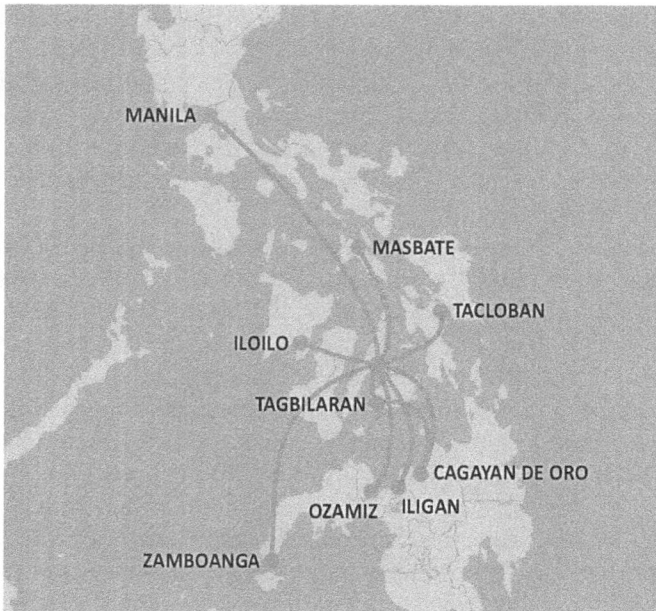

Figure 3.1.   Ports and routes of the Trans-Asia Shipping Line.

nation as a unified whole by interconnecting its disparate parts. In this sense, "trans"-nation (going across the nation) results in "pan"-nation (uniting the nation). In this regard, the name of this company, Trans-Asia Shipping Lines, is a misnomer: it should have been called Trans-Philippines Shipping Lines.

Of course, the project of trans-Asia is not focused on the nation; on the contrary, it aims to go beyond it and transcend—and from a critical point of view, problematize—the nation as a self-sufficient space. As Koichi Iwabuchi (chapter 1, in this volume) points out, a key focus of trans-Asia approaches is "the study of trans-Asia flows and connections of capital, people and media culture in Asia" and "how the intensification of cross-border cultural flows and human mobilities have been newly engendering trans-local dialogues, connection, association, rivalry and antagonism in Asian . . . contexts." He also stresses the importance of "transnationally shared issues [which] cannot be well dealt with by the existing framework of the nation-state." That is, the trans-Asian project is expressly transnational: it does not only bring different Asian nations in connection with each other, for example, through comparative inter-Asian referencing, but aims to go beyond individual nations to establish a perspective that is intrinsically deconstructive of (national) borders. Seen this way, Asia has to be imagined not so much as a borderless region, but a region where borders are constantly crossed and transcended, although never entirely dissolved. Asia here should be conceived as a trans-national space of flows, linking up, to paraphrase Castells, different localities and countries around shared functions, meanings, or even identities, while subduing or suppressing the experience of uniqueness in the space of local places. But would this "trans-Asia" (going across Asia) result in a "pan-Asia" (uniting Asia)? Would that even be possible or desirable?

"TRANS-EUROPE" AND "PAN-EUROPE"

To address this question, let me now turn to "Europe" as a counterpoint to "Asia." The case of Europe is interesting because its construction as a region goes beyond the realm of ideas and has been subject to sustained, real-world high-level politics and policymaking, represented today by the geopolitical reality of the European Union.[19] This political and economic union, which began with the establishment of a European Economic Community of six Western European nation-states (Belgium, France, Germany, Italy, Luxemburg, and The Netherlands) in the 1950s, has since expanded its boundaries beyond these foundation nations and as of 2019 consists of twenty-eight European countries, including ten former communist, Eastern European countries, who joined in 2004. The coming into being of this ambitious geopolitical regional unification was the work of some visionary European politicians, who, in the aftermath of the devastation of the Second World War, saw the establishment of a regional structure of cooperation and community-building as a way of preventing future wars and securing peace and prosperity for the region as a whole. In other words, the establishment of what is now the European Union was facilitated by a powerful foundation myth: that the unification of European countries economically and politically is an expression of the desire for peace.[20]

The word "union" in "European Union" (EU) articulates that what is envisaged here is the creation of a unified pan-Europe: individual nation-states are brought together in a kind of supra-national entity, integrated by a standardized system of laws that apply to all member states. The making of the EU is a work in progress, a continuing political and bureaucratic project: one aspect of this work has been the creation of a number of official symbols to signify a common European identity. These symbols include a European flag (a circle of twelve gold stars on a blue background, standing for the ideals of unity, solidarity, and harmony among the peoples of Europe), a European motto ("United in Diversity"), an annual Europe Day (May 9, to celebrate peace and unity), and a European anthem (Beethoven's "Ode to Joy"). All these official EU symbols are meant "to promote an image of Europe as strong, united and beneficial to all," but, as Johan Fornäs argues, they also point to tensions in the projection of a shared European identity: "One such tension runs between the strong hopes that shared symbols would strengthen the European project and their striking lack of success so far."[21] Indeed, there are no occasions when we can witness any enthusiastic waving of the European flag, and surveys have shown that awareness of Europe Day is almost nonexistent among European citizens. In other words, the making of Europe as an integrated regional entity, of "pan-Europe," is a protracted, contradictory, and incomplete process. In particular, the willful creation of a European identity—a common European imagined community—has proved to be strongly hampered by people's attachment to pre-existing national identifications: national identity, then, is a great obstacle to supra-national European integration.[22]

But the successful construction of a pan-Europe is not simply a matter of symbolic identification; more importantly, it depends strongly on enhancing the robustness of institutionalized trans-European interconnections; that is, the production of Europe as a space of flows. Throughout the years the EU has developed a whole range of policies and measures to stimulate such trans-European flows. Central to this is the construction of the EU as an internal single market, which refers to "the EU as one territory without any internal borders or other regulatory obstacles to the free movement of goods and services."[23] Underpinning this single market are what are the so-called four freedoms: the free movement of goods, services, capital, and persons. All member states of the EU are required, at least in principle, to guarantee to uphold all these four freedoms: to remove obstacles to ensure that goods, services, capital, and people can move around freely within the single market area.

Here we see the close connection between pan-Europe and trans-Europe: the free movement of goods, services, capital, and people (within the boundaries of pan-Europe as a single market) effectively encourages the dynamic development of trans-European routes and trajectories, thus linking disparate parts of Europe into an increasingly dense network of shared functions, meanings, and activities. In other words, trans-European flows are meant to eliminate barriers erected by national borders in the interest of smooth cross-border transactions and interactions across pan-European space. A crucial tool in this regard has been the introduction of a common currency, the euro, which came into existence in 1999 and began to circulate in 2002. As a symbol of European identity, a common currency is more forceful and practical than other symbols such as flag, anthem, motto, or day, because it literally enters into the daily lives of all citizens in countries where the currency has been introduced.[24] At the same time, the euro has an instrumental function in economic and financial management, facilitating trade in the trans-European Eurozone sphere by removing barriers such as exchange rate volatility. The European Commission mentions a diverse range of benefits of the euro, including more choice and stable prices for consumers, greater security, and more opportunities for businesses, more integrated financial markets, and a stronger presence for the EU in the global economy.[25]

However, as the tangible expression of an overarching European identity, the euro represents in a very direct way how the promotion of trans-European flow seeks to deconstruct national boundaries within pan-Europe. The euro replaced individual national currencies such as the German mark, the French franc, and the Italian lire, which had to cease operating as valid payment systems once these countries embraced the euro. Not all twenty-eight member states of the EU have accepted (or were allowed to participate in) this takeover of the national currency by a pan-European currency, designed to oil the easy trans-European flow of money. At present, the common currency is shared by nineteen countries, together forming the so-called Eurozone.

RESISTING TRANS-EUROPE, ENFORCING PAN-EUROPE

The United Kingdom was not one of these countries; instead, it chose to hold on to its own currency, the pound. Although reasons stated by the British government to opt out of the euro were mainly economic, the decision can be read more broadly as a declaration of national autonomy, in line with persistently large public opinion majorities who were against joining the euro, an expression of long-standing British Euroskepticism. Menno Spiering argues that this British Euroskepticism has a long cultural history: indeed, the British, or more specifically, the English, have long defined themselves as different from Europe.[26] For centuries, "Europe" and the Europeans functioned as the significant Other in the English quest for a national self. Toward the end of the nineteenth and beginning of the twentieth century, Britain was the most powerful nation in the world, commanding control over a vast global Empire. In this context, Britain did not need Europe. Feelings of detachment from Europe, enhanced by the geographical reality that Britain is an "island nation," were also intensified by historical events such as the Second World War, when Britain was the only European country that was not invaded by the Nazis. It sent its troops across the English Channel to help liberate, along with American, Canadian, Russian, and other Allied troops, the continent of Europe from Nazi occupation. This sense of separateness from Europe was an important reason why the United Kingdom resisted becoming part of an integrated Europe—that is, the EU—when it was first established in the 1950s. When it finally did, in 1973, it was to a large extent for economic reasons: joining the EU was a way of stopping its relative economic decline after the loss of its Empire.[27]

Indeed, economic historians agree that becoming part of pan-European space, the European single market, has contributed significantly to British prosperity by boosting trade, foreign direct investment, productivity, and innovation.[28] For example, EU membership has made it dramatically easier for companies to sell products without border checks within the European single market, where barriers to such trans-European trade have been removed through harmonization of regulations and a customs union. However, ambivalence toward being part of Europe has remained a strong strand of British attitudes, exemplified by the country's decision not to embrace the euro. The UK also opted out of the so-called Schengen Agreement, a landmark EU accord that enabled free travel for people across twenty-six European countries, which agreed to abolish passport and all other types of border control at their mutual borders.[29] In other words, although the UK did become a member of the EU—and thus incorporated itself into the pan-European space—it did not agree to abolish all borders between it and the rest of Europe, putting a significant break on the loosening up of trans-European flow.

More recently, a referendum in the country in June 2016, which resulted in a popular vote for Britain to leave the EU altogether, has set in train a complex process by which Britain aims to excise itself completely from the EU, a process which has come to be known as Brexit. Those who voted Leave (the EU) outnumbered those who voted Remain by 51.9 percent to 48.1 percent, signifying how divisive the issue has been in the country. One of the Leave campaign's most potent slogans was "Take back control of our borders," and it was squarely targeted at popular disquiet about one dimension of the four freedoms of European single market: the free movement of people. This EU principle stipulates that EU citizens from any country should have the right to live and work in any other EU country. In other words, free trans-European movement should not only apply to goods, but also to people. In the UK, this resulted in a significant increase of EU immigration, especially from East European countries who joined the EU in 2004. In 2015, 29 percent of EU immigrants into the UK were from Poland.[30] Many people were concerned that this influx of immigrants would lead to lower pay and less job opportunities for locals, and that they would make undue claims to welfare benefits. In fact, research has shown that such fears are unfounded: EU immigrants in the UK tended to be more educated, young, and more likely to be in work than their UK-born counterparts. They also pay more in taxes than they take out in welfare and use of public services, thus contributing to replenishing the financial coffers of the UK state. This research foreshadowed that a fall of EU immigration after Brexit would likely lead to lower living standards in the UK.[31] That such rational, evidence-based cost–benefit analysis tends to fall on deaf ears, however, suggests that concern about immigration—resulting from the principle of free movement of people—has more to do with social

and cultural fears than with economic anxieties.[32] More specifically, it resonates with the sentiment that the national culture is "under threat" due to the
influx of immigrants—from both inside and outside the EU—who are seen
as outsiders.[33] In this regard, the vote for Brexit was arguably at least in part
an act of xenophobic nationalism, motivated by a desire to keep the national
borders closed to foreigners. It was a vote to maintain Britishness as separate
from Europeanness—arguably to be attained by putting up obstacles to free
trans-European flow—despite evidence of the enormous economic benefits
of being part of the pan-European space that is the EU. The incongruous,
inconsistent nature of this desire was amply displayed by the utter paralysis
of the British government in deciding *how*—under which conditions and at
what cost—the country should cut its ties to the EU.

Sentiments against trans-European flow, especially when it concerns the
free flow of people, are not only apparent in Britain, but have also been rising in other European nation-states. But anti-immigrant feeling throughout
Europe has been fueled not so much by internal EU people flow, but by the
flow from outside pan-European space. This became clear particularly in the
fallout of the so-called refugee crisis that hit Europe in 2015, and continues to
this day, as asylum seekers fleeing war and poverty from the Middle East and
Africa keep attempting to enter Europe to seek refuge. While initially these
migrants were welcomed once they had arrived in the space of pan-Europe,
especially under the leadership of German Chancellor Angela Merkel, who
championed an open-border policy by welcoming hundreds of thousands of
refugees into Germany, a subsequent backlash saw several countries, especially in the Balkans and Central Europe, where migrants arriving through
Greece sought to find their path to the richer nations of northwestern Europe,
to erect barriers on their national borders to stem the free flow of migrants—
in direct contradiction with the core principle, ensconced in the Schengen
Agreement, of borderless trans-European passage across pan-European space
(see figure 3.2). Hungary, for example, dramatically used barbed wire fenc-
ing to block off its border with Serbia and Croatia, leaving thousands of
migrants stranded there. For the Hungarian prime minister Victor Orbán, the
goal was "to defend the borders [of Europe] and to control who is coming
in."[34] Fortified by a civilizational rhetoric that pits a Christian Europe against
Islam and Muslims, Orbán's hardline anti-immigration stance has gradually
become more influential across the EU and has helped shift the debate on
migration from a humanitarian stance (with an emphasis on accommodating
and integrating refugees and resettling them across the continent) to devising
measures to stop refugees from entering pan-European space at all.[35] That is,
what is proposed here is the creation of a "fortress Europe," a "gated continent" that keeps the non-European other out.[36] In Orbán's reasoning, it is only
by sealing the vast border around pan-Europe, a protectionist standpoint at

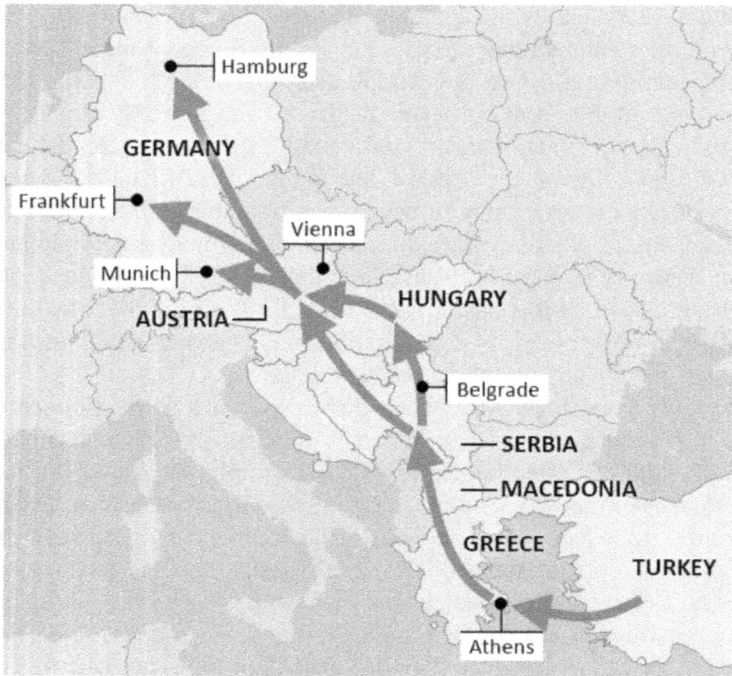

Figure 3.2.   Migrant routes through Europe (2016).

a regional scale that imposes a sharp demarcation line between Europe and non-Europe (and who does and does not belong to it), that the freedoms of trans-European flow (within the boundaries of pan-Europe) can be secured. "We would like to save the liberties . . . including the free movement inside the European Union," he says, by fixing and taking control of its porous external borders.[37] In other words, whereas in Britain debate has centered on whether it should belong to Europe, in Hungary its own belonging to Europe is not in question, but it wants to lock out those it considers outsiders to Europe. At the same time, as Europe as such becomes a magnet from the global poor and destitute—as shown in the continuing migrant crisis of the past few years—countries such as Hungary, but also others throughout Europe, are increasingly susceptible to populist, Euroskeptic political forces, who are defying the border-dissolving tendencies of the EU and wish to reassert national boundaries and identity.[38]

   This discussion of the geopolitical project of the EU shows that it involves a political imaginary that ties "trans-Europe" and "pan-Europe" closely together: trans-Europe can only be secured in a bounded "pan-Europe." Moreover, the politics of this project involves the constant negotiation and contestation of borders—sometimes aiming toward their erasure (such as in the Schengen Agreement), at other times focusing on their reinstatement (as in the Brexit case) or their reinforcement (as in calls to strengthen border patrols to prevent migrants from entering Europe at all). The rise of conservative nationalist populism in many countries in Europe today, as we have seen in both Britain and Hungary, exemplifies the complex politics related to "trans" in a regional context. In transcending borders, national or otherwise, the politics of trans-Europe is often favored for economic reasons, as it stimulates trade and prosperity, but it is simultaneously questioned culturally, because it deconstructs nationally bounded notions of place, identity, and (imagined) community. At the same time, the pursuit of unencumbered trans-European traffic within the EU is counterposed by a hardening of the borders around the regional space of pan-Europe, thereby producing—at least in the imagination—a clear demarcation between what is and what is not Europe.

The case of the EU illuminates that such struggles over borders are underscored by economic, political, and cultural dynamics that shape the fluctuating ways in which passages of people, money, and things throughout the region are managed, calibrated, and governed. So what can we learn from this detour through Europe for our considerations of "trans-Asia"?

TOWARD "TRANS-ASIA" AND BEYOND

Efforts to nurture trans-Asian approaches, as this volume seeks to do, are fundamentally focused on challenging the spatial boundedness of much knowledge and understanding of Asia. This bias toward spatial boundedness can occur at multiple scales. Most prominently, it takes place at the national scale, reproducing the methodological nationalism[39] that has been hegemonic in theory and research, including in cultural studies; but it can also occur at lower, subnational scales, such as those of cities. What the invocation of trans-Asia does not question, however, is the spatial boundedness associated with the notion of "Asia" itself. Indeed, a (strategic) essentialism at the regional scale is adopted here to pull together various studies and perspectives under the rubric of the trans-Asian project. In other words, we need to hold on to some idea of "Asia" as a whole—that is, of a virtual *pan*-Asia—in order to explore the possibilities of *trans*-Asian approaches.

This virtual pan-Asia, however, does not at present have its articulation in the real world of global geopolitics, unlike in the European context. The establishment of the EU (as the material institutionalization of the idea of pan-Europe) was made possible by the unique peculiarities of an historical moment, in a continent ravaged by the destructions of the Second World War, when the vision of a united, supra-national Europe took hold to avoid future conflict and secure peace and prosperity. In Asia, which was similarly devastated by the war, adverse political forces prevented the emergence of a similar pan-regional vision; instead, decolonizing struggles in different parts of Asia led to the prioritization of national sovereignty and nation-building as the key political project across the region. Even the establishment of the Association of Southeast Asian Nations (ASEAN), which can be described as a partial pan-Asian project, was based on a framework of regional cooperation aimed to strengthen, rather than weaken, the powers of the participating nation-states.[40] Meanwhile, regional visions have been persistently trumped by nationalist concerns in Northeast Asia, where Cold War politics, postcolonial resentment, and competitive international rivalry are more dominant in China, Japan, and (South) Korea than desires for mutual cooperation, let alone convergence.[41] In other words, throughout Asia the borders that matter most, and that continue to be most forcefully guarded, are national borders— a situation that is not offset, as has been the case in Europe, by the blurring of such national borders through the official enactment of an overarching, pan-regional border regime, within which trans-regional flow is facilitated. In this regard, the effort to nurture trans-Asian approaches acquires its *critical* purchase: it has to be pursued in the absence of a real-world pan-Asia.

At the same time, the European situation shows how problematic the transcendence of national borders is even in a context where free cross-border movement is legitimized and encouraged (mostly as a productive means of economic advancement). As the cases of Brexit and the European migration crisis demonstrate, opposition to such free movement is particularly intense when it concerns the flow of *people*. It is therefore in relation to transnational migration that the dismantling of borders is most vehemently resisted. Stronger still, it is against the perceived "invasion" of the nation by the migrant other that borders are either fortified or newly erected by states or, increasingly in Europe, by the supranational state of pan-Europe, the EU. Of course, this does not happen only in Europe; President Trump's wall along the U.S.– Mexico border is a case in point. In Asia, where trans-Asian labor migration has burgeoned in the past decades in an increasingly globalized economic world, policy arrangements between nation-states have enforced the obligatory return of migrants to their home countries after periods in another country, effectively nationalizing transnational mobility and naturalizing the strictly national belongingness of subjects.[42] The quest for trans-Asian approaches and perspectives has to argue persistently against such naturalized national boundaries and modes of identification, while recognizing that the divide of national selves and others is arguably the most difficult—and perhaps impossible—to break down.

Finally, the fact that a regionalized imagination does not only have a liberating potential by dissolving internal borders, but can also have exclusionary effects by tightening its external borders, is dramatically exposed by the "fortress model of border enforcement"[43] that is increasingly favored by the EU against asylum seekers from other, less affluent parts of the world, including Asia. This holds a last lesson for the critical pursuit of trans-Asian approaches: ultimately, such approaches will have to embrace not just trans-nationality, but also, eventually, trans-regionality: it has to go beyond the demarcation of "Asia" as the unquestioned orbit of discourse. That is, it has to transcend Asia itself.

NOTES

1. Koichi Iwabuchi, "Trans-Asia as Method: Exploring New Potentials of 'trans-Asian' Approaches," call for papers, international conference on June 12–13, 2017 at Monash Asia Institute, Monash University, Prato Centre, Italy, July 28, 2016, http://artsonline.monash.edu.au/mai/trans-asia-as-method-exploring-new-potentials-of-trans-asian-approaches/.

2. Chua Beng Huat, "Inter-Asia Referencing and Shifting Frames of Comparison," in *The Social Sciences in the Asian Century*, eds. Carol Johnson, Vera Mackie, and Tessa Morris-Suzuki (Canberra: ANU Press, 2015), 67–80.

3. Ibid., 78.

4. United Nations Statistics Division, "UNSD Statistical Databases," The United Nations Statistics Division of the Department of Economic and Social Affairs (DESA), https://unstats.un.org/unsd/databases.htm.

5. Ibid.

6. Ien Ang, "Australia, China and Asian Regionalism: Navigating Distant Proximity," *Amerasia Journal* 36, no. 2 (2010): 127–140.

7. Etienne Balibar, *Politics and the Other Scene* (London: Verso, 2002), 79.

8. Sandro Mezzadra and Brett Neilson, *Border as Method, or, the Multiplication of Labor* (Durham, NC and London: Duke University Press, 2013), 3.

9. Ibid., 7.

10. Chua, "Inter-Asia Referencing," Ananya Roy and Aihwa Ong, eds., *Worlding Cities: Asian Experiments and the Art of Being Global* (Chichester: Wiley-Blackwell, 2011).

11. Chua, "Inter-Asia Referencing," 78.

12. Trans Asia Group, "Home," tassgroup.com, accessed October 1, 2018, http://tassgroup.com/index.php?menu=Home.

13. Trans-Asia Shipping Lines Incorporated, "Today's Schedule," transasiashipping.com, accessed October 1, 2018, https://www.transasiashipping.com/.

14. Trans-Asia Shipping Lines Incorporated, "Destinations," transasiashipping.com, accessed October 1, 2018, http://www.transasiashipping.com/destinations.html.

15. Frank Dobbin, *Forging Industrial Policy: The United States, Britain, and France in the Railway Age* (Cambridge: Cambridge University Press, 1994); Ian Carter, *Railways and Culture in Britain: The Epitome of Modernity* (Manchester: Manchester

University Press, 2001); Matthew Beaumont and Michael Freeman, eds., *The Railway and Modernity: Time, Space and the Machine Ensemble* (Bern: Peter Lang, 2007); Richard White, *Railroaded: The Transcontinentals and the Making of Modern America* (New York & London: Norton, 2012).

16. Maria Fusaro, Bernard Allaire, Richard Blackmore, Tijl Vanneste, and Michael Dunford, eds., *Law, Labour, and Empire. Comparative Perspectives on Seafarers, c. 1500–1800* (Houndsmills: Palgrave Macmillan, 2015); Laxman D. Satya, "British Imperial Railways in Nineteenth Century South Asia," *Economic and Political Weekly* 43, no. 47 (2008): 69–77.

17. John Urry, *Mobilities* (Cambridge: Polity Press, 2007).

18. Manuel Castells, "Informationalism and the Network Society," in *The Hacker Ethic and the Spirit of the Information Age,* ed. Pekka Himanen (Random House, New York, 2001), 155.

19. John McCormick, *Understanding the European Union: A Concise Introduction*, 7th ed. (London: Palgrave Macmillan, 2017).

20. Johan Fornäs, *Signifying Europe* (Bristol: Intellect, 2012).

21. Ibid., 251.

22. Sean Carey, "Undivided Loyalties: Is National Identity an Obstacle to European Integration?" *European Union Politics* 3, no. 4 (2002): 387–413; Neil Fligstein, Alina Polyakova, and Wayne Sandholtz, "European Integration, Nationalism and European Identity," *Journal of Common Market Studies* 50, no. 1 (2012): 106–122.

23. European Commission, "The European Single Market," policies, information and services, accessed October 1, 2018, https://ec.europa.eu/growth/single-market_en.

24. Fornäs, *Signifying Europe*.

25. European Commission, "The Benefits of the Euro," policies, information and services, accessed October 1, 2018, https://ec.europa.eu/info/about-european-commi ssion/euro/benefits-euro_en.

26. Menno Spiering, *A Cultural History of British Euroscepticism* (Basingstoke: Palgrave Macmillan, 2015).

27. Nauro Campos and Fabrizio Coricelli, "Why Did Britain Join the EU? A New Insight from Economic History," *Vox*, CEPR Policy Portal, February 3, 2015, https://voxeu.org/article/britain-s-eu-membership-new-insight-economic-history.

28. Chris Giles, "What Has the EU Done for the UK?" *Financial Times*, March 31, 2017, https://www.ft.com/content/202a60c0-cfd8-11e5-831d-09f7778e7377.

29. Francesca Zampagni, "Unpacking the Schengen Visa Regime. A Study on Bureaucrats and Discretion in an Italian Consulate," *Journal of Borderland Studies* 31, no. 2 (2016): 251–266.

30. Jonathan Wadsworth, Swati Dhingra, Gianmarco Ottaviano, and John Van Reenen, *Brexit and the Impact of Immigration on the UK*, CEP Brexit Analysis No. 5, Centre for Economic Performance, London School of Economics and Political Science, May 2016, http://cep.lse.ac.uk/pubs/download/brexit05.pdf.

31. Ibid.

32. James Dennison and Andrew Geddes, "Brexit and the Perils of 'Europeanized' Migration," *Journal of European Public Policy* 25, no. 8 (2018): 1137–1153.

33. "Majority of Britons Think Minorities Threaten UK Culture, Report Says," *The Guardian*, May 25, 2017, https://www.theguardian.com/world/2017/may/25/majority-of-britons-think-minorities-threaten-uk-culture-report-says.

34. Matthew Kaminski, "All the Terrorists Are Migrants," *Politico*, December 2, 2015, https://www.politico.eu/article/viktor-orban-interview-terrorists-migrants-eu-russia-putin-borders-schengen/.

35. Angela Dewan, "Hungary's Orban Warns of Backlash against Immigration in European Parliament Vote," *CNN*, July, 28, 2018, https://edition.cnn.com/2018/07/28/europe/viktor-orban-hungary-european-parliament-intl/index.html.

36. Matthew Carr, *Fortress Europe: Dispatches from a Gated Continent* (New York: The New Press, 2016).

37. Kaminski, "All the Terrorists."

38. Robert Harmsen and Menno Spiering, eds., *Euroscepticism: Party Politics, National Identity and European Integration* (New York and Amsterdam: Brill, 2016).

39. Andreas Wimmer and Nina Glick Schiller, "Methodological Nationalism, the Social Sciences, and the Study of Migration: An Essay in Historical Epistemology," *The International Migration Review* 37, no. 3 (2003): 576–610.

40. Shaun Narine, "State Sovereignty, Political Legitimacy and Regional Institutionalism in the Asia-Pacific," *The Pacific Review* 17, no. 3 (2004): 423–450; Lee Jones, *ASEAN, Sovereignty and Intervention in Southeast Asia* (Houndsmills, UK: Palgrave Macmillan, 2012).

41. Samuel S. Kim, ed., *The International Relations of Northeast Asia* (Lanham, MD: Rowman & Littlefield, 2003); Chen Kuan-Hsing, *Asia as Method: Towards Deimperialization* (Durham, NC and London: Duke University Press, 2010).

42. Biao Xiang, "Return and the Reordering of Transnational Mobility in Asia," in *Return: Nationalizing Transnational Mobility in Asia*, eds. Xiang Biao, Brenda S. A. Yeoh, and Mika Toyota (Durham, NC and London: Duke University Press, 2013), 1–20.

43. Carr, *Fortress Europe*, 255.

BIBLIOGRAPHY

Ang, Ien. "Australia, China and Asian Regionalism: Navigating Distant Proximity." *Amerasia Journal* 36, no. 2 (2010): 127–140.

Balibar, Etienne. *Politics and the Other Scene*. London: Verso, 2002.

Beaumont, Matthew and Michael Freeman, eds. *The Railway and Modernity: Time, Space and the Machine Ensemble*. Bern: Peter Lang, 2007.

Campos, Nauro and Fabrizio Coricelli. "Why Did Britain Join the EU? A New Insight from Economic History." *Vox, CEPR Policy Portal*, February 3, 2015. https://voxeu.org/article/britain-s-eu-membership-new-insight-economic-history.

Carey, Sean. "Undivided Loyalties: Is National Identity an Obstacle to European Integration?" *European Union Politics* 3, no. 4 (2002): 387–413.

Carr, Matthew. *Fortress Europe: Dispatches from a Gated Continent*. New York: The New Press, 2016.

Carter, Ian. *Railways and Culture in Britain: The Epitome of Modernity*. Manchester: Manchester University Press, 2001.

Castells, Manuel. "Informationalism and the Network Society." In *The Hacker Ethic and the Spirit of the Information Age*, edited by Pekka Himanen, 155–178. Random House, New York, 2001.

Chen, Kuan-Hsing. *Asia as Method: Toward Deimperialization*. Durham, NC and London: Duke University Press, 2010.

Chua, Beng Huat. "Inter-Asia Referencing and Shifting Frames of Comparison." In *The Social Sciences in the Asian Century*, edited by Carol Johnson, Vera Mackie, and Tessa Morris-Suzuki, 67–80. Canberra: ANU Press, 2015.

Dennison, James, and Andrew Geddes. "Brexit and the Perils of 'Europeanized' Migration." *Journal of European Public Policy* 25, no. 8 (2018): 1137–1153.

Dewan, Angela. "Hungary's Orban Warns of Backlash against Immigration in European Parliament Vote." CNN, July 28, 2018. https://edition.cnn.com/2018/07/28/europe/viktor-orban-hungary-european-parliament-intl/index.html.

Dobbin, Frank. *Forging Industrial Policy: The United States, Britain, and France in the Railway Age*. Cambridge: Cambridge University Press, 1994.

European Commission. "The European Single Market." Policies, information and services. Accessed October 1, 2018. https://ec.europa.eu/growth/single-market_en.
———. "The Benefits of the Euro." Policies, information and services. Accessed October 1, 2018. https://ec.europa.eu/info/about-european-commission/euro/benefits-euro_en.

Fligstein, Neil, Alina Polyakova, and Wayne Sandholtz. "European Integration, Nationalism and European Identity." *Journal of Common Market Studies* 50, no. 1 (2012): 106–122.

Fornäs, Johan. *Signifying Europe*. Bristol: Intellect, 2012.

Fusaro, Maria, Bernard Allaire, Richard Blackmore, Tijl Vanneste, and Michael Dunford, eds. *Law, Labour, and Empire. Comparative Perspectives on Seafarers, c. 1500–1800*. Houndsmills: Palgrave Macmillan, 2015.

Giles, Chris. "What Has the EU Done for the UK?" *Financial Times*, March 31, 2017. https://www.ft.com/content/202a60c0-cfd8-11e5-831d-09f7778e7377.

Harmsen, Robert, and Menno Spiering, eds. *Euroscepticism: Party Politics, National Identity and European Integration*. New York and Amsterdam: Brill, 2016.

Iwabuchi, Koichi. "Trans-Asia as Method: Exploring New Potentials of 'trans-Asian' Approaches." Call for papers. International conference on June 12–13, 2017 at Monash Asia Institute, Monash University, Prato Centre, Italy. July 28, 2016. http://artsonline.monash.edu.au/mai/trans-asia-as-method-exploring-new-potentials-of-trans-asian-approaches/.

Jones, Lee. *ASEAN, Sovereignty and Intervention in Southeast Asia*. Houndsmills, UK: Palgrave Macmillan, 2012.

Kaminski, Matthew. "All the Terrorists Are Migrants." *Politico*, December 2, 2015. https://www.politico.eu/article/viktor-orban-interview-terrorists-migrants-eu-russia-putin-borders-schengen/.

Kim, Samuel S., ed. *The International Relations of Northeast Asia*. Lanham, MD: Rowman & Littlefield, 2003.

"Majority of Britons Think Minorities Threaten UK Culture, Report Says." *The Guardian*, May 25, 2017. https://www.theguardian.com/world/2017/may/25/majority-of-britons-think-minorities-threaten-uk-culture-report-says.

McCormick, John. *Understanding the European Union: A Concise Introduction*. 7th ed. London: Palgrave Macmillan, 2017.

Mezzadra, Sandro, and Brett Neilson. *Border as Method, or, the Multiplication of Labor*. Durham, NC and London: Duke University Press, 2013.

Narine, Shaun. "State Sovereignty, Political Legitimacy and Regional Institutionalism in the Asia-Pacific." *The Pacific Review* 17, no. 3 (2004): 423–450.

Roy, Ananya, and Aihwa Ong, eds. *Worlding Cities: Asian Experiments and the Art of Being Global*. Chichester: Wiley-Blackwell, 2011.

Satya, Laxman D. "British Imperial Railways in Nineteenth Century South Asia." *Economic and Political Weekly* 43, no. 47 (2008): 69–77.

Spiering, Menno. *A Cultural History of British Euroscepticism*. Basingstoke: Palgrave Macmillan, 2015.

Trans Asia Group. "Home." Tassgroup.com. Accessed October 1, 2018. http://tassgroup.com/index.php?menu=Home.

Trans-Asia Shipping Lines Incorporated. "Today's Schedule." Transasiashipping.com. Accessed October 1, 2018. https://www.transasiashipping.com/.

———. "Destinations." Transasiashipping.com. Accessed October 1, 2018. http://www.transasiashipping.com/destinations.html.

United Nations Statistics Division. "UNSD Statistical Databases." The United Nations Statistics Division of the Department of Economic and Social Affairs (DESA). https://unstats.un.org/unsd/databases.htm.

Urry, John. *Mobilities*. Cambridge: Polity Press, 2007.

Wadsworth, Jonathan, Swati Dhingra, Gianmarco Ottaviano, and John Van Reenen. *Brexit and the Impact of Immigration on the UK*. CEP Brexit Analysis No. 5. Centre for Economic Performance, London School of Economics and Political Science. May 2016. http://cep.lse.ac.uk/pubs/download/brexit05.pdf.

White, Richard. *Railroaded: The Transcontinentals and the Making of Modern America*. New York & London: Norton, 2012.

Wimmer, Andreas, and Nina Glick Schiller. "Methodological Nationalism, the Social Sciences, and the Study of Migration: An Essay in Historical Epistemology." *The International Migration Review* 37, no. 3 (2003): 576–610.

Xiang, Biao. "Return and the Reordering of Transnational Mobility in Asia." In *Return: Nationalizing Transnational Mobility in Asia*, edited by Xiang Biao, Brenda S. A. Yeoh, and Mika Toyota, 1–20. Durham, NC and London: Duke University Press, 2013.

Zampagni, Francesca. "Unpacking the Schengen Visa Regime. A Study on Bureaucrats and discretion in an Italian Consulate." *Journal of Borderland Studies* 31, no. 2 (2016): 251–266.

Chapter 4

Toward Asian Independence: The Transpacific and Inter-Asian Trajectories of Taraknath Das

Chih-Ming Wang

In August 2007, in preparation for revising my PhD dissertation into a book, I was leafing through *The Chinese Students' Monthly*, a periodical edited by and for Chinese students in the United States, published between 1905 and 1931.[1] I was utterly surprised—in fact, puzzled—to come across the name Taraknath Das, who published three articles in the *Monthly* on the following topics: "Asian Independence and World Peace" (1927), "Afghanistan in World Politics" (1928), and "The Political Future of India" (1930), topics that are gravely important but seemingly remote to the concerns of overseas Chinese students, then as today. Though the *Monthly* did have a wide coverage of interests and a vast network of contributors from Chinese students and scholars to American professors and politicians, it was still fairly unusual for a Chinese student publication to include works by an Indian scholar whose tie to the Chinese student circle seems tangential and even ungrounded. I cannot help wondering: How did Das tap into the Chinese student network in the United States in the early twentieth century? How did the Chinese students then perceive and understand the significance of his articles? In addition, how was his notion of "Asian independence" understood in his time and place, and what implications does it entail for us today? In the genealogies and networks of pan-Asianism in the early twentieth century, what place did Das occupy and what role did he play?

I feel compelled to begin my chapter with such a personal anecdote because Das, and the pan-Asianist lineage and minor transnational networks he represents, has a particular valence to the projects I have been engaging with: Asian American history and culture that began as a form of civil rights movement and posited a political identity based on the pan-ethnic vision of Asianism on the one hand, and the movement of inter-Asia cultural studies that takes decolonization in the realm of knowledge production as its primary task on the other. Both projects affirm a vision of independence couched in the discourse of justice and equality, and a future of decolonization for which Asia, and Asian identity, is but a means to, not an end of, political liberation. An Indian revolutionary in exile seeking to terminate the British rule in India and a civil rights activist in North America fighting against racial exclusion, Das represents a unique and precise combination of the two projects, linking at once decolonizing efforts in Asia to anti-racist campaigns in North America, and embodying a nexus of transpacific and inter-Asian trajectories which grounded Asianism in both the international order of the 1920s and the assertion of an ethnic and political identity in the 1960s. His connection with the Chinese student circle, moreover, demands a critical inquiry into the state of inter-Asian connections in the early twentieth century—through the civilizational discourses of Rabindranath Tagore and Okakura Tenshin, to the political visions of Sun Yat-Sen and Li Dazhao, and down to the devious circuits of Japanese imperialism, among others.[2] The puzzles around Das instruct me that not only such demarcations of Asian American studies, where he is regarded as an immigrant fighter,[3] and Asian studies, where he was deemed an Indian nationalist,[4] cannot adequately account for the complex history and politics that Das brought together. A critical investigation into the deep linkages that Das embodies between racial identity, imperial geopolitics, and diasporic attachments in the early twentieth century moreover presents us an opportunity for theorizing "trans-Asia as method" that Koichi Iwabuchi in this volume defines as a "tactical approach" to critically engage with the "transnational circulation of capital, people and culture and [the] uneven connections it engenders" to go "beyond a mutually exclusively demarcated understanding of region and nation," and to strive toward "an open and dialogical social relation" in and beyond Asia. As Das's story below will unveil, trans-Asia stands for "minor transnational" practices[5] that defy Western universalism by deviating from and rearticulating the global circuits it has created, to reclaim as well as reconfigure Asia in motion. But first, who is Taraknath Das?

THE TRANSPACIFIC FIGHT

According to Tapan K. Mukherjee (see Figure 4.1), Taraknath Das was born on June 15, 1884, in a lower-middle class family in a village north of Calcutta. He is the youngest of three siblings and since early on shows outstanding intellect and patriotism, as evinced in his essay on "Indian Universities, Present Educational System and Its Sustainability to the Indian People," which was written in response to Lord Curzon's plan to reform India's educational system in 1902, a plan that aimed at suppressing Indian nationalism by

Figure 4.1. Cover image of Taraknath Das's biography written by Tapan K. Mukherjee.

derecognizing and regulating _ndigenous institutions of learning.[6] The essay drew the attention of Bengali ɔarrister Pramathonath Mitra of Calcutta High Court who then recruited him into the original cadre of Anusilan Samiti, a gymnastic organization that trained students in wrestling, sword, and stick playing. Mukherjee indicates that the purpose of Anusilan Samiti was "to build a cell of physically strcng, brave young men who would eventually form the base of a disciplined and dedicated national liberation army"[7] and it soon evolved into a secret society dedicated to seeking freedom for India. Das became a core member and key organizer of Anusilan Samiti and plotted terrorist bombings against Curzon's plan to partition Bengal as announced in 1903, to support and expand the Swadeshi movement, which by protesting partition and boycotting foreign goods generated a national campaign for self-rule.[8]

Das was quickly put on the hunting list of the British India. Worrying that his revolutionary activities would put his family at risk, Das left for Japan in 1905. Japan had just won a war against Russia and immediately gained respect from fellow Asians suffering the yoke of white supremacy and Western imperialism. Impressed by Japan's victory, Das hoped to acquire advanced training in industrial technology there to modernize India, only to realize soon after his arrival that Japan is assisting the British to track him down. Unable to stay in Tokyo, Das decided to move again, this time to the United States. He landed in Seattle in July 1906 and then moved to San Francisco, where he enrolled in the University of California, Berkeley as a "special student" in the College of Chemistry. With a foothold in the Bay Area, Das began organizing the Hindu students there: he formed the California Hindu Students Association in Berkeley and established the Indian Independence League with Hindu laborers settled around San Francisco. He even started an evening school in Oakland to teach English and American history to Hindu laborers to help them apply for U.S. citizenship. Das himself applied for U.S. citizenship in 1906 but was rejected because the Bureau of Immigration and Naturalization ruled that Indians while belonging to the Caucasian race do not qualify as "white" and are thus ineligible for citizenship. Partly because of this rejection, and partly because of the racial riot in the U.S.-Canadian border affecting South Asian immigrants, Das went up to Vancouver in September 1907 to organize the Punjabi community there; within months he formed a Hindustani Association and started publishing in April 1908 *Free Hindustan* (see Figure 4.2), a bimonthly that in its subheading claims: "Resistance to tyranny is obedience to God."

The leading article of the inaugural issue is "A Strong Protest against British Injustice," which criticized the Canadian government's attempt to legalize exclusion of Indian immigration—enacted on April 10, 1908 in the name of "continuous journey regulation."[9] It argues that the Canadian exclusion laws against Indians would not only prevent Indians from entering Canada, but also cause the United States to follow suit. Besides pleading Indian leaders to take action against this legislation in Canada, this article challenges the Western standard of equality by pointing to white racist treatment against Asians, exemplifies the spirit of defiance, and underscores migration to British colonies as an inalienable right of Indians as *British* subjects. Such an emphasis on migration as the right of British subjects that was abrogated by racism and the inequality of British rule reveals the transpacific and trans-Asian nature of Das's activism. Besides designating the route of escape for Das, the transpacific here also connotes his deliberate endeavor to connect British imperialism in India with white supremacy in North America where exclusionary legalization made India a transpacific entity and South Asians—Sikh and Punjabi included—a trans-Asian figure of discrimination. Thus, the call for freedom, as espoused in the title of this leading article, is not only meant for South Asian laborers in Canada to safeguard their freedom to immigrate, but rather for the greater Indian community at home and abroad to demand liberation from the British rule. As Canadian secret agent Thomas McInnes rightly noted,

Figure 4.2. The inaugural issue of *The Free Hindustan*.

[*Free Hindustan*] is intended for whites to read. . . . Its object is to create the impressions among Canadians that there will be a serious danger to the Empire if Hindus are shut out of Canada as they are shut out of Australia. It seeks to make the government hesitate in any policy of exclusion or even restriction by threat of revolt in India.[10]

Das's effort to organize Indian diaspora and connect it to homeland politics was a typical move of Asian revolutionaries in the early twentieth century. Whereas the homeland was politically stifled by feudalism and imperialism, the diaspora was both a space of relative freedom and a site where political support for homeland freedom could be more easily organized. The freedom to immigration is not merely a token of justice but a ticket to safety and political activism. Like the Chinese revolution led by Sun Yat-sen from Honolulu, Tokyo, and Southeast Asia, the Indian diaspora had been a critical site for organizing and articulating national independence campaign—from Har

Dayal's Ghadar Party first formed in London to Subhash Bose's Indian Army based in Tokyo—linking demands for national liberation with transnational aspirations for migration as equal rights. Thus, fighting for immigration rights and organizing diasporic community was for Das a necessary first step.

As *Free Hindustan* was soon banned by the British Indian government, and the Canadian pressure to stifle his political activism increased, Das had to figure out other plans. In May 1907, he left Canada to enroll in the military college in Vermont, but after a year he was discharged from the college due to British pressure, and returned to the Seattle–Vancouver border to organize and work with the Sikh community there. In 1909 he started correspondence with Leo Tolstoy, using the letter form as an international medium to publicize British tyranny in India and to win international support, but the exchange was a hit and miss, because the nonresistance philosophy of the Russian sage crossed the revolutionary zeal of the young rebel who instead found the emerging Ghadar movement led by Hal Dayal, a beacon of hope.

Though Mukherjee argues[11] that "Das never joined the Party as a formal member,"[12] he was intimately associated with the Ghadar movement. Meaning revolt, the Ghadar movement encompassed a wide range of ideologies from nationalism to anarchism and socialism, but its call for an armed struggle against British India stitched together the vast Indian diaspora across the globe and inspired them to return home in 1915 to seek Indian liberation by force.[13] Taking the Revolt of 1857 as the predecessor of, and necessary path to, independence struggle, the Ghadar movement represents the radicalization of Indian nationalism that separated itself from the moderate approach led by the Congress Party.

With the Ghadar mutiny of 1915 ended in failure, Das and his fellow nationalists realized that their power was too small, compared to the British, and hence it would be vital to seek help from Britain's enemies. Germany that was at war with Britain in the First World War gave them great hope. In October 1914, a month before setting out for Germany, Das wrote an article published in *Sunset*, a prestigious California monthly, where he argues:

> It is evident that there is every possibility of having serious uprisings, if not a revolution, in India. Its success will depend upon many factors and most important of them are the successful German resistance against the allied force, and the attitude of Turkey towards Great Britain. If Germany, by diplomacy or any other means, can get Turkey to declare holy war against Great Britain, then in this juncture there will be uprisings in Egypt, Persia, and India where the Mohammedan population is over sixty million, and other parts of the Mohammedan world such as Algeria, Tripoli, and Morocco which will keep the Allies busy.[14]

This passage reveals two key elements in Das's revolutionary thinking at this stage: a keen interest in international politics as the analytical ground for seeking national liberation, and the hope that Pan-Islamism would create a trans-regional anti-British alliance.[15] While Pan-Islamism would soon be replaced by Pan-Asianism in his action and thinking, the imagination of a trans-regional, transracial, anti-imperial resistance—within and beyond Asia—based upon an understanding of international politics would become the signature of his work for many years to come.

THE INTER-ASIAN LINK

Frustrated with his work in Germany, Das returned to Japan in 1916 to work with Japanese intellectuals, including Tokutomi Iichiro and Okawa Shumei; but soon after, he went to China, first to Beijing, then Shanghai, to expand the Pan-Asiastic movement that Japanese had initiated. According to Mukherjee, in Shanghai, with the help of Japanese, Das formed the Oriental Ancient Literature Society with the hope of creating a library of Oriental philosophies and translating the philosophical texts into English.[16] These are interesting activities in and of themselves, but little is known about the society and its activities, and there is no evidence to indicate success or failure of the pan-Asiatic movement, except that Das managed to publish *Is Japan a Menace to Asia?* (see Figure 4.3) in Shanghai in 1917. This political pamphlet includes an introduction by Tang Shaoyi—the first prime minister of the newly established Republic of China—and a short piece by Tokutomi Iichiro, Japanese pan-Asianist who was later listed as a Class A criminal in the Tokyo Tribunal, in the appendix. It was later translated into Japanese by Okawa Shumei, a leading pan-Asianist in Japan who held a strong interest in Indian culture and history, but it was banned by the British. Mukherjee indicated that Das's main mission in East Asia was to "teach and preach the doctrine of Asia for Asiatics" and to form an organization with Indians, Chinese, and Japanese, hoping that "once the organization became strong it would be possible to send through the Yunnan province [of China], or even by sea route, anything that the revolutionaries needed in India."[17] As it is throughout his pan-Asianist career, Das always had Indian independence in mind.

It is important to consider the role of East Asia—namely, Japan and China—in the development of Das's pan-Asianism. With the exception of Thailand, China and Japan are the only two countries that were not fully colonized in Asia. While China was weak and vulnerable to colonial aggression, Japan was the beacon of hope. Whereas Chinese intellectuals and revolutionaries, such as Sun Yat-sen, sought assistance from Japan to reform and modernize China, Japanese intellectuals, such as Miyazaki Toten, also viewed China as the place for initiating global transformation. As fondly recalled in his memoir *Thirty Three Years of Dream*, Miyazaki himself not only aided but also participated in Sun Yat-sen's revolutionary activities in the 1900s because he believed that it was the path toward worldwide revolution.[18] Miyazaki wrote in his memoir that he chose China as the site for pursuing his ambition and joined China's revolution "as Chinese" because China is big and populous, and the call for revolution is urgent: "If I could replace them, or enable like-minded people to establish the foundations of a nation according to my ideals, and from there to command the world, my ambitions may perhaps be realized."[19] Miyazaki's words, while aiming to portray a sense of urgency or zeal for world revolution in his life, betrays a deep-seated imperial tendency in Japan's pan-Asianism which Das himself had to struggle with and eventually detach from.

Indeed, against his hope that Japan would cooperate with China and India to lead Asia toward political independence, Japan expedited its course to world domination by intensifying military aggression in China in the 1930s. *Is Japan a Menace to Asia?* was thus remembered as an ironical statement of pan-Asianism, given our hindsight of Japanese imperialism between the 1920s and 1940s.[20] Cemil Aydin points out that Das in an article submitted to *The New Asia*—a pan-Asianist journal established in 1939 and edited by Okawa Shumei—expressed dissatisfaction with Japan's effort for Asian solidarity and skepticism over the motivations behind Japan's "return to Asia" in the 1930s.[21] But in 1917, the world was still mired in war and shifting alliances with no clear signs of the future in sight, and Japan, thriving in the period of "Daisho democracy" (1912–1926), had yet to fully reveal its imperialist nature. That Das should have pinned his hope for Asian independence on Japan is not only understandable in his time and place, but also has a promissory quality that should be recuperated from our pessimistic hindsight.

Das's mission in Asia came to an abrupt end in the summer of 1917, because the U.S. government was hunting him down for his involvement with the Ghadar Party. He was given the option of running off to live a life of exile or returning to the United States to face the trial, and he determinedly took the latter option. The Hindu-German conspiracy trial, also known as the Ghadar Conspiracy trial, began on November 20, 1917, and Das was found guilty and sentenced to prison for twenty-two months. After released from prison, Das continued to work for the cause of Indian independence and began a scholarly career in Georgetown University, New York University, and Columbia University. After India gained its independence in 1947, Das twice visited India, but was deeply disappointed by it. He passed away in 1958, survived by his Caucasian wife, Mary Keatinge Morse, and the Taraknath Das Foundation at Columbia University dedicated to the educational exchange between India and the United States.[22]

DEFENSIVE REALISM: DAS'S PAN-ASIAN THINKING

As an activist and a scholar of international politics, Das wrote several pamphlets and books concerning Asia: *Isolation of Japan in World Politics* (1918), *Indian and World Politics* (1923), *Sovereign Rights of Indian Princes* (1924), *British Expansion in Tibet* (1927), *Foreign Policy in the Far East* (1936), and *The War Comes to India* (1942), to name a few major works. Of all his publications, *Is Japan a Menace to Asia?* (1917) occupies a special place not only because it was "dedicated to the cause of Asian independence" and accredited as the "magnum opus of the Pan-Asiatic Movement"[23] but also because of its perceptive analysis and vision of Asia and the world, delivered with both passion and a cool, at times cruel, pragmatism. His vision of Asian independence is based on a mixture of racial solidarity, cultural affinity, and political necessity seeking a better world liberated from Western imperialism. In his thinking, Asia is a category of cultural substance, political alliance, and intermediary force that commands world-transforming potentials. It is both a medium by which Indian independence is to be achieved and the project to which Indian independence must make a contribution. Asia in this sense is both one and all, a "method"[24] for, or a tactical approach to, decolonization.

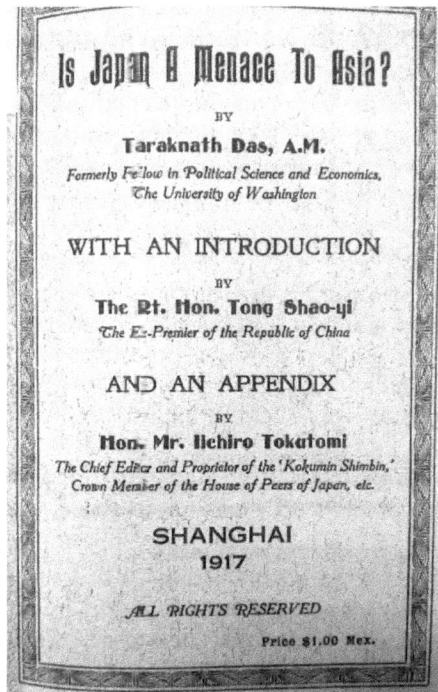

Figure 4.3. Cover image of *Is Japan a Menace to Asia?*

Is Japan a Menace to Asia? begins with a plea to Asian youths to strive toward the "Assertion of Asia":

> Our method of assertion should not be mere imitation of the West. Our ambition is to draw our inspiration from the glorious past of Asia and rising above its present degraded condition, preserving the best of our ancestral treasures from the attacks of vandals and assimilating the best of all that the modern world has to give to Humanity, to build up something higher than the best products of Modern civilization.[25]

Das's simple but emphatic statement indicates that the assertion of Asia emerged with both a rejection of imitation of the West and a claim of ancestral treasure which must be married with modernity for a higher civilization to arrive. Although this may sound like a grand but empty slogan, it embodies the critical energy of pan-Asianism, at once a race-based proposition for opposition and a movement for transforming the political order of the world. As Tang Shaoyi aptly summarizes in his introduction, "Political assertion of Asia will make Europe and America more tolerant and respectful towards human rights," and that requires "a solid Asiatic unity."[26] Writing at a time of Western colonialism on all fronts of Asia, Das believes that the degraded condition of Asia was caused mainly by its political—rather than cultural—weakness, and the ascent of Japan as a power to be reckoned with illuminated for him and his contemporaries a great hope of defiance, upheld in the principle of "Asia for Asiatic."

"Asia for Asiatic" is a critical but problematic principle. It is a racial expression of the will against colonial domination. It also conveys the desire for national sovereignty and autonomy. It was a reflection of America's Monroe Doctrine that Japan wished to appropriate to justify her action in Asia. As Das puts it himself,

> Japan's assertion in Asia and the driving out of the special privileges of the Europeans in Asia . . . is certainly a challenge to European authority in Asia. This challenge of Japan inspires confidence in the mind of other Asiatic nations about the future possibility of holding their own like Japan in the field of economic and political rivalry with European nations.[27]

It is for the possibility of holding up like Japan that the principle gained recognition and support by such Asianists as Das. Asia, as articulated in this anticolonial context, is a distinctly pragmatic notion in that it is meaningful *only in so far* as an intermediary identity and interactive platform for pursuing racial equality and national independence. Das's analysis and defense for Japan, therefore, must be viewed with a spin of political pragmatism.

The title is a rhetorical question that seeks to dispel the worry that a strong and powerful Japan is a menace to Asia. Its objective is to prove otherwise by presenting a perceptive analysis of the political situation in Asia by contending that Japan has the strength and will to lead Asia toward independence because it cannot exist otherwise. The relationship between Japan and Asia is one of mutual dependence. Das believed, because despite its victory over Russia, Japan "has since been taught that the citizenship of the world belongs to the whiteman and to the whiteman alone and that Japanese destiny lies in Asia and nowhere else."[28] Hence, it would be of great stake for Japan to ally with Asia, rather than to imagine itself as outside or beyond Asia, because creating a hostile environment in Asia would not only be detrimental to Japan's growth as a regional power but also hurt the cause of Asian independence for which Japan was to be the champion. Fellowship and cultural affinity are moreover important reasons for creating an Asiatic alliance, especially if Japan wishes to establish a "community of interests between all the yellow races."[29] Das maintained furthermore that it is important to consider Asiatic alliance through the perspective of "practical politics."[30] If colonialism is a game of plunder and survival, then unless respective Asian countries could be strong enough to fend for themselves, each of them would be preyed by Western powers one after another. Following this logic, Das tried to defend Japan's aggression in Asia—particularly its annexation of Korea—as an act of self-preservation rather than a colonial attempt: because if Korea were left to defend itself, it would fall prey to Russia, and become a menace to Japan. Das quoted a British scholar to draw an analogy:

> [Korea's] incorporation by a strong military and aggressive Western Power would be as great a threat to the independence and national security of Japan as would Ireland, independent or under the influence of a hostile power, be to the safety of the British Empire.[31]

By the same logic, Das argues that "Japan for the sake of self-preservation must adopt sure preventive measures against European aggressions in China, even if these measures be very much resented by China."[32] In a nutshell, self-preservation provided Japan with an impetus for Asian integration even at the expense of Chinese sovereignty and Korean independence. The result is not the harmonious Asia that Das preferred of course, but this crude geopolitical analysis was compelling and convincing as a rhetorical device to persuade Japan to change her policy "so that China can give her adequate support in maintaining with the position of both countries in the field of world-politics."[33]

On the surface, Das's analysis of Japan resembles the theory "defensive realism" built on Robert Jervis's work on the security dilemma and Kenneth

Waltz's "balance-of-power" theory, which posit that the international order is an anarchy and it therefore encourages individual states to pursue defensive or moderate policies to obtain security. Different from "offensive realism" pioneered by John Mearsheimer, which believes that states, to obtain hegemony so as to maximize its security, must adopt "offenses" against others, defensive realism interprets the state's actions as necessary attempts at maintaining security without asserting and aspiring hegemony.[34] While offensive realism differs from defensives realism in many areas, particularly the assumption of the priority of the state: to survive or dominate, the concern with security is shared by both camps and can sometimes cause defense to blend into offense. Das's geopolitical analysis of the 1910s Japan contains a curious mixture of defensive and offensive realisms in today's political hindsight. In perceiving that Japan's moves are acts of self-preservation against Western powers, Das's defense of Japan slid to an acceptance of Japan's offensive colonization of Asia. However, it is important to underscore that his emphasis on self-preservation was couched in the pan-Asianist project in which the inter-Asian alliance was to be created, not for expansion and hegemony (as predicted by offensive realism), but for resistance to the offense of Western imperialist expansion. Whereas contemporary debates over structural realism in international relations tend to obfuscate the foundation on which these theories were articulated, our revisit to Das's pan-Asianist proposal lends us critical insights into the ideological and geopolitical foundation of "international relations": a world of anarchy created by colonialism where one must fend for itself. It is for the sake of Asia's self-preservation as a whole that Das's defense for Japan was justified as a first step toward a global political transformation.

Das's analysis is of course controversial and problematic because it anticipated the Japanese discourse of Greater East Asianism, which became a form of imperialism in the 1930s that plagued Asia and installed roadblocks for inter-Asian reconciliation after 1945. Nonetheless, Das was neither naïve nor oblivious about Japan's colonial policy in Formosa (Taiwan), Korea, and Manchuria, as he admitted that Asia for Asiatic "is a very hard policy to fight, for it expresses itself in pseudo-European terms."[35] Moreover, he pointed out that "Japan's action in Korea and Eastern Asia were in the past, and would be in the future, a mere reflex of the world-policy of the European Powers and America."[36] This is a keen and honest observation because Japan's aggression was in every way an imitation of the West, namely, the reproduction of the imperialist logic that pushed Japan away from Asia by shedding her "Asian skin" so to speak. This is what Takeuchi Yoshimi had critiqued in 1948 regarding the absence of resistance in Japan. Without resistance to the logic of imperialism, Takeuchi believed, Japan had fallen into decadence and rendered herself neither Asian nor European. In the attempt to become the master of Asia, Japan had reaffirmed the logic of the imperial master and implicated herself in the position of the slave. That is why Takeuchi contended that "Japan's progress is the slave's progress; its diligence is the slave's diligence."[37] Aware of Japan's will to imperialism, yet still hoping to bring Japan closer to Asia, Das wrote the following lines of critique that regretfully continue to ring true:

> It must be admitted, however, that this feeling of antipathy and distrust on the part of the Chinese, has been heightened by the haughty attitude of some of the Japanese, and the jingoists of the military party of Japan have also done much to foster it. These people seem to think that the Japanese are more European than Asiatic and so they must look to the Asiatic people with contempt as Europeans do. These people are a real menace to Asia and Japan.[38]

The co-articulation of Asia with its national constituents is instrumental to Das's thinking of Asia, for in his mind, Asia is an integral unity that emerges in friendship, cooperation, and mutual dependence. The enunciation of Asia is both whole and partial because Asia does not exist by itself nor merely in opposition to the West, but crucially in the coming together as an independent assemblage of differences. This is what Das had in mind when he iterated the "cause of Asian Independence" and why he believed in 1917, perhaps with a bit of idealism, if not naiveté, that Japan had no such ambition as to overlord Asia with might. Pan-Asianism, as Das understood it, is an inter-Asian collective for resistance that has the potential to transform itself as well as the world at large. It is a world-making project so to speak that had anticipated the Third World non-alignment movement in the 1950s and the revival of the Global South today.[39]

Therefore, it is all too easy to contend from our hindsight that Das was wrong in his analysis, because Japan had indeed become a menace to Asia in the 1930s, and that the vision of pan-Asian alliance, to our dismay, was an ideological prop of imperialism. Instead, it would be more productive to reconsider Das's analysis as prophetic of the disaster to come and his defense of Japan as a form of defensive realism, attempting to wrest Japan away from the spell of imperialism. As I have discussed earlier, Das was well aware of the imperialist tendency in Japan, yet he chose to believe in the usefulness of the notion of Asian independence because its emphases on cultural affinity, racial solidarity, and a shared sense of deprivation of sovereignty may be mobilized not only for liberating darker nations from the yoke of the West but also for overcoming the imperialist modernity that produced the idea of Asia in the first place. As we witness the rise of China as the next global hegemon, as the editors of this volume observe, especially in relation to Hong Kong, how to "de-imperialize" the rising power, and to transform her into a benevolent leader, so as to create a fair and just international order on the principles of independence and equality, is arguably the most valuable challenge that Das has left us today.

CONCLUSION

One of the distinctive characteristics of Taraknath Das's life and work is his vision of Asia as a space of linkage, mediation, interaction, and transformation emerging from practical politics and urgent desire for independence. For Asia never existed by itself, nor was it ever one to begin with, but has emerged in relation to the West and the heterogeneous constituents within. Asia is a synecdoche—a partial representation that is also a provisional yet productive symbol for something both smaller and greater. It is a messy concept for solidarity and comparison, as the editors of this volume suggest, that is rife with paradoxes and slippages. Yet, as a symbol of the lived experience of minor transnationals like Das, it both resists and demands representation to transform itself and the world that gave it its name. For this reason, it must be a totality that refuses to be totalitarian.

The articulation of Asian independence in Das's work is an attempt to achieve complete autonomy: not as the privilege of Asia, but as a fundamental human right that Asians, like whites and blacks, are entitled to enjoy. Put differently, Asian as an identity, both in Asia in the 1920s and in the United States in the 1960s, is but an articulation of the desire for independence and equality, rather than a specific kind of independence and equality available only to Asians. In linking to other projects of liberation, "Asian" is, and has to be, represented in a variety of specific struggles as they had happened in China, India, Korea, Taiwan, Japan, etc., where they intersected and became mutually constitutive—as minor transnational networks that haunt the imperialist and capitalist circuits—to stake a global vision of a better future. The question of Asia is therefore more than a matter of representation; as "lived experience," it is created in the complex and inter-crossing itineraries of life and politics, as Das traveled and travailed within and between East, South, and West Asias, across the Pacific, and beyond. In this view, Asia is not only a cognitive category but a *trans*portable and *trans*formative affective frame of mind that urges one to attend to crosscurrents, conjunctures, and unexpected encounters where "the *trans* and *inter* converge and diverge, overlap and differ."[40] As a pan-Asianist who dedicated his life and work to the cause of Indian independence, Das demonstrated that Asia is never simply a place of dwelling, but an intermediating multiplicity and transformative agency that takes the world as its target—a tactical intervention that we may call "trans-Asia."

Such a reading of Das's life and work moreover enables us to rearticulate the discussion of Asia in both Asian American studies and Asian studies. Das is a product of both Asia and America, a pioneer straddling both continents for the transformations of not only his own community and homeland but also the world at large. In this vein, pan-Asianism is not merely an *Asian* discourse for solidarity but a figure of the greater desire for decolonization. As Vijay Prashad contends, "the Third World is a project,"[41] a project that can trace its roots to the conferences on anti-imperialism and the divergent framings of pan-movements in the early twentieth century and connect with the aspirations of the nonalignment movements in the 1950s and 1960s, anticipating an alternative to the world created by colonialism and Cold War geopolitics. In this vibrant and diverse genealogy, such categories as Asian, African, and Latin American are more symbolic and affective than geographically fixated and immovable; they register more of the desire for recognition and compassion than the allegiance to the past. The rise of China and India in the new millennium especially renewed this aspiration into what Giovanni Arrighi calls the "New Bandung" that can "mobilize and use the global market as an instrument of equalization of South-North power relations."[42] While the change seems more economic than political on the surface, the ascent of China as a contender of global hegemon clearly suggests that a political transformation is also under way, as China exerts its power through the "Belt and Road" initiatives and takes leadership role in the new Trans-Pacific Partnership without the United States. These changes seem to imply that the days of Western imperialism are on the wane, and the revival of Asia is no longer just a projection. Yet the very Asia we speak of is even more intricately articulated with other continents through the trans-regional flows of desire, capital, and people, as indicated in Kim's, Ferrari's, and Zhang's chapters in the volume. A singular, pure Asia untouched by the West and kept to itself is already an impossibility, not to mention the dynamic interaction within Asia itself. The vision of Asian independence that Das dedicated his life to can only be a starting point for the work of decolonization today. In the era of bio-political, neo-liberal infiltration through Facebook, WeChat, and other techno-social media, the task of independence is a challenge of global reconfiguration. To revisit Das and his pan-Asianist work in the intertwining transpacific and inter-Asian axes hence compels us not only to recover legacies from the past but also to re-engage with the politics of liberation with cautionary tales.[43]

Moreover, in our "age of anger" and global revolt that achingly shows the limits of Western democracy and modernity, entangled with the upsurge of devious forms of populist nationalism and xenophobic conservatism around the world, Taraknath Das, though a minor figure in both the history of pan-Asianism and Asian America, literally embodies what Pankaj Mishra calls an "alienated young man of promise" whose passion for transforming the world overnight might have resulted in the creative destruction we witness today.[44] The point though is not to take sides or blame the enemy, but to reflect critically on the history that produced the present as such in order to release the charge of emotion from failed revolution and missed opportunities, and to consider what it means and takes to be "independent" in this world of complex entanglements.

NOTES

1. For an introduction to the *Chinese Student Monthly*, see Wang (2013), Chapter 2.
2. For the inter-Asian connections in early twentieth century pan-Asianism, see Sun (2001); Bharucha (2006); Zachmann (2007); Wang (2007); Hotta (2007); Zhang (2008).
3. Gary Hess, "The Forgotten Asian Americans: The East Indian Community in the United States," *Pacific Historical Review* 43, no. 4 (1974): 576–596; Kornel Chang, *Pacific Connections: The Making of the U.S.-Canadian Borderlands* (Berkeley, CA: University of California Press, 2012); Amy Bhatt and Nalini Iyer, *Roots and Reflections: South Asians in the Pacific Northwest* (Seattle, WA: University of Washington Press, 2013).
4. Tapan K. Mukherjee *Taraknath Das: Life and Letters of a Revolutionary in Exile* (Calcutta: National Council of Education, Bengal, 1998); Sohan Singh Josh, *Hindustan Gadar Party: A Short History*, 2nd ed. (Jalandhar: Desh Bhagat Yadgar Committee, 2007); Seema Sohi, *Echoes of Mutiny: Race, Surveillance and Indian Anticolonialism in North America* (New York: Oxford University Press, 2014); Giovanni Arrighi, *Adam Smith in Beijing: Lineages of the Twenty-First Century* (London: Verso, 2007); Maia Ramnath, *Haj to Utopia* (Berkeley: University of California Press, 2011).
5. Shu-mei Shih and Francois Lionnet, eds., *Minor Transnationalism* (Durham, NC: Duke University Press, 2005).
6. For a critical yet brief discussion of this plan enacted in the Universities Act of 1904, see Jayapalan (2000, 73–78).
7. Mukherjee, *Taraknath Das*, 2.
8. For a succinct account of the Swadeshi Movement, see Chapter 10 in Bipan Chandra et al. (1989, 124–134).
9. Because India, like Canada, was part of the British Empire, Canadian government could not restrict Indians from coming; moreover, given the previous experiences of anti-immigration riot in Australia, South Africa, and New Zealand, the Canadian government wished to be cautious with its exclusion, and thus decided to indirectly halt Indian immigration by declaring "continuous journey regulation." It prohibited immigrants who did not come to Canada by a *continuous* journey. In practice this applied only to ships that began their voyage in India, as the great distance usually necessitated a stopover in Japan or Hawaii. This was discriminatory to Indians

who could not travel directly to Canada and has resulted in the notorious Komagata Maru Incident of 1914 in which passengers on the ship—mostly from India—were denied entry to Canada.

10. Mukherjee, *Taraknath Das*, 15. Bipan Chandra et al. (1989, 147) moreover pointed out that imposing restriction on Indian immigration was not merely a Canadian response to populism, the British Indian government too had its own reasons for it, for it worries that "close familiarity of Indians with White which would inevitably take place in America was not good for British prestige," that "the immigrants would get contaminated by socialist ideas," and that experience of racial discrimination "would become the source of nationalist agitation in India."

11. Mukherjee, *Taraknath Das*, 47.

12. Other scholars however hold different views on this point. See for instance Stolte (2012, 90).

13. On the historical formation and various ideologies of the Ghadar Party, Ramnath (2011) and Josh (2007).

14. Quoted in Mukherjee, *Taraknath Das*, 65.

15. Between 1914 and 1916, Das sought cooperation with Germany and with German's help, went on various missions to the Suez Canal, Kabul, and Turkey to seek alliance and coalition with pan-Islamist groups to struggle against the British Empire. These missions almost cost his life, but the achievement was minimal. However, Das's prognosis of the world situation and his adventures into the Middle East and Eurasia can be said to represent an earlier moment of Third Worldism.

16. Mukherjee, *Taraknath Das*, 96.

17. Ibid.

18. Miyazaki Toten, *Sanshisan nian zhi meng* (*Thirty Three Years of Dream*), trans. Qiyan Lin (Guilin: Guangzhou shifan daxue chubanshe, 1902/2011).

19. Ibid., 18. My translation.

20. In contrast, Das's pamphlet *Isolation of Japan in World Politics* (1918), published in Tokyo, reads more like an urgent proposition to Japan, urging her not to tread on the imperialist road of the West and to form solidarity with Asian nations so as to avoid isolation in world politics. In our hindsight, it also reads like the last call for caution from Das, who drifted from Japan soon after the pamphlet was published.

21. Cemil Aydin, *The Politics of Anti-Westernism in Asia: Visions of the World Order in Pan-Islamic and Pan-Asian Thought* (New York: Columbia University Press, 2007), 176.

22. Due to space limit, the discussion to follow will focus on Das's pan-Asianist writing in the 1920s. His later writings and return visits to India after 1945 are to be explored in elsewhere.

23. Mukherjee, *Taraknath Das*, 102.

24. Chen Kuan-Hsing, *Asia as Method* (Durham, NC: Duke University Press, 2010).

25. Taraknath Das, *Is Japan a Menace to Asia?* (Shanghai: The Author, 1917), unpaged.

26. Shao-Yi Tang, "Introduction," in *Is Japan a Menace to Asia?*, by Taraknath Das (Shanghai: Author, 1917), iii.

27. Das, *Is Japan a Menace*, 77.

28. Ibid., 32.

29. Ibid., 33.

30. Ibid., 70.

31. Ibid., 50.

32. Ibid., 70.

33. Ibid., 54.

34. For a discussion of the differences between offensive realism and defensive realism (also known as structural or contingent realism), see Mearsheimer (2001) and Taliaferro (2000/01).

35. Das, *Is Japan a Menace*, 34.

36. Ibid., 54.

37. Takeuchi Yoshimi, *What Is Modernity?: Writings of Takeuchi Yoshimi*, ed. and trans. Richard F. Calichman (New York: Columbia University Press, 2005), 66.

38. Das, *Is Japan a Menace*, 43.

39. For a critical genealogy of anti-imperialist and anti-racist reworlding movements from the early twentieth century to the present, see Prashad (2007, 2012).

40. See Gladys Pak Lei Chong, Yiu Fai Chow, and Jeroen de Kloet's introduction to this volume.

41. Vijay Prashad, *The Darker Nations: A People's History of the Third World* (New York: New Press, 2007), 1.

42. Giovanni Arrighi, *Adam Smith in Beijing: Lineages of the Twenty-First Century* (London: Verso, 2007), 384.

43. Chinese Muslim writer Zhang Chengzhi (2008), in his book of essays written at the dawn of Beijing Olympics, recounts the history of pan-Asianism as a way to interrogate the rise of China, to warn China against the errors and pitfalls of a rising power.

44. Pankaj Mishra, *Age of Anger: A History of the Present* (New York: Farrar, Strauss, and Giroux, 2017), 29.

BIBLIOGRAPHY

Arrighi, Giovanni. *Adam Smith in Beijing: Lineages of the Twenty-First Century.* London: Verso, 2007.

Aydin, Cemil. *The Politics of Anti-Westernism in Asia: Visions of the World Order in Pan-Islamic and Pan-Asian Thought.* New York: Columbia University Press, 2007.

———. "Taraknath Das: Pan-Asian Solidarity as a 'Realist' Grand Strategy, 1917–1918." In *Pan-Asianism: A Documentary History Vol. 1: 1850–1920*, edited by Sven Saaler and Christopher W. A. Szpilman, 305–309. Lanham, MD: Rowman & Littlefield, 2011.

Bharucha, Rustom. *Another Asia: Rabindranath Tagore and Okakura Tenshin.* Oxford: Oxford University Press, 2006.

Bhatt, Amy, and Nalini Iyer. *Roots and Reflections: South Asians in the Pacific Northwest.* Seattle, WA: University of Washington Press, 2013.

Chandra, Bipan, Miridula Mukherjee, Aditya Mukherjee, Sucheta Mahajan, and K. N. Panikkar. *India's Struggle for Independence*. Gurgaon: Penguin India, 1989.

Chang, Kornel. *Pacific Connections: The Making of the U.S.-Canadian Borderlands*. Berkeley, CA: University of California Press, 2012.

Chen, Kuan-Hsing. *Asia as Method: Toward Deimperialization*. Durham, NC: Duke University Press, 2010.

Das, Taraknath. *Is Japan a Menace to Asia?* Shanghai: The Author, 1917.

—[as an Asian Statesman]. *Isolation of Japan in World Politics*. Tokyo: The Asiatic Association of Japan, 1918.

Hess, Gary R. "The Forgotten Asian Americans: The East Indian Community in the United States." *Pacific Historical Review* 43, no. 4 (1974): 576–596.

Hotta, Eri. *Pan-Asianism and Japan's War 1931–1945*. New York: Palgrave, 2007.

Jayapalan, N. *History of Education in India*. New Delhi: Atlantic, 2000.

Josh, Sohan Singh. *Hindustan Gadar Party: A Short History*. 2nd ed. Jalandhar: Desh Bhagat Yadgar Committee, 2007.

Mearsheimer, John. *The Tragedy of Great Power Politics*. New York: Norton, 2001.

Mishra, Pankaj. *Age of Anger: A History of the Present*. New York: Farrar, Strauss, and Giroux, 2017.

Miyazaki, Toten. *Sanshisan nian zhi meng* (*Thirty Three Years of Dream*). trans. by Qiyan Lin. Guilin: Guangzhou shifan daxue chubanshe, 1902/2011.

Mukherjee, Tapan K. *Taraknath Das: Life and Letters of a Revolutionary in Exile*. Calcutta: National Council of Education, Bengal, 1998.

Prashad, Vijay. *The Darker Nations: A People's History of the Third World*. New York: New Press, 2007.

———. *The Poorer Nations: A Possible History of the Global South*. London: Verso, 2012.

Ramnath, Maia. *Haj to Utopia*. Berkeley, CA: University of California Press, 2011.

Shih, Shu-mei, and Francois Lionnet, eds. *Minor Transnationalism*. Durham, NC: Duke University Press, 2005.

Sohi, Seema. *Echoes of Mutiny. Race, Surveillance and Indian Anticolonialism in North America*. New York: Oxford University Press, 2014.

Stolte, Carolien. "Imagining Asia in India: Nationalism and Internationalism (ca. 1905–1940)." *Comparative Studies in Society and History* 54, no. 1 (2012): 65–92.

Sun, Ge. *Yazhou yiwei ze shenme?* (How Does Asia Mean?). Taibei: Juliu, 2001.

Takeuchi, Yoshimi. *What Is Modernity?: Writings of Takeuchi Yoshimi*. ed, and trans. by Richard F. Calichman. New York: Columbia University Press, 2005.

Taliaferro, Jeffrey W. "Security Seeking under Anarchy: Defensive Realism Revisited." *International Security* 25, no. 3 (2000): 128–161.

Tang, Shao-Yi. "Introduction." In *Is Japan a Menace to Asia?*, by Taraknath Das, i–vi. Shanghai: Author, 1917.

Waltz, Kenneth N. *Theory of International Politics*. New York: McGraw-Hill, 1979.

Wang, Chih-ming. *Transpacific Articulations: Student Migration and the Remaking of Asian America*. Honolulu, HI: University of Hawaii Press, 2013.

Wang, Hui. "The Politics of Imagining Asia: A Genealogical Analysis." *Inter-Asia Cultural Studies* 8, no.1 (2007): 1–33.

Zachmann, Urs Matthias. "Blowing up a Double Portrait in Black and White: The Concept of Asia in the Writings of Fukuzawa Yukichi and Okakura Tenshin." *Positions* 15, no. 2 (2007): 345–368.

Zhang, Chengzhi. *Jingzhong yu xibie: zhi riben* (Respect and Farewell to Japan). Beijing: Zhongguo youyi chubanshe, 2008.

Chapter 5

On *Exile Trilogy*: Trans-Asia Trajectory

Soyoung Kim

HEART OF SNOW, HEART OF BLOOD

The sign emerges as one drives along the route 7 on the east coast of South Korea. It reads Asian Highway: Korea-China-Kazakhstan-Russia. It is a puzzling sign when there is no such highway when North Korea stands as a blockage from South Korean perspective. It is not possible to travel by land to China, Kazakhstan, and Russia. When the indexical road sign turns into a fantasmatic one, my documentary practice titled *Exile Trilogy* tries to follow a turbulent trajectory of Korean diaspora in Russia and Central Asia.

My engagement with Trans-Asia project is rooted in the still unresolved post–Cold War situation in which I have viscerally felt captive since my childhood under the military dictatorship. We cannot go to other parts of Asia by land beyond DMZ. Writing Asia via documentary making is made possible by the highly negotiable framework of Trans-Asia and Inter-Asia beyond the Cold War division. *Exile Trilogy* is composed of *Heart of Snow, Heart of Blood* (2014), *Sound of Nomad: Koryo Arirang* (2016), and *Goodbye My Love, North Korea* (2017). *Kim Alex's Place: Ansan-Tashkent* is a preamble to *Heart of Snow, Heart of Blood* (2014). The trilogy looks at the issues of translation, intermediality, art practice of diaspora, and writing history of collective trauma, which will build into a diaspora archive. It encourages one to understand Trans-Asia trajectory as mediatic-historical-affective events. Trans-Asia also moves toward other Asia questions such as North Korea, Central Asia, or Soviet Asia also known as Global Subaltern area, which will be inclusive of Eurasia, the other side of Cold War from the capitalist perspective.[1] *Exile Trilogy* is set in Central Asia, Russia and Ansan, South Korea. My concerns with Koryo people started in Ansan known as the multicultural city, where migrant workers congregate. South

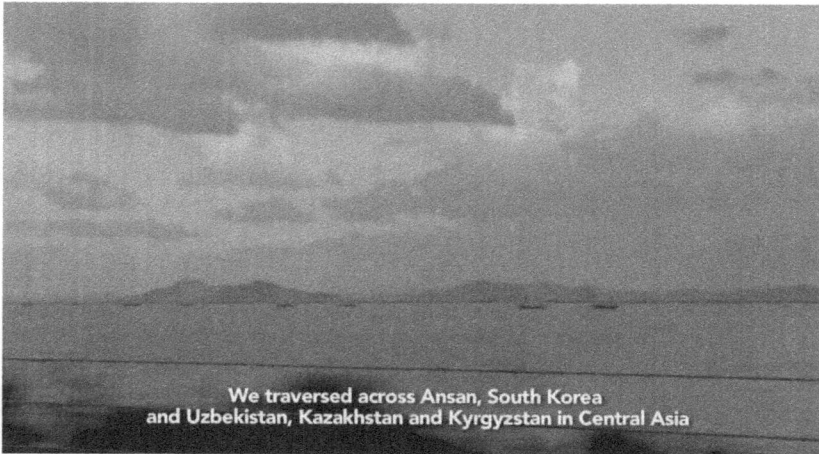

We traversed across Ansan, South Korea
and Uzbekistan, Kazakhstan and Kyrgyzstan in Central Asia

Figure 5.1. Trans-Asian trajectory of Korean diaspora (Koryo saram). *Heart of Snow, Heart of Blood* **(dir. Soyoung Kim (a.k.a. Jeong Kim), 98 min., documentary, 2014).**

Korea, putatively a homogeneous and monolingual nation, has entered an era of unprecedented "multiculturalism" brought about by migrant workers and marriage migration. This has opened up a multitude of issues concerning globalization. I was particularly interested in the Koryo people who had come back to South Korea after 150 years of migration. Koryo people started crossing the Dooman River at the border of Korea and Russia around 1860. Their numbers increased significantly after the Japanese colonization of the Korean peninsula. They settled in the Ussuriysk and Vladivostok areas, poor but skillful rice farmers. Soviet Communist Party general secretary and late premier, Josef Stalin, deported 180,000 of them to Central Asia. Despite deaths and injuries, Koryo people made themselves as leaders of Kolhoz (collective farms). They set up a Koryo theater and newspaper that preserved the Korean language. Soviet artists such as the writer Anatoly Kim (born 1939) and the Soviet rock legend Viktor Tsoi (1962–1990) are part of this Koryo diaspora art scenes. After the collapse of the Soviet Union, the situation of racial minorities in many former Soviet areas worsened, particularly in Uzbekistan, where the authoritarian post-Soviet government confiscated assets and imposed the Uzbek language. The story of Kim Alex and Hu Sveta in *Heart of Snow, Heart of Blood* emerged from the aftermath of the rise of Uzbek authoritarian nationalism. Initially, I didn't know that my research interests would materialize as a documentary trilogy.

This encounter is my second phase of "trans" Asian moment since I set up Trans Asia Screen Culture Institute in 2000.[2] The second time fell in the period of unbearable passing of five of my beloved ones within three years.

Perhaps the time of mourning was in need of a place elsewhere. When they all vanished from the earth, the words were leaving me. I picked up my camera and left for Kyrgyzstan. I was looking for an old woman with a shroud as I previously saw a striking photo in which a Koryo saram granny hanged a long traditional white *Hanbok* shroud on the wall. The woman in the photo turned out to have gone but I met Yevgenia Chegay, the second generation of Koryo saram who kept her shroud in Hanbok style in Bishkek, Kyrgyzstan. Encountering a Koryo diaspora woman over ninety years old resonated with a recollection on my grandmother in the first part of *Women's History Trilogy* titled *Koryu: Southern Women, South Korea* (2000). In the film, the double meanings of Koryu (居留 as dwelling, 去留 as life and death) were evoked for the women's lives in pre-modern and modern Korea. The collective writings of eulogy written in vernacular Korean at the threshold of pre-modern and modern times were redeemed for women's mode of expression.

Succeeding *Women's History Trilogy* including *Koryu: Southern Women, South Korea*, *Exile Trilogy* is partly a eulogy for Koryo diaspora who were subject to mass deportation in 1937 by Stalin. *Heart of Snow, Heart of Blood* has its Korean title, *Heart of Snow: The Place Where the Sadness Takes Us* (seulpumi urirul daeryeoganeumgot), which is suggestive of the eulogy form. Toward the end of editing, I was able to find Victor Tsoi's (half ethnic Koryo) song called *The Sadness* for the final music.

A bird visited us when I practiced a modest ritual for my father on the lunar New Year's Day on the snowy hills In Bishkek, Kyrgyzstan. I bought a dried brownish cod from the local Korean grocery, an essential food material for the ritual and wrote a poem for my father. The bird flew into the ritual scene and made light noises.

The camera pointing at the heart of the snow bled into memory. The relations between the living and the dead and the natural and the technological

Figure 5.2. Reading Eulogy, Koryu: *Southern Women/South Korea* **(dir. Soyoung Kim, 75 min., documentary, 2000).**

Figure 5.3.   The ending scene of *Heart of Snow, Heart of Blood* (2014). From the lyrics of Victor Tsoi's *The Sadness*, a border between Kyrgyzstan and Uzbekistan.

Figure 5.4.   Ritual for my late father at the heart of Kyrgyzstan, *Heart of Snow, Heart of Blood* (dir. Soyoung Kim, 98 min., documentary, 2014).

found ways in the last sequence with a wishing tree. An interior somatic place of memory seems to exceed a documentary apparatus, an extra somatic site of digital memory, and a prosthesis. The affective rhythm brings forth to *Exile Trilogy* in dialogue with Trans Asia trajectory reaching Central Asia with compassion. It also made me acknowledge a lack of understanding toward the post-Soviet Asia. Koryo people in Central Asia who speak Koryo (Korean dialect) language as well as Russian played the role of a cultural, historical

Figure 5.5. *Heart of Snow, Heart of Blood* (dir. Soyoung Kim, 98 min., documentary, 2014).

Figure 5.6. Encountering horses. *Heart of Snow, Heart of Blood* (dir. Soyoung Kim, 98 min., documentary, 2014).

translator for me. It is a brief encounter, but still offers a possibility of re-Worlding based on a different historical configuration.

The documentary features Kim Alex and his partner Sveta as main characters, and has a double structure that switches back and forth between South Korea and Uzbekistan and Kyrgyzstan in Central Asia. The pair are representative of fragmented histories.

I myself was raised and academically trained in South Korea and the United States during the Cold War. I have entered the Koryo community

무슨 죄를 지었다고 그렇게 많은 아이들이 죽어야 했을까요
What sins did they commit that so many of them had to die?

Figure 5.7.   Kim Alex at the assembly of prayers for Sewol ferry incident, soon to turn into a political one. Most of the victims are from Ansan, where he runs his restaurant Tashkent for the Koryo (ethnic Koreans in Central Asia and Russia) community and others. *Heart of Snow, Heart of Blood* (dir. Soyoung Kim, 98 min., documentary, 2014).

Figure 5.8.   Kim Alex. *Heart of Snow, Heart of Blood* (dir. Soyoung Kim, 98 min., documentary, 2014).

of post-Soviet Central Asia, where they mostly speak Russian (a language I do not understand) and Koryo dialect, as well as local languages, particularly since the collapse of the Soviet Union. To most Koreans, the continent stretching west from the Korean peninsula is only China and Russia. The historical trajectory of the Koryo diaspora might help correct this geographical blockage. The dispersion and dissemination might trigger a productive reorientation of all sense of sovereignty centered on Korean peninsula, which has been the stage of a protracted turf war between the big powers of China, Russia, Japan, and the United States.

Currently, Central Asia partly falls into Chinese government initiative "One Road One Belt." As briefly introduced before, Gayatri Spivak argued that CIS (The Commonwealth of Independent States, formed when the former Soviet Union totally dissolved in 1991; at its conception it consisted of ten former Soviet Republics: Armenia, Belarus, Kazakhstan, Kyrgyzstan, Moldova, Russia, Tajikistan, Turkmenistan, Ukraine, and Uzbekistan) should be seen as an emergence of global subaltern calling for critical regionalism.[3]

From the gaze of global media, Central Asia is displaced, shadowy, and misinformed area as it comprises the other side of post–Cold War. I find it thankful that I was guided and informed by the ethnic Korean diaspora (Koryo ethnic) community in Central Asia about the region.

SOUND OF NOMAD: KORYO ARIRANG

The blue train was curving out to the outskirts of the city Almaty, Kazakhstan. Koryo Theater, which was founded in Vladivostok, Russia in 1920s, is not far from this train spotting site. Tall trees surround the theater. I met the actors of Koryo Theater and watched the rehearsals of the trainees. At the time, I was producing a film that would be titled *Kim Alex's Restaurant*.

I stood in the Hall of Koryo Theater and watched the photos of Koryo actors and performers on the wall. The evening was approaching. The photos

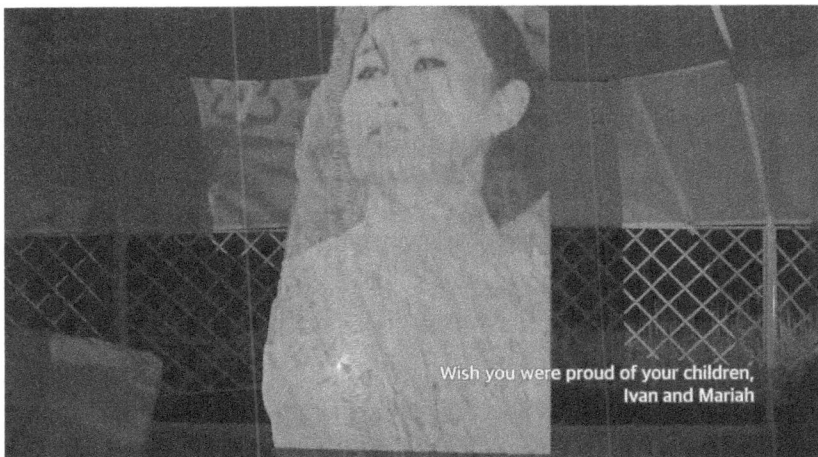

Figure 5.9.   Bang Tamara, Diva of Arirang Ensemble, Koryo Theater. *Sound of Nomad: Koryo Arirang* (dir. Soyoung Kim, 87 min., documentary, 2016).

Figure 5.10. *Sound of Nomad* **poster. The film was released in theaters nationwide in 2017.**

Figure 5.11.   A poem by a Kory poet. *Sound of Nomad: Koryo Arirang* **(dir. Soyoung Kim, 87 min., documentary, 2016).**

were painted in the dark red color of the sun setting in Almaty. I wanted to hear the songs of female singers. I was longing for the sound. I was able to find relevant footage of Koryo Theater at a private archive. I was fascinated by Bang Tamara in particular. I heard her young voice in the archival materials first and then met her in person. It felt like her walking out of the archive when I started filming her. *Sound of Nomad: Koryo Arirang* starts with her looking at the archive materials that she never knew existed. She is a diva of a tragic family history related to a history of migration. The film is a testimonial—a witness to injustice and tragedy, but it is also a declaration of survival—a survival that is not static but transformative. The trains that displace, the deserts that separate from one harsh horizon but within that limit, against it and across it are people, are a culture, not escaping but flourishing unofficially with the affective majesty of a melody, a rhythm, Arirang.

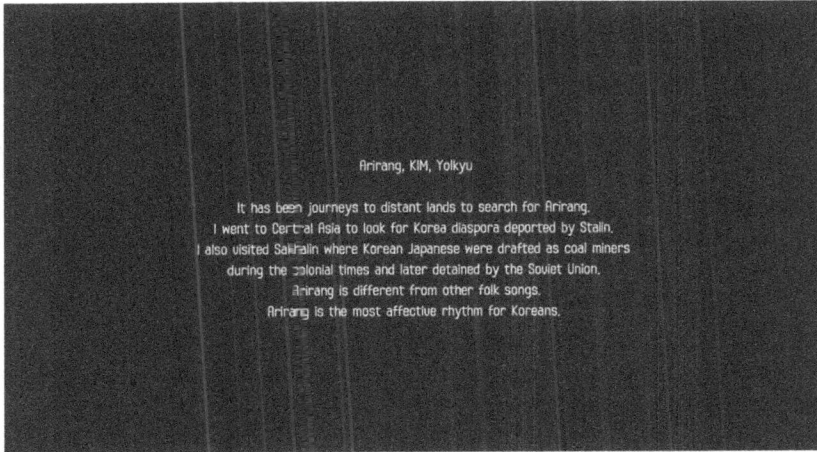

Arirang, KIM, Yolkyu

It has been journeys to distant lands to search for Arirang.
I went to Central Asia to look for Korea diaspora deported by Stalin.
I also visited Sakhalin where Korean Japanese were drafted as coal miners
during the colonial times and later detained by the Soviet Union.
Arirang is different from other folk songs.
Arirang is the most affective rhythm for Koreans.

Figure 5.12. **My father wrote extensively on Arirang sung by Koryo people in Central Asia and Russia after he made a research trip to the area once he completed a book on Arirang in the Korean peninsula.** *Sound of Nomad: Koryo Arirang* **(dir. Soyoung Kim, 87 min., documentary, 2016).**

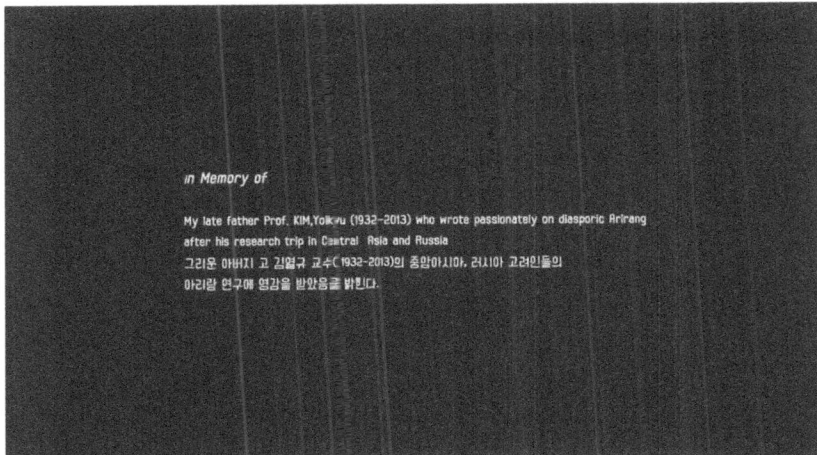

in Memory of

My late father Prof. KIM,Yolkyu (1932-2013) who wrote passionately on diasporic Arirang
after his research trip in Central Asia and Russia
그리운 아버지 고 김열규 교수(1932-2013)의 중앙아시아, 러시아 고려인들의
아리랑 연구에 영감을 받았음을 밝힌다.

Figure 5.13. **My father wrote extensively on Arirang sung by Koryo people in Central Asia and Russia after he made a research trip to the area once he completed a book on Arirang in the Korean peninsula.** *Sound of Nomad: Koryo Arirang* **(dir. Soyoung Kim, 87 min., documentary, 2016).**

Sound of Nomad: Koryo Arirang is the second of *Exile Trilogy* on the survivors and descendants of Stalin's forced transfer of the Korean population of far eastern Russia into Central Asia. The Koryo people are victims of history, as they settle into lives and rebuild communities in Central Asia, they re-enter history as agents, as the generations preserve, adopt, adapt, and synthesize the culture, and they become the historical memory and the historically described present. This documentary engages in a dialogue with the found footage reanimating the sound and image of the nomadic past of Koryo people. The documentary practice particularly approximates diaspora archive.

When we put diaspora and archive together, it becomes rather an intriguing idea than a description. They almost cancel out each other as archive drives toward storage and diaspora moves toward dispersion. The resultant double erasure ironically evokes the traces of the collective memory of ethnic minorities converging on the "subaltern cosmopolitanism" of Koryo Theater. They travelled and performed for all walks of people throughout the Soviet Union. Diaspora archive in its dynamics and turn challenges the existing meanings of both. This set of entity points to a lack or an excess in each: a lack in diaspora and an excess in archive.

The documentary production also functions as a response/responsibility to diaspora archive in becoming. In the second documentary, the archival footage is re-animated with aleatory encounters. The deeply inspiring documentary *Koryo Saram* by the second generation Koryo filmmaker Song Lavernti features fluent speakers of Koryo language who are not ethnic Koryo people. Multifarious possibilities of assemblage and editing of archival footage with live footage render this kind of documentary practice Worlding, a complex and dynamic assemblage of ever-renewing realities, sensations, and perceptions through which we must constantly work our way through to hold open "the open of the world."[4] Put in another way, Worlding is "a historical process of taking care, setting limits, entering into, making world horizons come near and become local, situated, in/formed, cared for;

The Beijing treaty was drawn between Russia and Qing dynasty and a maritime province became part of Russia

Figure 5.14.   A photo of Korean neighborhood, Vladivostok, Far East Russia. *Sound of Nomad: Koryo Arirang* (dir. Soyoung Kim, 87 min., documentary, 2016).

Figure 5.15.   Koryo Theater members, including Lee Hamdeok appearing as "People's performer," in *Sound of Nomad: Koryo Arirang* (dir. Soyoung Kim, 87 min., documentary, 2016).

Figure 5.16.   The first settlement site of Koryo people, Ushtobe, Kazakhstan. *Sound of Nomad: Koryo Arirang* (dir. Soyoung Kim, 87 min., documentary, 2016).

instantiated as an uneven/incomplete material-cultural process of world-making and world-becoming."

GOODBYE MY LOVE, NORTH KOREA: APPROACHING THE VANISHED

The film is an interlocking portrait of eight North Korean men who went to Moscow Film School in 1952 and sought political asylum in 1958 after denouncing Kim Ilsung. Three of them became filmmakers in Kazakhstan and the Soviet Union. Choi Kukin, in particular, established himself as an acclaimed director with *The Year of The Dragon* (1980) and a voice of solidarity with the resistance movement of the Uighur. Han Jin became a writer at the Koryo Theater for ethnic Koreans in Central Asia. The film stands as a memorial for the people who met their last moment in a foreign land.

Figure 5.17.   Quotes from Han Jin, a North Korean writer in exile at Kazakhstan.

Figure 5.18.   Quotes from Han Jin, a North Korean writer in exile at Kazakhstan.

Figure 5.19.   Quotes from Han Jin, a North Korean writer in exile at Kazakhstan.

People who vanished from official history are brought back through the *Exile Trilogy*. I find documentary practice in this case a search for technology of and for the dead. In making the third film, *Goodbye My Love, North Korea*, I lost one of the last interviewees during filming. The film is about eight people who defected to the Soviet Union—nine have now passed away as of 2016. When we are shooting with a Blackmagic camera and editing footage of people who vanished from this world, we are in fact working with the dead. This might be the first layer of what I mean by technology of/for the dead. Herein the technology signifies the concrete and the actual. Even when you lose your interviewee during a shoot, you keep her/him alive in your images.

In the oft-cited essay "Theses on the Philosophy of History," Walter Benjamin evokes Paul Klee's "Angelus Novus"—the angel of history—and tells us, "He wants to stay and awaken the dead and make whole what has been smashed."[5] As we know, the storm called progress propels the angel into the future to which his back is turned, while the debris piles skyward before him. While a wish for redemption following an awakening of the dead is disrupted in Benjamin's essay, film as an apparatus is also partial to awakening the dead.

It is certainly very challenging to face and trace eight people who traversed from North Korea to the Soviet Union and then Central Asia over a half century. They were young elites from North Korea studying mostly at Moscow Film School in 1950s. Once defected to the Soviet Union after criticizing Kim Ilsung, they had to struggle themselves to find their new work and homes. Some of them have made their names as filmmaker, cinematographer, and writer. Others die poor and anonymous. Documentary practice will be a way

Figure 5.20. "*Goodbye My Love North Korea,* What a frighteningly beautiful film! It is fiercely cinematographical melancholy. It is ultimately both jubilantly commemorative (faithful to the parts of the interviews that redouble the reminisces' faith in/aspirations toward ethnic identity and unity) and discomfiting (the final steps of the film along several geographical, luminous, psychic, and metanarrative precipices turn it into an act of grief that threatens to displace the political romanticism and documentary linearity that had previously anchored most of the preceding 70 or so minutes)." Walter K. Lew (poet). *Goodbye My Love, North Korea* (dir. Soyoung Kim, 80 min., documentary, 2017).

Figure 5.21.   Photo taken by Yang Wonsik at VGIK.

to awaken the nine dead men and let them speak in various modes. Seven out of eight were already gone when we started our documentary project. One out of two survivors passed away and there is only one left now—the last survivor of and witness to Korean War, Partition, and Kim Ilsung as well as Stalin. These eight people are testimonies to yet untold history of Cold War. Mobilizing the archival materials against the great landscape of Central Asia, this filmmaking will look at the ways in which the youths rebelled against the power in order to find their voices resonant with the rest of the world.

With *Exile Trilogy* I have explored modes of convergence within and across migration and social practices across Central Asia and Korea, along with the idea of subaltern cosmopolitanism by invoking the prismatic fragments of history, gender, and artistic imagination. Working across Central Asia, I have increasingly found myself at the over-determined intersection and entanglements. To hold open "the open of the world" beyond the confinement of nation-state, I'd like to end my note therefore with a call for Inter/Trans-Asia collaboration for aleatory encounter with other Asias, re-Worlding the world.

To awaken the dead and to piece together what has been smashed

Figure 5.22. *Goodbye My Love, North Korea* (dir. Soyoung Kim, 80 min., documentary, 2017).

Figure 5.23. The final scene of *Goodbye My Love, North Korea* (dir. Soyoung Kim, 80 min., documentary, 2017).

NOTES

1. Chakravorty Gayatri Spivak, *Other Asias* (Oxford: Blackwell, 2008). Spivak addresses Soviet Central Asia as Global Subaltern in a book titled *Other Asias* in which she draws the readers' attention to Armenia and Afghanistan.

2. The "trans" (易) stands as a threshold crisscrossing and highlighting multilayered signifying processes. "Trans" in Trans Asia Screen Culture shares a meaning of "trans" in transnational which go beyond national. "Trans" in particular throws a meaning of translation and transformation into a relief when the dominant use of "trans" as a prefix at the time was a flow of transnational capital. I chose the Korean-Chinese term 역(易), similar to the one in 周易 (the Book of Change).

3. Spivak, *Other Asias*.

4. Martin Heidegger, *Poetry, Language, Thought*, trans. Albert Hofstadter (New York: HarperCollins, 1971), 45.

5. Walter Benjamin, *Illuminations* (New York: Schocken Books, 1968), 257–258.

BIBLIOGRAPHY

Benjamin, Walter. *Illuminations*. New York: Schocken Books, 1968.

Goodbye My Love, North Korea. Directed by Soyoung Kim (Jeong Kim). 2017. South Korea: Privately Published, 2017.

Heart of Snow, Heart of Blood. Directed by Soyoung Kim (Jeong Kim). 2014. South Korea: Privately Published, 2014.

Heidegger, Martin. *Poetry, Language, Thought*. Translated by Albert Hofstadter. New York: HarperCollins, 1971.

Kim Alex's Place: Ansan-Tashkent. Directed by Soyoung Kim (Jeong Kim). 2014. South Korea: Privately Published, 2014.

Rob Wilson and Christopher Leigh Connery, eds., *The Worlding Project: Doing Cultural Studies in the Era of Globalization*, Berkeley and Santa Cruz, CA: North Atlantic Books and New Pacific Press, 2007.

Sound of Nomad: Koryo Arirang. Directed by Soyoung Kim (Jeong Kim). 2016. South Korea: Privately Published, 2016.

Spivak, Chakravorty Gayatri. *Other Asias*. Oxford: Blackwell, 2008.

Chapter 6

Asian Theatricalities in the Transpacific: The Hispanophone Transculturation of Nick Rongjun Yu's *The Crowd* or, Performing the Chinese Cultural Revolution in Peru

Rossella Ferrari

RE-ROUTING TRANS-ASIAN TRAFFIC

"Frequently, large metropolitan cities have subway services that extend from suburban neighborhoods to the center; however they do not offer connecting service between the suburban subcenters themselves. This is an analogy for what occurs in intercultural dialogue."[1] The problem of occluded peripheral connections that Enrique D. Dussel identifies in the above quote typifies the dynamics of intercultural transit wherein movement is steered from the vantage point of traffic controllers positioned within a dominant geolinguistic intersection—most frequently Euro-American, and most frequently Anglophone. This kind of centrist circulatory pattern leaves limited scope for crossings and collisions that unfold along tangential routes and circumvent the metropolitan centers of the global English-speaking West/North. Thus, my inquiry into the Trans-Asia project's potential for critical "*trans*-formation," which Jeroen de Kloet, Yiu Fai Chow, and Gladys Pak Lei Chong outline in the introduction to this volume, explores the application of trans-Asian methodologies in the analysis of transversal pathways of interculturality between so-called peripheries (to an Anglo-Western-centric standpoint) within a performance studies framework. The purpose is to reveal uncharted patterns of inter-referential dialogism that can "de-compartmentalize,"[2] decolonize, and deflect the discourse of/on Asian performance cultures away from prevailing West–East/North–South vectors of circulation and comparison.

The rationale for this expansive approach to Trans-Asia is to assist a decolonial rerouting of intercultural politics and practice, and to harness the capacity of what I designate as trans-Asian theatricalities to capture performative contacts within and outside the boundaries of geopolitical Asia. On the one hand, trans-Asian theatricalities underscore the relational matrix of Asian performance production in contexts of transnational and transcultural mobility. On the other hand, they probe the potential of inter-referencing lived and performed experience to elicit the significance of horizontal—East–East, East–South, South–South—relations that evade the mediation of normative and often (post-/neo-) colonial epistemologies.

Embryonic Asian-Latin American performance connections will be explored through tracing the transculturation trajectory of Nick Rongjun Yu (aka Yu Rongjun)'s *The Crowd* (2015) from the Sinophone to the Hispanophone geolinguistic sphere. A parallel contextual reading of the original Chinese production and its Spanish-language version, *La multitud*, premiered in Lima in 2016, elucidates the bearing of the text and its performances both domestically—as a dramatization of minor histories of the Cultural Revolution (1966–1976)—and transnationally, as the first local production of a contemporary Chinese play in Latin America. Moreover, *La multitud* marks the first Spanish production of a play by the Shanghai-based author, who is the most prolific and most frequently produced living Chinese dramatist and, possibly, the most widely translated and staged internationally.[3]

The investigation of *The Crowd*'s transpacific voyage along the Sino-Hispanophone route adopts a broad spectrum approach to the definition of trans-Asian theatricalities to account for multiple realms of performance (re)production—namely, stage productions and reproduced behaviors.[4] Taking the Asian-transpacific axis "as a dialogic communicative space,"[5] the exploration of the text's Latin American *trans*-formations reveals how postsocialist China and post-conflict Peru inhabit contiguous affective realms shaped by comparable histories of violence and sustained by a long record of Sino-Peruvian interchange which predates China's contemporary rise as a prominent economic actor in the region. This condition of emotive contiguity in the sphere of mundane experience and the text's mnemonic resonance within the local sociohistorical context are likely to have assisted its transmission and "extraordinary" reception.[6] The analysis thus considers the artistic re-enactment of China's radical past on the Limean stage alongside the performative repurposing of propaganda imageries and political rituals in the transculturation—or ideological transperformance—of Maoism in Peru.

The acknowledgment of nascent Sino-Hispanophone theatrical connections affirms the validity of a theoretical alignment of trans-Asian and transpacific methodologies to foreground a comparable thrust toward the "dislocation of the West" from its normative position of implicit arbiter and standard of cultural legitimacy. Notwithstanding, the critical investigation of these connections should also be cognizant of the metamorphic—even performative—properties of "the West" as a shifting ideological construct.[7] Put differently, this is a proposal for an inclusive trans-Asian epistemology, which expands the scope of Asia (or trans-East-Asia) "as method"[8] beyond existing definitions and applications to validate the generative capacity of new transversal alliances and vectors of relational comparison, thereby further destabilizing entrenched epistemological hierarchies between the West and the (Asian-Latin American) rest. It thus resonates with this volume's research agenda in "recogniz[ing] the importance of 'Asia' as an affective and imagined framework" yet refraining from "drawing fixed boundaries" and restricting "epistemological potentials."[9] However, while scrutinizing the "*possibilities*" of Trans-Asia as an epistemological and political "*project*," the global extension of the conceptual reach of both the "trans-" and of "Asia" should also be alert to the "*paradoxes*" that such redrawing of boundaries may engender.[10] Specifically, the possibility for paradox that might result from valorizing fruitful sites of encounter across the Asian-Latin American transpacific rests in the production of alternate scenarios wherein Asia (China, in this instance, whose growing economic traction in Latin America has been contentious) recasts herself in the role of the West, thereby adding an extra dimension to the politics of performance (re)production—namely, the potential reconstitution of existing power structures within different geocultural settings.[11] Nonetheless, the prospect of dissonant comparisons and "unequal constellations"[12] should not detract from their value as meaningful objects of inquiry. Far from being invariable and static, such emergent trans-Asian formations bring into relief "the struggles and cacophonies that take shape around these changing relations" in the global economies of culture.[13]

TRANS-ASIAN THEATRICALITIES WITHIN AND BEYOND ASIA: INTER-ASIAN AND TRANSPACIFIC TRAJECTORIES

The intellectual project of Asia as method has thus far attended primarily to inter-Asian relations within East Asia. Elsewhere, I have explored intercultural collaborations that unfold through rhizomatic networks and radicant performances in journey-form, and engaged the propositions of Asia as method—along with its critique of "the West as method"—in the investigation of inter-Asian projects that resonate with its tripartite agenda of "decolonization, deimperialization, and de-Cold War"[14] of performance practices and epistemologies. It is within this framework that formulations of Asia as method can productively intersect with theorizations of "minor transnationalism" in a combined effort to elicit the significance of translocal, transversal, and transcolonial alliances.[15] A critical mapping of multiple articulations and interactions of trans-Asian theatricalities captures the distinctive mechanisms of performative acts that are not only circumscribed to the theater stage but also impinge on the realm of the quotidian and on the spheres of affect and mundane behavior. This equally meaningful component of trans-Asian theatricalities is embedded in intercultural practices that reflect social and scholarly endeavors to reinforce grassroots solidarities and assist people-based processes of transregional integration.[16]

But there are benefits to expanding the critical domain of the trans-Asian. How can we magnify the cartographies of trans-Asia? How can we envision augmented perspectives that can fruitfully interrogate received understandings of trans-Asia's conceptual boundaries? How can existing trans-Asian approaches enter into relational dialogue with new cultural, political, and geolinguistic trans-dimensions? One way of extending the empirical reach of trans-Asian theatricalities would be not only to consider work that is devised and disseminated through trans-East-Asian networks, but also to undertake a more sustained examination of performance relationalities between Northeast and South/Southeast Asia. In addition to revealing new vectors, voices, and conversations, a lateral investigation of alternate inter-Asian theatrical trajectories would fulfill the vision of pioneers of Asia-focused methodologies such as Takeuchi Yoshimi, who advocated the valorization of autonomous patterns of inter-Asian modernization through a trilateral comparison of China, Japan, and India as early as the 1960s.[17]

A further step toward expanding the latitudes of trans-Asian theatricalities would be to begin unraveling embryonic and hitherto largely uncharted linkages between Asia, Africa, and Latin America, so that the trans-Asian approach could productively intersect with critical South–South perspectives to attain a more inclusive ecology of Asian relationalities in performance. The conceptual imaginaries of the "trans-" might thus extend to comprise a notion of trans-ing as not only the act of traversing borders *across, through,* or, indeed, *within* Asia (inter-Asia) but also as one that gestures at alternate configurations of movement *beyond* naturalized geopolitical boundaries, and toward a definition of transcontinental and transoceanic Asia. Yet other underexplored avenues of Trans-Asia would be disclosed by probing intersections with Trans-Europe[18] and Asian America,[19] Australasian pathways,[20] and diasporic routes linking up global subaltern realities and post–Cold War experiences from Northeast to Central Asia.[21] In the context of emergent solidarities between geolinguistic constituencies, which, historically, have played a peripheral role in the global economies of cultural production, the performance of glocalized experience—namely, the localized re-enactment of global issues—works toward de-provincializing Asia by way of transversal alliances that bypass (geopolitical) Euro-American (linguistic) Anglophone, and (ethnic) Caucasian brokerage. Trans-Asian theatricalities so understood are transnational as much as translational; they transmute language, translate experience, and transpose behavior along local-to-local trajectories, interlacing the Asian experience with the affective textures of indigenous cultures.

The Crowd's Latin American journey presents a seminal instance of East-to-South transculturation that assists the theoretical rerouting of well-trodden East–West/North–South itineraries, in an attempt to dispel the hegemonic "spectres of the West" that loom large on the histories of comparative, intercultural, and area studies.[22] In this context, it resonates, as well, with recent explorations of the transpacific as an emergent comparative methodology. As Andrea Bachner and Pedro Erber maintain, "Asia and the Americas no longer occupy the disconnected extremes of an imagined map. Nor do they continue to embody the antipodes of East and West, framing Europe as the symbolic center. Rather, accelerated by recent geopolitical and global economic shifts, the transpacific has emerged as a space of intense transcultural movement and exchange."[23] Their view of Asian–Latin American interactions as "unstable constellations rather than fixed relationships" pinpoints the significance of recognizing the value of "uneven dialogues" and productive inconsistencies alongside the celebration of "compelling analogies" and of the progressive potential of conversations that destabilize entrenched epistemological frameworks.[24]

The Crowd is a case in point. On the one hand, its Latin American transmission negotiates claims to normative authority within the global politics of intercultural and transnational circulation by forging multilingual relations between minor "cultural particularities,"[25] which sidestep Western-centric hegemonies. On the other hand, its transculturation dynamics intersect the operational tracks of the Asian major—namely, of the Chinese nation-state. This is not only because its author holds important administrative positions in government-sponsored organizations, as the vice president of SMG Shanghai Performing Arts Group and deputy general manager of the Shanghai Dramatic Arts Centre (SDAC), but also because the play's Hispanophone transmigration was mediated by official channels. The Regional Centre of Confucius Institutes for Latin America (Centro Regional de los Institutos Confucio para América Latina (CRICAL)) supported its Spanish translation and assisted the Peruvian production—the latter in partnership with the Pontifical Catholic University of Peru (Pontificia Universidad Católica del Perú (PUCP)) and the local Confucius Institute. My proposal to expand the remit of Trans-Asia is, consequently, also an attempt to look beyond the constitutive political thrust of Asia as method toward the valorization of grassroots, minor, and people-based alliances by thinking through the potential of trans-Asian approaches to apprehend anisomorphic formations, productive disjunctions, and uneven positions that unsettle neat distinctions between minor and major, peripheral and dominant, independent and institutional.

Since *The Crowd* confronts contested national histories and its transnational (re)productions—in Peru and elsewhere—were informed by comparable

narratives of national trauma; this case also compels us to consider the varying capacities, connotations, and scopes of intervention of the "trans-" with
respect to the continued and often conflictual relevance of the national within
the transnational. Additionally, it complicates binary understandings of the
"trans-" as an invariably minor, tensional, or outright resistant dimension
vis-à-vis the normativity of the nation as a major centripetal force, for it presents a meaningful instance of lateral trans-Asian collaboration that subscribes
to the politics of the minor while concurrently sharing in the strategies of the
major. Consequently, it does not only negotiate East–West and North–South
divides by redirecting the play's transmission along East-to-South routes but
also tests the validity of the minor/major binary as such, since "in reality the
minor and the major participate in one shared transnational moment and space
structured by uneven power relations."[26] These observations are relevant to
current debates on China–Latin American cultural and economic relations,
yet this project also challenges the assumption that the minor (independent) is
invariably progressive and the major (institutional) inevitably acquiescent or
hegemonic. As Françoise Lionnet and Shu-mei Shih note, the binary opposition of major/dominant versus minor/resistant and the assumption of antago-
nistic dynamics between these presumed polarities occlude "micropractices
of transnationality in their multiple, paradoxical, or even irreverent relations
with the economic transnationalism of contemporary empires."[27] Accordingly, the play and its productions show that the minor can exist within the
major as a dialectical negotiating force.

THE CROWD FROM CHINA TO PERU, VIA HONG KONG

The Crowd was coproduced by the SDAC and the Hong Kong Arts Festival
(HKAF). The HKAF originally commissioned an adaptation of Henrik Ibsen's
An Enemy of the People (1882) that would reflect aspects of contemporary
China–Hong Kong relations. Yet, after researching historical events and current news stories that resonated with the Ibsenian themes of mass fanaticism
and crowd behavior, Yu ended up writing an original script that explores the
nature of mass incidents and the relationship between the individual and the
collective, along with notions of responsibility and guilt. Moreover, both
texts address the question of truth—how truth can be concealed or distorted—
and engage themes of (self-)censorship and systemic corruption, exposing the
collusion of media, corporate powers, and political authority.[28] Hong Kong
director Wai-kit Tang directed the world premiere on March 27–29, 2015, at
the Hong Kong Cultural Centre with a production team from Hong Kong and
performers from the SDAC. The Mandarin Chinese version was subsequently

staged in Shanghai, Beijing, Chengdu, Chongqing, Hamburg, and Sibiu. Readings in Norwegian, English, and Rumanian were held between 2015 and 2017, and Japanese and Portuguese translations were also commissioned.

The 2016 Spanish premiere was co-presented by the Performing Arts Department and the Confucius Institute of PUCP with the support of CRI-CAL. *La multitud* enjoyed thirty-two commercial performances (May 12— June 27) in a 294-seat auditorium inaugurated on this occasion at the Centre of Sino-Peruvian Friendship (Centro de la Amistad Peruano China) in Lima.[29] The award-winning production received extensive and vastly positive media coverage and was broadcast on national television. Before traveling to Peru to attend the opening, Yu also gave lectures at two Confucius Institutes in Chile to mark the publication of the first Spanish-language collection of his plays, to be distributed in Chile, Peru, Argentina, and Mexico.

The year 2016 marked both the China–Latin America and Caribbean Cultural Exchange Year and the 45th anniversary of the establishment of Sino-Peruvian diplomatic relations. *La multitud* was not part of the official programs, being an independent project which director Marissa Béjar, who is also a professor at PUCP, and Rubén Tang, the head of the PUCP Confucius Institute, had initiated already in 2014. Nonetheless, a high-profile exchange involving a prominent Chinese dramatist and a cast of renowned Peruvian actors to unveil a newly built, Chinese-funded venue in Peru's capital city surely presented a positive opportunity for cultural diplomacy in the aftermath of the 2015 China-CELAC 5-year cooperation plan,[30] and prior to the release of China's Policy Paper on Latin America and the Caribbean. The latter was sanctioned by President Xi Jinping's visit to the Asia-Pacific Economic Cooperation Forum in Lima in November 2016.

Considering the potentially sensitive content of the script, such tensional intersections of national and transnational, major and minor, are remarkable. *The Crowd* is noteworthy within Sinophone theater because it re-enacts a momentous yet marginalized chapter of China's revolutionary historiography— the Chongqing armed fights of 1967–68, whose victims have been stigmatized in official accounts of the Cultural Revolution.[31] Furthermore, it resurrects contested memories of progressive social movements such as the 1989 Tiananmen Square demonstrations and the 2014 Umbrella Movement. Thus, it is also notable as an early (perhaps the earliest) Mainland Chinese literary response to the Hong Kong protests.[32]

Through the personal history of a man seeking revenge for the unprovoked murder of his mother in the armed fights, *The Crowd* investigates the psychological dynamics that bring individuals to relinquish integrity, morality, and reason and abandon themselves to the destructive impulses of the mob. It explores notions of memory, trauma, and alienation while touching on issues of individual and institutional corruption, culpability, and (self-)justice. In addition to reflecting the ambivalent nature of social movements and a notion of history as the accumulation of collective and often uncontrolled mass incidents, the text addresses the implications of crowd psychology in the digital public sphere, the vicious force of online anonymity, and the power of the Internet to influence individual ethics and group behavior in the age of history 2.0.

THE CROWD: CHINESE PRODUCTIONS

The Crowd navigates multiple locales and temporalities over more than four decades of Chinese history to tackle momentous mass events and mnemonic landmarks in the national unconscious, ranging from the collective excesses of Maoism to civil disobedience in contemporary Hong Kong. The Cultural Revolution and the Umbrella Movement bookend a forty-year record of personal and public chronicles, as the narrative spans through the post-revolutionary trials of the late 1970s, oblique yet persistent allusions to the Tiananmen Square massacre of 1989 (purposely misdated in the script to occur in June 1987), stampedes on millennium night in 2000, petitions to the authorities during the 2008 Beijing Olympics, public square dancing during the Shanghai Expo 2010, and virtual assassinations in the cyber realm. Consistent with Haun Saussy's description of modern Chinese history as "an Age of Crowds, punctuated by explosions of crowd energy,"[33] the play's epic scope foregrounds the transhistorical reverberations of the psychology of the crowd as a fundamental historical subject and transformative social agent. Yu's crowd is Janus-faced, as his text references both emancipatory and destructive mass phenomena to underline a fundamental ontological tension between "the Loner and the Crowd"—to reiterate a well-known Chinese literary trope.[34] Moreover, it reveals how the extremist tendencies of crowd behavior have been amplified in the contemporary age by the participatory dimension of the new media ecologies and by the congenital performativity—and performability—of the mob, so that mass gatherings and collective actions come to function as extended theatrical happenings.

The play begins with a metadramatic prologue set in a theater at the time of the performance followed by descriptions of sit-ins, cordoned streets, and crowds gathered on a square, under the rain, in Hong Kong in 2014. These scenes conjure memories of Occupy Central and the Umbrella Movement but also the more distant specters of the "riotous spring" and "melancholic, hushed summer" of 1989.[35] Sixty-year-old Wang Guoqing sits alone in a hotel room, haunted by nightmares and homicidal hallucinations. The action then switches to the 1967 armed fights. The sectarian conflict between rival factions of student Red Guards and radicalized laborers escalated into a bona fide civil war in Chongqing, as each group engaged in "competitive performances" of revolutionary devotion to the Maoist doctrine.[36] The fight was particularly fierce and the death toll exceptionally high in the Southwestern Chinese city because of the wide availability of firearms in its arsenals and ammunition factories.[37] Significantly in the context of a China–Hong Kong collaboration, 1967 was also the year of violent leftist riots in Hong Kong between pro-communist organizations and the British colonial establishment.

Chongqing's "people's war"[38] is the theater of the primal murder scene that triggers Wang's forty-year-long revenge drama. As a thirteen-year-old Wang and his mother are fleeing to safety to the countryside, the latter is hit by a stray bullet that worked Ding Jianguo—a young recruit into the armed struggle—fires carelessly while testing a new gun he acquired through a firearms exchange between allied factories. The woman bleeds to death on the dry and dusty soil of the clearing between two arsenals, where fights between rival groups are taking place. She falls beneath a "savage" and "venomous" sun[39]—a likely reference to the cult of Mao as China's Red Sun—surrounded by a flock of crows under her son's petrified gaze. Crows appear as symbolic devices throughout the play, as the black cloaks the performers wear in various scenes of both the Chinese and Peruvian productions suggest. As a Greek-style chorus that comments on the action and connects actors and audiences, the crows may signify a crowd but, individually, they are alter-egos to those who—like the protagonist—stray from, are forsaken by, or fight against it.[40] Yu depicts the senseless murder of Wang's mother as a hallucination, prefiguring the hallucinatory visions that will accompany him through his lifelong pursuit of justice, up until the shabby hotel room of his final destination, Hong Kong. The dry and dusty landscape of the no man's land where the mother falls—hit by scorching sunlight and encircled by crows craving for water—is written as a wasteland where no sanctuary can be found.

In 1979, Wang returns from being sent down to the countryside for ideological re-education and marries a fellow "educated youth,"[41] as China enters a new era of optimism and relative prosperity. Upon hearing in court that Ding has been sentenced to merely three years of imprisonment, Wang resolves to seek his own justice, despite his family's intimations to forgive and forget the past, based on the argument that collective fanaticism diminishes individual responsibility. Hence the decade since his mother's death—"Ten whole years. Blood all over the ground."[42]—comes to signify the savagery of an entire nation

Wang chases Ding relentlessly, from place to place. In June 1987, he tracks him down at a Shanghai hospital, but Wang's brother alerts Ding of Wang's revengeful intentions, enabling the culprit to vanish once again into the safe anonymity of the crowd. The brother's betrayal shows the deterioration of domestic and interpersonal relationships resulting from the collective trauma of a violent upheaval, and so does Wang's father's deathbed revelation that he—a former militant in the Chongqing struggles—gave Ding the gun who killed Wang's mother.

On New Year's Eve 2000, Wang finds Ding's son, Liming, among reveling crowds on the Shanghai Bund. Upon stalking him, Wang discovers that Liming, a successful judge, is implicated in a maze of bribery and vice. After petitioning his case in Beijing to no avail, Wang plots the judge's virtual assassination by posting a video on the Internet of his encounter with a sex worker in a shady nightclub frequented by corrupt officials. Shortly, the video is shared hundreds of times. The faceless cyber crowd is "ready to dash out, to bite,"[43] and savagely tears Liming's reputation apart in the dog-eat-dog showground of online anonymity. The text underscores the close relationship between new digital technologies, participatory media platforms, and performative online behaviors, and the social consequences of the rise of "virtual communities gathered online from disaggregated private spaces."[44] The contemporary emergence of such phenomena as cyber bullying and netizen vigilantism has given novel dimensions to the psychology of the crowd, to the extent that certain Chinese Internet activists have been portrayed as "21st Century successors to the Red Guards."[45]

Another scene depicts the pervasive spectacle of square dancing as an additional illustration of modern-day mass gatherings that have brewed social conflict and occasionally involved physical violence, as citizens compete over claims to privacy and use of public space. The dancers' seizing of the square summons the ghost of another occupied square—Tiananmen—which *The Crowd* invokes obliquely, yet persistently, echoing Dai Jinhua's view of the shifting connotations of the Chinese term for "square" in post-1989 China. As the memory of the 1989 demonstrations was rendered invisible and replaced in the collective psyche with a hedonistic and far more innocuous type of public activism—marketplace consumption—the term changed from signifying a sphere of radical politics to denoting a consumerist shopping plaza[46]; or, indeed, a theater for public dancing.

Eventually, the action returns to Hong Kong in 2014. Wang meets Ding but chooses to forsake his revengeful plan, while on the streets the crowds disperse in the aftermath of a failed protest.[47] Although Occupy Central had already started at the time of writing, the version of the script published and produced in Hong Kong in March 2015 was completed in July 2014, hence before the Umbrella Movement of September–December 2014. However, the manner in which it does not explicitly differentiate the progressive nature of Hong Kong's civil disobedience from the devastating extremism of the armed fights caused criticism after the premiere.[48] Some critics in Hong Kong maintained that the play infers negative associations between the Cultural Revolution and the Umbrella Movement, considering that some local public figures had previously drawn questionable analogies between the Red Guards and the student activists.[49] *The Crowd*'s chief concern is, however, not a comparison of any specific movement, but the exploration of group dynamics, the unfolding of history through mass events, and the ways in which the collective performs and produces history—often violently. The director of the Hong Kong production likewise identifies "the relationship between the individual and the masses" as its thematic core, stating that Yu "didn't set out to write a political play."[50] Meaningfully, however, *The Crowd* travelled to Peru in the year coinciding with the 50th anniversary of the Cultural Revolution.

LA MULTITUD: PERUVIAN (RE)PRODUCTIONS

As mentioned above, *La multitud* marks a historic occurrence in the Hispano-phone context of Latin America as the first production of a contemporary Chinese play by a local director with a local cast. Significantly, the Latin American premiere took place in a country with a long history of Asian connections that precedes the recent intensification of official relations between China and Peru. A prominent Chinese Peruvian (*tusán*) community has emerged since the mid-nineteenth century settlement of Chinese indentured laborers, producing influential public figures and an established literary tradition.[51] Successive migratory waves caused an expansion of Peru's Chinese population to become the largest and culturally "most significant in Latin America."[52] Moreover, China shaped the ideological horizon of Peruvian communism, from José Carlos Mariátegui's (1894–1930) early reflections on Chinese politics and Chinese cooleism in Peru to the vehement Maoism of Abimael Guzmán, leader of the insurgent guerrilla organization known as the Shining Path (Sendero Luminoso).

Director Marissa Béjar chooses neither to adapt her production to the local context nor to make explicit references to Peru's political history. The setting and characters are Chinese, and the script follows the CRICAL-commissioned translation, except for some lexical modifications to adjust the language to Limean Spanish.[53] Yet, with its poignant imagery, dark irony, magical realist allegories, and hallucinatory atmospheres, Yu's text resonates with unsettling domestic realities that are still vivid in Peru's social memory.

An internal armed conflict ravaged the nation in the 1980s and 1990s, beginning with a terrorist attack by Sendero in 1980 on the eve of the first elections in over a decade. Guzmán and other *senderistas* attended Chinese training camps at the height of the Cultural Revolution in the 1960s, embracing the Maoist principles of people's war and prolonged, rural-based revolutionary struggle. As Matthew Rothwell comments, "the factional struggles that broke out among Peruvian Maoists resembled the rhetorical battles between Red Guard factions in China, with each side hurling quotations from Mao Zedong at each other and claiming to be the true bearers of Mao's line."[54] In all likelihood, the violent sectarian infighting which *La multitud* re-enacted on the Peruvian stage restored a recognizable experiential horizon wherein actors and audiences were cast as a testimonial community of witnesses and depositaries of transnational experiences of comparative violence, shared affects, and traumatic postmemory.

Megan Ferry maintains that Latin American reincarnations of Chinese visual propaganda were instrumental in shaping popular imaginations and "a common ideological space for a transnational Maoism" bonded by political affinity and comparable histories of imperialism and economic inequality. The global circulation of local (Chinese) revolutionary imagery fashioned localized (Latin American) iconographies and utopian sites for everyday rituals that fulfilled specific needs within the receiving communities.[55] In Peru, not only did Sendero re-rehearse Mao's ideas but also re-enacted his public image, personality cult, and political performances. With the outbreak of the internal conflict, Guzmán styled himself as "the fourth sword of Marxism,"[56] prophet of Marxism-Leninism-Maoism-Gonzalo Thought, and true heir of Mao's legacy in consequence of what he viewed as Deng Xiaoping's betrayal of socialist ideology and reactionary opening to capitalism. Going by the *nom de guerre* of Presidente (Chairman) Gonzalo, or Doctor Puka Inti (Quechua for "Red Sun"—Mao's epithet), Guzmán rose as the chief architect of an increasingly radicalized, dogmatic, and ruthless movement. A personality cult flourished around this elusive rebel of semi-mythical stature while Maoist-inspired propaganda spread across the Sierra region, where Sendero's core operations were located, comprising posters, graffiti, and slogans that mimicked those of the Cultural Revolution and portrayals of Guzmán wearing a Mao suit and emulating Maoist gesturality.[57] The ideological transperformance of Maoism in Peru thus unfolded through a repertoire of reiterations and reproductions of "restored" or "twice-behaved behaviour."[58]

Sendero's re-enacted Maoism escalated into a theater of violence as the group became responsible for countless atrocities among the indigenous communities of the Andean highlands, in addition to assassinations and terrorist attacks in Lima and other cities in the second decade of the conflict. Additionally, the state armed forces under successive corrupt governments (especially the Alberto Fujimori regime of 1990–2000) perpetrated multiple human rights violations on civilians over a twenty-year-long war that the Peruvian Truth and Reconciliation Commission (TRC) described as "the most intense, extensive and prolonged episode of violence in the entire history of the Republic."[59] As with the most destructive phases of the Chinese Revolution, the internal conflict caused immense material and human loss (about 70,000 deaths and disappearances between 1980 and 2000) and widespread social disruption, bearing long-lasting consequences on the political unconscious and affective configuration of a nation torn by brutality, retaliation, and fear. Following Guzmán's incarceration in 1992, Sendero's influence declined, just as the Cultural Revolution's radical politics lost momentum after Mao's death. Nonetheless, residual factions are still active and were responsible for an attack in central Peru on the eve of the April 2016 presidential elections, just weeks before the opening of *La multitud* in Lima.[60]

Correspondences between the Chinese and Peruvian experiences were not missed by the local media at the time of the performances. One reviewer writes that *La multitud* paints "a devastating view of the individual consequences of a political event such as the Chinese Cultural Revolution—or the internal armed conflict in Peru—and a portrait of the tragic dimensions of a human passion like revenge."[61] Béjar herself notes the play's universal relevance in several interviews, describing it as a humanistic reflection on the meaning of being an individual and, simultaneously, part of a group. Hence the protagonist's vicissitudes can resonate with different communities transnationally and transhistorically. Béjar brings the examples of the French Revolution and Nazi Germany, but also mentions the 50th anniversary of the Cultural Revolution to note the text's exposure of political processes that the Peruvian people have, likewise, withstood: the terror, the anarchy, and the trauma of loss—of human life, but also of a sense of social and individual justice.[62]

Such views on the text's transmnemonic bearing reflect former TRC president Salomón Lerner Febres's remarks on the Commission's collaboration with Grupo Cultural Yuyachkani, a local theater ensemble, in collecting testimonies of the conflict through performance: "[T]he case of Peru is far from unique, and hardly incomparable to others. It is useful therefore to bear the example in mind in broader international reflections on art and memory in the aftermath of violence."[63] For instance, the themes of collective responsibility, institutional corruption, and inadequate justice in postsocialist China pertain equally to post-conflict Peru, where it was felt that sentences were assigned unfairly, with many in the government and the military escaping punishment despite accusations of corruption and abuses while innocent victims were neither rehabilitated nor adequately compensated, and their remains never found. Lerner Febres's assertion that the re-performance of memories of the conflict eased the "reversal of two principles that facilitated the horror—namely, silence and forgetting,"[64] echoes Yu's commitment to his play as a necessary intervention in resisting collective amnesia of unsettling, yet unrecognized, facets of China's past. "The greatest guilt is not discussing it enough," he said of the Cultural Revolution to a Peruvian newspaper; but only preserving the memory of the horror can prevent the horror from happening again.[65]

128 *Chapter 6*

Assessing the Latin American transculturation of Maoist visual culture, Ferry argues that China was perceived as both a "socialist utopia" and an exotic paradise. It embodied the essence of revolution, but also signified essential alterity and mystique.[66] Likewise, a combination of familiarity and otherness—of thematic resonances at the level of content paired with defamiliarizing aesthetics at the level of form—appears to characterize the reception of *La multitud*. As with the tacit yet tangible associations to local history, the subtle accents of Chineseness in the sound, set, and costume design are more suggestive than stereotypical and skillfully integrated with indigenous elements (see figure 6.1). Nowhere does the production steer toward exoticism, yet many reviews underscore its "Brechtian" effects and unusual aesthetics, if compared to the predominantly realistic offerings of Lima's theater scene.[67]

Possibly to bridge cultural distance, *La multitud* opens with a brief contextualization of the work and clarifications, by the actors, of the multirole personas they embody. Interestingly, whereas local commentaries relate Yu's non-naturalistic dramaturgy to Brecht, the playwright ascribes certain rhythmic and compositional features to Pingtan—a Chinese folk performance genre that combines singing and storytelling. These include the script's requirement that the actors declaim technical notations such as "silence" and "pause" regularly throughout the performance, interspersed with dialogues, monologues, third-person narration, and music.[68] Unlike the Chinese productions, in which a musician plays a prepared piano to accompany the acting, the Peruvian version features a syncretic music score. The performers use a

Figure 6.1. Umbrellas allude to the 2014 Hong Kong protests in *La multitud* (2016), directed by Marissa Béjar. Photo credits: Gabriel Olaya.

range of instruments including a rainstick, a kalimba, and a modified Andean panpipe as both sound sources and stylized weapons, hence as ambiguous implements of symbolic violence (see figure 6.2).

The play's episodic structure, distancing techniques, and multiperspective approach to acting are distinctly foregrounded by six versatile performers that step in and out of numerous roles across generations, genders, and species (humans, animals, plants) in addition to doubling up as narrators. In the Peruvian version, the sense of emotional distance is enhanced by the frequent disassociation of voice and body, so that as one actor "speaks" an action (e.g., narrates the act of killing) another acts it out (e.g., makes the gesture of raising a weapon). The production design is symbolic and minimalistic, with basic set and costume changes—such as rapid furniture rearrangements or swapping coats, hats, and small props in view of the audience—signaling changes in locations and roles. It makes abundant use of digital animations (e.g., of a tree, crows, rain, online chatrooms, architectural landmarks) and heightened corporeality (e.g., group figures and arm movements to suggest leaves and branches on a tree) to recreate the sceneries of the real and virtual dimensions of Wang's drama (see figure 6.3).

The break with realism in favor of narrative episodicity and affective detachment is relevant to the text's potential for transcultural inter-referencing. The rationality that it appears to advocate at the level of content—with a critique of the crowd's irrational tendencies—breaks down at the level of form once one is "faced with the challenge of narrating the unspeakable"

Figure 6.2. Peruvian musical instruments used as stylized weapons in *La multitud* (2016), directed by Marissa Béjar. Photo credits: Gabriel Olaya.

Figure 6.3.   A scene of *La multitud* (2016), directed by Marissa Béjar, set in Chongqing during the armed fights of 1967–68. Photo credits: Gabriel Olaya.

and portraying "the unthinkable," as Lerner Febres has described the TRC's task of documenting the Peruvian conflict.[69] In their refusal to sensationalize violence, combined with the attempt to make it universal, the text and its performances rely on stylization, metaphors, and metatheatrical methods that expose the performative nature of the writing to articulate structures of feeling which cannot be explained by naturalistic conventions and rational language. The repeated pauses and spoken stage directions interject the emotional flow to engender an objective space for audiences to stand as witnesses. Concomitantly, as audiences are themselves a crowd, it forces them to think of their real-life behavior. Thus, to a degree, it also makes them complicit.

Béjar's direction accentuates the individual-crowd conflict by creating clear visual and spatial contrasts between an individual, such as Wang or Ding, and the rest of the ensemble. The ethical value of the juxtaposition is, however, fundamentally ambiguous. Since all actors portray numerous characters, moral distinctions are far from neat, as if to suggest that everyone is ambivalent, and everyone is potentially accountable in the social theatre of history.

THE ASIAN–LATIN AMERICAN TRANSPACIFIC AS ARCHIPELAGIC ASSEMBLAGE

Since the 1950s, informal cultural exchanges that preceded, or run alongside, the establishment of diplomatic institutions have been paramount in reinforcing Sino-Latin American ties and central to China's pursuit of national priorities in strategic areas of politics, economics, and international relations.[70] The circulatory dynamics of *The Crowd* signal an intention to continue—and possibly intensify—China's transpacific connections through culture, since the play's translations and stage production were supported by a PRC-sponsored local infrastructure and the regional Confucius Institutes as national vehicles of cultural diplomacy relying on the symbolic capital of prominent academic institutions transnationally. The relevance of *La multitud* as a transcultural operation is, therefore, enhanced by the recent increase in strategic agreements between the two regions and might serve as a stepping-stone for more sustained circulations and reproductions in the future.[71]

Large-scale Chinese investments in the territory can be viewed as a symptom of a "power flux inversion" in Sino-Latin American relations and of a potentially radical shift "in global imageries and recognition" for China in broader transnational terms.[72] However, the transpacific passage of such a multidimensional text as *The Crowd* also attests to the porousness of boundaries between national policies and transnational negotiations. It shows that in the same manner as the transnational can help strategically circumvent national constraints, the national can, likewise, shape the transnational dimensions of cultural production by assisting generative acts of deterritorialization, reterritorialization, and cross-fertilization.

China may as well be a rapidly expanding global power and a hegemonic political force, but her growing economic traction has not yet translated into corresponding cultural capital. Neither the Sinophone nor the Hispanophone is yet a dominant player in the cultural-artistic world order. The naturalized centers of cultural authority are still firmly situated within the Euro-American Anglophone, which dictates what constitutes culture for global consumption and circulation. Hence, *The Crowd*'s transculturation trajectory—whereby a text migrates laterally from a local (Sinophone Asian) to a local (Hispanophone Latin American) setting—highlights transversal dialogues between *culturally* decentered particularisms within a predominantly Western-centric realm.

It might be fitting, in this context, to invoke the operational metaphor of the archipelago to envision the Asian–Latin American transpacific as a fluid space of relations that connects seemingly disconnected (is)lands of disparate morphologies and magnitudes. There is no assumption of relational symmetry in the archipelago; its constitutive units are simultaneously independent and interdependent from one another, and it does not postulate equality in size, power, and prestige between components. What matters in the archipelago are the connections. Hence, an archipelagic contact zone can account for both horizontal networks and comparisons as well as for tensions and collisions on potentially uneven playing fields. The Asian–Latin American archipelago comprises an acentered "pluriverse" of interconnected formations that are not homologated into a homogenic or hegemonic cultural uni-verse, and can contain "all of those aspects that are situated 'beyond' (and also 'prior to') the structures valorised by modern European/North American culture."[73] In this perspective, the definition of "trans-" as "movement beyond" encompasses not only transborder travel and linguistic transfers but also an epistemological turn toward comparative decoloniality.[74]

The East-to-South transculturation of *The Crowd* elucidates possible modalities of resignification and reproduction of performance texts and performative behaviors between archipelagic assemblages constituted by contiguous experiential horizons in the expanded relational space of transpacific Trans-Asia. It reveals the functions of "the trans- of performance" as "a temporary and mobile framework that enables rather than confirms or fixes knowledge about the world."[75] Furthermore, the convergence of inter-Asian and transpacific trajectories onto *The Crowd*'s multiple pathways of theatrical and ideological transperformance from China to Peru, via Hong Kong, encapsulates the significance of a reconfigured conceptual reach for Trans-Asia that transcends fixed boundaries.

Expanding the maps of Trans-Asia to include alternate geolinguistic sites and cultural players signifies an attempt to pluralize the remit of trans-Asian methodologies by foregrounding emergent affinities, unstable connections, and productive gaps. The valorization of uncharted counter-cartographies and horizontal itineraries ultimately reveals emergent sites of knowledge production, which are bound to become increasingly substantial as Chinese cultures expand—for better or worse—across new latitudes.

NOTES

1. Enrique D. Dussel, "Transmodernity and Interculturality: An Interpretation from the Perspective of Philosophy of Liberation," *Transmodernity: Journal of Peripheral Cultural Production of the Luso-Hispanic World* 1, no. 3 (2012): 54.

2. See Koichi Iwabuchi's chapter 1 in this volume.

3. Yu authored more than 50 stage and screen dramas between 2000 and 2016. For an introduction see Claire Conceison, "Behind the Play: The World and Works of Nick Rongjun Yu," *Theatre Journal* 63, no. 3 (2011): 311–321.

4. Richard Schechner, "Performance Studies: The Broad Spectrum Approach," *TDR: The Drama Review* 32, no. 3 (1988): 4–6.

5. See Iwabuchi's chapter 1 in this volume.

6. Teresina Munoz Najar, "El rostro de *La multitud*," *Integración* 8, no. 39 (2016): 44.

7. Naoki Sakai, "Dislocation of the West and the Status of the Humanities," *Traces* 1 (2001): 71–94.

8. See Kuan-Hsing Chen, *Asia as Method: Toward Deimperialization* (Durham, NC: Duke University Press, 2010), and Koichi Iwabuchi, "Trans-East Asia as

Method," in *Routledge Handbook of East Asian Popular Culture*, eds. Koichi Iwabuchi, Eva Tsai, and Chris Berry (London: Routledge, 2017), 276–284.

9. See Gladys Pak Lei Chong, Yiu Fai Chow, and Jeroen de Kloet's introduction to this volume.

10. Ibid.

11. Junyoung Verónica Kim, "Asia—Latin America as Method: The Global South Project and the Dislocation of the West," *Verge: Studies in Global Asias* 3, no. 2 (2017): 101. Views on the rising profile of China in Latin America range from a discourse of solidarity that challenges the global economic supremacy of advanced capitalist nations to neocolonialist interpretations of the PRC's investment strategy in the region. While some support a framework of South–South cooperation against Euro-U.S. economic hegemony, others maintain that China is forging asymmetric "center–periphery" relations and creating the conditions for an economy of Sino-dependency. See James M. Cypher and Tamar Diana Wilson, "Introduction. China and Latin America: Processes and Paradoxes," *Latin American Perspectives* 42, no. 6 (2015): 5–26.

12. Andrea Bachner and Pedro Erber, "Remapping the Transpacific: Critical Approaches between Asia and Latin America," *Verge: Studies in Global Asias* 3, no. 2 (2017): ix.

13. Kim, "Asia—Latin America as Method," 100.

14. Chen, *Asia as Method*, 212, 216.

15. Françoise Lionnet and Shu-mei Shih, "Introduction: Thinking through the Minor, Transnationally," in *Minor Transnationalism*, eds. Lionnet and Shih (Durham, NC: Duke University Press, 2005), 1–23.

16. See Rossella Ferrari, "Journey(s) to the East—Travels, Trajectories, and Transnational Chinese Theatre(s)," *Postcolonial Studies* 13, no. 4 (2010): 351–366, and "Asian Theatre as Method: The Toki Experimental Project and Sino-Japanese Transnationalism in Performance," *TDR: The Drama Review* 61, no. 3 (2017): 141–164.

17. Yoshimi Takeuchi, "Asia as Method," in *What Is Modernity? Writings of Takeuchi Yoshimi*, ed. and trans. Richard F. Calichman (New York: Columbia University Press, 2005), 149–165.

18. See Ien Ang's chapter 3 in this volume.

19. See Chih-Ming Wang's chapter 4 in this volume.

20. See Iwabuchi's chapter 1 in this volume.

21. See Soyoung Kim's chapter 5 in this volume.

22. Naoki Sakai and Yukiko Hanawa, eds., "Special Issue: Specters of the West & Politics of Translation," *Traces* 1 (2001). See also Yiu Fai Chow and Jeroen de Kloet, eds., "Special Issue: Cultural Studies, Europe, and the 'Rise of Asia,'" *European Journal of Cultural Studies* 17, no. 1 (2014).

23. Bachner and Erber, "Remapping," vi.

24. Ibid., xi, xiii.

25. Lionnet and Shih, "Introduction," 2.

26. Ibid., 7.

27. Ibid.

28. Rongjun Yu, "Nimen zenme neng da yige guanzhong de lian? (How could you slap an audience in the face?)" *Juben* 2 (2016): 49–51. Comparisons have also been

drawn between Yu's play and Gustav Le Bon's *The Crowd: A Study of the Popular Mind* (1895).

29. Inaugurated in 2014, the Centre was built with a Chinese government donation of RMB 20 million.

30. CELAC stands for Comunidad de Estados Latinoamericanos y Caribeños (Community of Latin American and Caribbean States).

31. Everett Y. Zhang, "Grieving at Chongqing's Red Guard Graveyard: In the Name of Life Itself," *The China Journal* 70 (2013): 26.

32. Wayne C. F. Yeung (Chaofeng Yang), "Cong wenge dao yusan yundong: yi Yu Rongjun ji Huang Biyun pouxi qunzhong xinlixue, minzhu yu zhengzhi ziyou (From the Cultural Revolution to the Umbrella Movement: An Analysis of Mass Psychology, Democracy and Political Freedom in Yu Rongjun and Huang Biyun)," *Weipi Paratext*, December 14, 2016, http://paratext.hk/?p=292.

33. Haun Saussy, "Crowds, Number, and Mass in China," in *Crowds*, eds. Jeffrey T. Schnapp and Matthew Tiews (Stanford, CA: Stanford University Press, 2006), 256.

34. Leo Ou-fan Lee, *Voices from the Iron House: A Study of Lu Xun* (Bloomington, IN: Indiana University Press, 1987), 69–88.

35. Rongjun Yu, *Wuhe zhizhong/The Crowd*, trans. Gigi Chang (Hong Kong: Hong Kong Arts Festival Society Ltd., 2015), 153. This bilingual edition includes the 2014 version of the script, which contains explicit mentions of Tiananmen Square. These are replaced with generic references to Beijing in subsequent versions. The predated "riotous spring," "melancholic, hushed summer," and "June 1987" are maintained in all versions. Yu completed the first draft on July 10 and the second on July 19, 2014. The revised third and fourth drafts were completed on February 11, 2015, and February 23, 2016, respectively. For the version published in Mainland China see Rongjun Yu, "Wuhe zhizhong," *Juben* 2 (2016): 18–48; 51. I have also consulted the 2015 Spanish translation by Demetrio Ibarra Hernández, the 2016 updated English translation by Gigi Chang revised by Claire Conceison (unpublished), and video recordings of the Hong Kong, Shanghai, and Lima productions.

36. Guobin Yang, *The Red Guard Generation and Political Activism in China* (New York: Columbia University Press, 2016), 19.

37. Xujun Eberlein, "Another Swimmer," in *Chinese Characters: Profiles of Fast-Changing Lives in a Fast-Changing Land*, eds. Angilee Shah and Jeffrey Wasserstrom (Berkeley, CA: University of California Press, 2012), 68.

38. Yu, *The Crowd*, 124.

39. Ibid., 118, 121.

40. The play's Chinese title, meaning "mob," "rubble," or "motley crew," originates from *Guanzi*, wherein Guan Zhong (c. 720–645 BC) uses the image of a flock of crows to refer to an unruly crowd or multitude. The play also references Aesop's "The Crow and the Pitcher."

41. The armed fights ended in 1968 when Mao ordered the dissolution of Red Guard factions and their re-education among the peasants.

42. Yu, *The Crowd*, 139.

43. Ibid., 191.

44. Anup Grewal and Tie Xiao, "Did Someone Say "Crowd"? The Dis/Appearance of the Political Mass in Contemporary China," *Modern Chinese Literature and Culture* 25, no. 2 (2013): 9.

45. Carrie Gracie, "The New Red Guards: China's Angry Student Patriots," BBC News, May 26, 2017, http://www.bbc.co.uk/news/world-asia-39996940.

46. Jinhua Dai, "Invisible Writing: The Politics of Mass Culture in the 1990s," in *Cinema and Desire: Feminist Marxism and Cultural Politics in the Work of Dai Jinhua*, eds. Jing Wang and Tani E. Barlow (London: Verso, 2002), 213–234.

47. In the 2016 revised version, Wang discovers in a hallucinatory encounter with Ding Liming that Ding Jianguo committed suicide in June 1987, presumably overcome by guilt.

48. The scenes set in Hong Kong are dated "July 2014" in the Hong Kong published script (Yu, *The Crowd*) and "September 2014" in the 2015 and 2016 updated versions.

49. Yeung, "Cong wenge."

50. Bei Hu, "Crowd Work," *Global Times*, March 5, 2015, http://www.global times.cn/content/910371.shtml.

51. Ignacio López-Calvo, *Dragons in the Land of the Condor: Writing Tusán in Peru* (Tucson, AZ: University of Arizona Press, 2014).

52. Jae Park, "Cultural Artefact, Ideology Export or Soft Power? Confucius Institute in Peru," *International Studies in Sociology of Education* 23, no. 1 (2013): 5. See also Isabelle Lausent-Herrera "Tusans (*tusheng*) and the Changing Chinese Community in Peru," *Journal of Chinese Overseas* 7, no. 1 (2009): 115–152. Chinese theatre, particularly Cantonese opera, has been practiced in Lima Chinatown since the early stages of Chinese immigration.

53. Marissa Béjar, email to author, March 18 and April 2, 2018.

54. Matthew D. Rothwell, *Transpacific Revolutionaries: The Chinese Revolution in Latin America* (London: Routledge, 2013), 57.

55. Megan M. Ferry, "China as Utopia: Visions of the Chinese Cultural Revolution in Latin America," *Modern Chinese Literature and Culture* 12, no. 2 (2000): 238.

56. Rothwell, *Transpacific Revolutionaries*, 48.

57. David Scott Palmer, "The Influence of Maoism in Peru," in *Mao's Little Red Book: A Global History*, ed. Alexander C. Cook (Cambridge: Cambridge University Press, 2014), 130–146. See Ferry, "China as Utopia," for illustrations and further analysis.

58. Richard Schechner, *Performance Theory* (London: Routledge: 2003), 324.

59. Comisión de la Verdad y Reconciliación, "Final Report: General Conclusions," Commission report, August 28, 2003, http://www.cverdad.org.pe/ingles/ifinal/conclusiones.php.

60. Colin Post, "Shining Path Ambush Kills 10 on Eve of Peru's Election," *Peru Reports*, April 12, 2016, http://perureports.com/2016/04/12/shining-path-ambush-kills-10-eve-perus-election.

61. Valentina Pérez Llosa, "'La multitud': Repercusiones personales de una revolución masiva," *LaMula*, May 26, 2016, https://redaccion.lamula.pe/2016/05/26/la-multitud-repercusiones-personales-de-una-revolucion-masiva/valentinaperezllosa/.

62. Ibid.; Hernán Hernandez, "Marissa Béjar: 'En Perú no se visibiliza la cultura china," *La República*, May 22, 2016, http://larepublica.pe/tendencias/940641-marissa-bejar-en-peru-no-se-visibiliza-la-cultura-china.

63. Salomón Lerner Febres, "Memory of Violence and Drama in Peru: The Experience of the Truth Commission and Grupo Cultural Yuyachkani," keynote speech, Brandeis University, December 1, 2011, https://www.brandeis.edu/ethics/peacebuild ingarts/pdfs/Lerner_Speech_Dec2011_EnglishTranslation.pdf.

64. Ibid.

65. Enrique Planas, "La autocensura es el problema del arte en China," *El Comercio*, May 12, 2016. N.p.

66. Ferry, "China as Utopia," 239.

67. Pérez Llosa, "'La multitud'"; Piero Miovich Bedregal, "La multitud," *Las fauces de la musa*, July 21, 2016, http://pieromiobe.blogspot.co.uk/2016/07/la-multi tud.html.

68. Nick Rongjun Yu, personal communication, October 27, 2017.

69. Lerner Febres, "Memory of Violence."

70. Ferry, "China as Utopia," 251; Rothwell, *Transpacific Revolutionaries*, 18–27.

71. There are plans to stage Yu's *The Eight Day of the Week*, which tackles the sensitive subject of the Great Famine of 1958–1961 and remains unproduced in China at the time of writing. Although the focus of this chapter is the China-to-Peru route, there are instances of Sino-Peruvian interchange in the opposite direction. Béjar herself taught at Shanghai Theatre Academy in 2017 and Miguel Rubio Zapata of Grupo Cultural Yuyachkani gave seminars in China in 1993.

72. Park, "Cultural Artefact," 14.

73. Dussel, "Transmodernity," 43.

74. See Walter D. Mignolo, "On Comparison: Who Is Comparing What and Why?" in *Comparison: Theories, Approaches, Uses*, eds. Rita Felski and Susan Stanford Friedman (Baltimore, MD: Johns Hopkins University Press, 2013), 99–119.

75. Amelia Jones, "Introduction: *Trans-ing* Performance," *Performance Research*, 21, no. 5 (2016): 5.

BIBLIOGRAPHY

Bachner, Andrea, and Pedro Erber. "Remapping the Transpacific: Critical Approaches between Asia and Latin America." *Verge: Studies in Global Asias* 3, no. 2 (2017): vi–xiii.

Bedregal, Piero Miovich. "La multitud." *Las fauces de la musa*, July 21, 2016. http://pieromiobe.blogspot.co.uk/2016/07/la-multitud.html.

Chen, Kuan-Hsing. *Asia as Method: Toward Deimperialization*. Durham, NC: Duke University Press, 2010.

Chow, Yiu Fai, and Jeroen de Kloet, eds. "Special Issue: Cultural Studies, Europe, and the 'Rise of Asia.'" *European Journal of Cultural Studies* 17, no. 1 (2014).

Comisión de la Verdad y Reconciliación. "Final Report: General Conclusions." Commission report. August 28, 2003. http://www.cverdad.org.pe/ingles/ifinal/conclusiones.php.

Conceison, Claire. "Behind the Play: The World and Works of Nick Rongjun Yu." *Theatre Journal* 63, no. 3 (2011): 311–321.

Cypher, James M. and Tamar Diana Wilson. "Introduction. China and Latin America: Processes and Paradoxes." *Latin American Perspectives* 42, no.6 (2015): 5–26.

Dai, Jinhua. "Invisible Writing: The Politics of Mass Culture in the 1990s." In *Cinema and Desire: Feminist Marxism and Cultural Politics in the Work of Dai Jinhua*, edited by Jing Wang and Tani E. Barlow, 213–234. London: Verso, 2002.

Dussel, Enrique D. "Transmodernity and Interculturality: An Interpretation from the Perspective of Philosophy of Liberation." *Transmodernity: Journal of Peripheral Cultural Production of the Luso-Hispanic World* 1, no. 3 (2012): 28–59.

Eberlein, Xujun. "Another Swimmer." In *Chinese Characters: Profiles of Fast-Changing Lives in a Fast-Changing Land*, edited by Angilee Shah and Jeffrey Wasserstrom, 67–78. Berkeley, CA: University of California Press, 2012.

Febres, Salomón Lerner. "Memory of Violence and Drama in Peru: The Experience of the Truth Commission and Grupo Cultural Yuyachkani." Keynote speech. Brandeis University, December 1, 2011. https://www.brandeis.edu/ethics/peace buildingarts/pdfs/Lerner_Speech_Dec2011_EnglishTranslation.pdf.

Ferrari, Rossella. "Journey(s) to the East—Travels, Trajectories, and Transnational Chinese Theatre(s)." *Postcolonial Studies* 13, no. 4 (2010): 351–366.

———. "Asian Theatre as Method: The Toki Experimental Project and Sino-Japanese Transnationalism in Performance." *TDR: The Drama Review* 61, no. 3 (2017): 141–164.

Ferry, Megan M. "China as Utopia: Visions of the Chinese Cultural Revolution in Latin America." *Modern Chinese Literature and Culture* 12, no. 2 (2000): 236–269.

Gracie, Carrie. "The New Red Guards: China's Angry Student Patriots." BBC News, May 26, 2017. http://www.bbc.co.uk/news/world-asia-39996940.

Grewal, Anup, and Tie Xiao. "Did Someone Say 'Crowd'? The Dis/Appearance of the Political Mass in Contemporary China." *Modern Chinese Literature and Culture* 25, no. 2 (2013): 1–20.

Hernandez, Hernán. "Marissa Béjar: 'En Perú no se visibiliza la cultura china.'" *La República*, May 22, 2016. http://larepublica.pe/tendencias/940641-marissa-bejar-en-peru-no-se-visibiliza-la-cultura-china.

Hu, Bei. "Crowd Work " *Global Times*, March 5, 2015. http://www.globaltimes.cn/content/910371.shtml.

Iwabuchi, Koichi. "Trans-East Asia as Method." In *Routledge Handbook of East Asian Popular Culture*, edited by Koichi Iwabuchi, Eva Tsai, and Chris Berry, 276–284. London: Routledge, 2017.

Jones, Amelia. "Introduction: *Trans-ing* Performance." *Performance Research* 21, no. 5 (2016): 1–11.

Kim, Junyoung Verónica. "Asia–Latin America as Method: The Global South Project and the Dislocation of the West." *Verge: Studies in Global Asias* 3, no. 2 (2017): 97–117.

Lausent-Herrera, Isabelle. "Tusans (*tusheng*) and the Changing Chinese Community in Peru." *Journal of Chinese Overseas* 7, no. 1 (2009): 115–152.

Lee, Leo Ou-fan. *Voices from the Iron House: A Study of Lu Xun*. Bloomington, IN: Indiana University Press, 1987.

Lionnet, Françoise, and Shu-mei Shih. "Introduction: Thinking through the Minor, Transnationally." In *Minor Transnationalism*, edited by Françoise Lionnet and Shu-mei Shih, 1–23. Durham, NC: Duke University Press, 2005.

Llosa, Valentina Pérez. "'La multitud': Repercusiones personales de una revolución masiva." *LaMula*, May 26, 2016. https://redaccion.lamula.pe/2016/05/26/la-multitud-repercusiones-personales-de-una-revolucion-masiva/valentinaperezllosa/.

López-Calvo, Ignacio. *Dragons in the Land of the Condor: Writing Tusán in Peru*. Tucson, AZ: University of Arizona Press, 2014.

Mignolo, Walter D. "On Comparison: Who Is Comparing What and Why?" In *Comparison: Theories, Approaches, Uses*, edited by Rita Felski and Susan Stanford Friedman, 99–119. Baltimore: Johns Hopkins University Press, 2013.

Najar, Teresina Munoz. "El rostro de *La multitud*." *Integración* 8, no. 39 (2016): 42–44.

Palmer, David Scott. "The Influence of Maoism in Peru." In *Mao's Little Red Book: A Global History*, edited by Alexander C. Cook, 130–146. Cambridge: Cambridge University Press, 2014.

Park, Jae. "Cultural Artefact, Ideology Export or Soft Power? Confucius Institute in Peru." *International Studies in Sociology of Education* 23, no. 1 (2013): 1–16.

Planas, Enrique. "La autocensura es el problema del arte en China." *El Comercio*, May 12, 2016. N.p.

Post, Colin. "Shining Path Ambush Kills 10 on Eve of Peru's Election." *Peru Reports*, April 12, 2016. http://perureports.com/2016/04/12/shining-path-ambush-kills-10-eve-perus-election.

Rothwell, Matthew D. *Transpacific Revolutionaries: The Chinese Revolution in Latin America*. London: Routledge, 2013.

Sakai, Naoki. "Dislocation of the West and the Status of the Humanities." *Traces* 1 (2001): 71–94.

Sakai, Naoki, and Yukiko Hanawa, eds. "Special Issue: Specters of the West & Politics of Translation." *Traces* 1 (2001).

Saussy, Haun. "Crowds, Number, and Mass in China." In *Crowds*, edited by Jeffrey T. Schnapp and Matthew Tiews, 249–269. Stanford: Stanford University Press, 2006.

Schechner, Richard. "Performance Studies: The Broad Spectrum Approach." *TDR: The Drama Review* 32, no. 3 (1988): 4–6.

———. *Performance Theory*. London: Routledge, 2003.

Takeuchi, Yoshimi. "Asia as Method." In *What Is Modernity? Writings of Takeuchi Yoshimi*, edited and translated by Richard F. Calichman, 149–165. New York: Columbia University Press, 2005.

Yang, Guobin. *The Red Guard Generation and Political Activism in China*. New York: Columbia University Press, 2016.

Yeung, Wayne C. F. (Chaofeng Yang). "Cong wenge dao yusan yundong: yi Yu Rongjun ji Huang Biyun pouxi qunzhong xinlixue, minzhu yu zhengzhi ziyou

(From the Cultural Revolution to the Umbrella Movement: An Analysis of Mass Psychology, Democracy and Political Freedom in Yu Rongjun and Huang Biyun)." *Weipi Paratext*, December 14, 2016. http://paratext.hk/?p=292.

Yu, Rongjun. *Wuhe zhizhong/The Crowd*, translated by Gigi Chang. Hong Kong: Hong Kong Arts Festival Society Ltd., 2015.

———. "Wuhe zhizhong (The Crowd)." *Juben* 2 (2016): 18–48; 51.

———. "Nimen zenme neng da yige guanzhong de lian? (How could you slap an audience in the face?)" *Juben* 2 (2016): 49–51.

Zhang, Everett Y. "Grieving at Chongqing's Red Guard Graveyard: In the Name of Life Itself." *The China Journal* 70 (2013): 24–47.

Chapter 7

Repeating Anime's Creativity across Asia

Stevie Suan

TRANS-ASIA AS METHOD: THINKING ACROSS ASIA

The transformative potential of knowledge production, where shifts in approach can substantiate changes in the way we view the world, underpins Chen Kuan-Hsing's work on "Asia as method." Providing alternative approaches to area studies, Chen implements a multilayered reading of the "Asia as Method" lecture given by Takeuchi Yoshimi in 1960. Takeuchi attempted to work through the affinity he felt towards China and the people's relation to modernity, an analysis that would in turn help him confront Japan's own relation to modernity.[1] Takeuchi's lecture is later rethought by Yūzō Mizoguchi in his work *China as Method* (1996 [1989]), upon which Chen builds, adapting Mizoguchi's conception of "base-entities." Sometimes altered by external forces, these "local spaces" are constantly shifting (nonessentialized), different from place to place, but with their own internal logics, contradictions, and social relations that are products of long histories.[2] Chen stresses the importance of inter-referencing, which would change the perspective on the base-entity, that a mutual "objectification" allows both points of departure to mediate one another and reach a different understanding: "to do area studies is not simply to study the object of analysis but also to perform a self-analysis through a process of constant inter-referencing . . . [R]elativizing the understanding of the self as well as the object of the study is a precondition for arriving at different understandings of the self, the Other, and world history."[3]

   Chen is part of a larger movement in Asian Studies, and to contribute to this inquiry, with the intent to conceptualize a "Trans-Asia as method," I would propose to think not only about the base-entities and inter-referencing to shift our understanding, but how and what is traversing across these local spaces. In other words, following Ani Maitra's and Rey Chow's advocation[4] of moving away from the area studies methodology of looking at "media *in* Asia," we might consider thinking through the flows *across*, not *into* different, parts of Asia. When the transnational is brought into play, we tend to think of cultural products like Japanese anime as it is brought *into* China, or how K-dramas are influential *in* Japan. This focus on popular cultural products is traditionally considered in relation to the nation. As an alternative, we might draw on the recent publication by Marc Steinberg and Jinying Li who, in part building on Thomas Lamarre's work[5] on media process geographies, consider regions as "produced by the medial effects of 'something coming into common' (as Lamarre puts it)," which may not align with established boundaries of a region.[6] They focus on media platforms, which circulate "tremendous amounts of contents, products, and transactions, which actualize the transmedial-transnational processes that, in turn, produce a feeling of regional affinity, intimacy, and proximity."[7]

Such media products, produced by the "creative industries," have been the focus of much attention as the different (East) Asian nations undergo shifts in the current stage(s) of global neoliberalism in a transition toward the creative economy. A diverse range of occupations are included under the rubric of creative industries, many of them associated with popular cultural products like commercial animation. Indeed, the South Korean and Chinese governments have been investing in their respective animation industries in recent years, and the output of animation has increased dramatically in volume.[8] However, in terms of global presence and recognizability, Japan's commercial animation industry, with anime as its emblem, appears at the forefront of the animation industry. Though usually parsed as "Japanese popular animation," what is normally considered anime is actually a type of animation that is usually termed *shinya* (or "late-night") anime, for the time it is broadcast in Japan. These works usually have a very recognizable aesthetic, utilizing similar design styles, narrative tropes, and animation techniques. Exploiting the institutional and methodological tendencies to use nation as a point of departure for examining culture, nation-branding campaigns like Cool Japan have helped sustain such an aesthetic as representative of Japan—in other words, there is an exclusive link between the media-form of anime (the repeated patterns in animation) and Japan.

However, anime production, which is usually thought of as located in Japan, has a long history of transnational production within Asia. Here I will be focusing on this creative industry *across* Asia, instead of focusing on Japan, in an attempt to rethink how transformations of our notion of creative production can alter the concepts we use to consider regionality through the media produced. For this, I will take a formalist approach, examining the mechanics of creativity as it applies to anime and engaging with the dynamics of anime's transnational system of production. We will analyze anime's recognizability, taking anime as a media-form with repeated patterns, showing how anime itself is sustained on a type of iterability with minor variation, providing an alternative to dominant conceptions of creativity, which valorize "originality" and departure from trend. I will then consider the implications of this in regard to recent transnational anime productions and propose how to (re)consider anime's history of outsourcing labor across Asia. While the focus will be mainly on recent works that relate to China's creative industries due to the current production practices in regards to anime, there will also be attention paid to other places in Asia that have been part of anime's transnational production network.

CREATIVITY AND COPYING

Interrogating the terms of "creative industry," the word "industry" implies an economic model and the regularity and controllability of production, which seems almost antithetical to the common usage of "creativity." As Justin O'Connor and Gu Xin espouse, "the term [creativity] feeds on a form of 'artistic' sensibility and practice—breaking the rules, 'thinking outside the box', 'coming from left field', etc.—which links to the aesthetic of the 'revaluation of all values', 'the shock of the new' and the agonistic struggle with the existing order which characterizes the modernist and avant-garde traditions."[9] Such an understanding of creativity is deeply connected to the largely Western notion of the individual artist,[10] where their interiority is externalized, one which ideally can affect substantial challenges to the social world. In other words, there is a valorization, in regards to artistic creative output, of the departure from established trend, which may conflict with the regimented, repetitive, and predictable outcomes presumed in industrial processes.

But as Laikwan Pang details in her seminal work on the creative industries, our understandings of creativity are "characterized by the tensions and dynamics between freedom and control, art and design, textuality and industrialism."[11] Pang contends "unpredictability and indocility make artistic creativity both resistant and germane to the modernity project"[12] and that the contemporary global creative economy (fueled by the creative industries) is the latest manifestation of this, following the logic of the individual artist in the regime of intellectual property rights (IPR).[13] As noted above, the creative industries often link up with nation-branding, where an intimate relationship between nation and creative production are made in the context of the global: the interiority of the individual artist (or company) is a stand in for a nation, whose unique cultural interior is externalized through the product and exported to the world where it can compete in the global market place as representative of the nation.

Furthermore, the promotion of the creative industries "draws precisely on the discourse of cultural modernization itself," which is "no longer a question of how to manage the rapid industrialization of a peasant society, it is now about promoting human creativity."[14] Such a shift is in part to meet the demands for "cultural" consumer goods, to move beyond the production of basic consumer goods towards a leisure economy, the "next stage" in economic development.[15] This, as O'Connor and Xin assert, "presents problems in East Asia generally, [and] it poses specific questions in China."[16] They raise the intriguing query of whether "China [can] develop an innovative entertainment and leisure sector without the artistic milieu, without that active modernist cultural sensibility."[17] In other words, is there a different model of creativity that fits the conditions of contemporary China and its "developing" creative industries?

Such a question is in consideration of the "the direct control of content and the resistance to any notion of an autonomous cultural sphere" in a country where maintaining social stability is paramount to the state.[18] Indeed, as Anthony Y.-H. Fung and Vicky Ho detail in their account of the animation industry in China, these are some of the criteria that guide the censorship and award system for domestic animation production: maintaining a harmonious society.[19] Fung and Ho maintain that, while there has been a quantitative increase in volume of animation production, there is a stifling of (artistic) creativity because animated works "ought not to be shocking or disruptive," restricted by the prevailing conceptual and policy views that animation is a child-oriented medium and works must be in line with the government agenda.[20] They also note how there has been a history of outsourcing of Japanese animation (namely, anime) in China, and that this has left a "lingering Japanese influence," where works of this type are sometimes lambasted as "copycat" works.[21] This can be a common reaction in Asia, where local animations produced with anime influence, for example, by South Koreans,[22] have also received similarly negative reactions.

The important point to note here is the reaction to imitation in the context of creativity. Placed in opposition to the modernist artistic creativity that is a departure from trend and normally valorized in discourses on creativity— even imbedded in the very notion of creativity, as Pang details—practices that follow trend, which result in "mere copies" are denigrated as derivative and lesser. Indeed, this is part of the dynamics of many accusations of mimicry applied to Asia, often in comparison to Western models.[23] Japan itself has often been characterized as a country of "copying" in various contexts, not least of which was imitating Western modernity itself.[24] China has been one of the recent targets of such accusations of "merely copying," without any "real innovation" in its modernization process. Animated productions are just one of the contemporary topics of the accusation that China (or Korea) is just imitating Japanese animation without any local flair—in other words, there has yet to be a decidedly "Chinese" (or "Korean") type of animation. But is this not replaying the same debates about the interplay between modernization, nation, and culture as in "national literatures or cinema"? Does every Asian nation necessarily have to create their own, unique type of animation? It is worth exploring how we might conceive of "copying" across Asia, specifically in regards to anime, and how this may inform or impede a conception of regionality, of "something coming into common."[25] With this in mind, we might have to rethink how we engage with the dynamics of copying and creativity in regards to anime production across Asia.

CITATIONALITY AND ANIME'S CREATIVITY: EXAMPLE 1

Before going any further, let me provide a recent example of anime from China: *School Shock* (2015), an anime made by the Chinese company Haoliners (owned by the media giant Tencent). Based on a popular manhua (comic) of the same name, the production was mainly done in China, but it received a Japanese dub, involving the highly popular voice-actress Kana Hanazawa in a lead role. Taking place in China, the narrative follows a high school student, Haoxuan Sun (Hōken Son), a special "Child of Eden," who is protected by a nanotechnology-enhanced Liu Li (Ruri), a human weapon who is transferred to Sun's school to guard him, her final mission before she gets "decommissioned." Though the anime contains specific designs, characters, and a world-setting, in many ways the animation appears as a "standard" TV anime from Japan, involving many of the common visual traits of characters (e.g., long limbs, hair colors, large eyes, pointed nose), conventionalized facial expressions (e.g., arched eyes for smiling, white orbs for shock), narrative tropes (e.g., mechanized female characters, a "wimpy" male protagonist who is a "chosen" person, female transfer student who has supernatural powers, female character with time limit on life), and voice-acting (in Japanese).

To give an example of the degree of similarity, there is a seemingly innocuous scene at the very end of episode two, where the main character, Sun, is daydreaming during school, thinking about his traumatic experience as a hostage where he was saved by Liu Li. Snapped out of his dream by the teacher scolding him, he obeys her instructions to close the window next to him, gazing out into the dirt soccer field below, where he sees Liu Li in the same school uniform, implying that she would be a transfer student to his school. It is not just the scene as such (reminiscing about the traumatic events at school), or the character designs, or the inclusion of a mysterious transfer student that is noteworthy. What is striking here is the placement of Sun's seat (by the window in the classroom) and the general layout of the school (the soccer field below). For a narrative supposedly set in China, the design and placement of the seating are strikingly similar to the images of schools in Japan in anime. In fact, the placement of the main character in that particular seat is a widely known trope in anime: the main character is almost always seated by the window, the blackboard in front of them (see figure 7.1).

How do we read such a scene, supposedly set in China, that is so closely related to imagery associated with Japan? It is clear that on multiple levels—character designs, animation techniques, background settings, narrative patterns, etc.—the above work, one of a growing number of productions, is reproducing the same recognizable conventions of Japanese anime. But this act may not be outside of the norm, even in Japan. Indeed, if there is such a recognizability to Japanese anime, that must imply that there is a certain degree of repetition already invoked in anime. This repetition is worth examining.

We might consider these reiterated conventions as "anime-esque"[26] performances, a topic that I have detailed elsewhere but will summarize below.[27] Such conventions are recognizable as anime-esque because of their very repetition in anime—they are the elements expected by the creators and consumers of the media product labelled anime. These anime-esque elements might be considered what Hiroki Azuma[28] labelled "*moe*-elements" in his theory of database consumption, where fans disassemble and reassemble different character "parts" (e.g., hair, eyes, clothes) to produce new characters, a concept that can be extended to other elements of anime (e.g., narrative, character types, facial expressions). These elements appear so anime-esque because of their regularity, built up over time, each with a history. Anime-esque elements might best be considered as "models," which are constantly cited in different combinations when producing anime. This does not mean

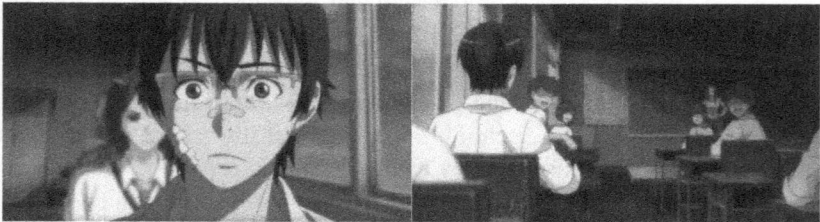

Figure 7.1.   Screenshots from *School Shock* showing the trope of the main character sitting by the window (left) with a similar structural layout of a classroom (right) used in anime set in Japanese schools.

there is some essential "core" to anime made up of such models. Rather, each citation is not *exactly* the same but minorly different, placed in differing contexts and combinations, which are in turn, disassembled and re-cited once more, inducing change and enabling diversity. Thus, what is anime-esque shifts over time, some citations becoming popular and continuing to become cited (felicity), others failing (often through poor sales, bad fan reception: infelicity), and left unrepeated. Furthermore, what may be considered anime-esque would differ from person to person, period to period, place to place; it is an act of interpretation, a manner of grouping together anime and selecting what you (the creators, the consumers) would see as characteristic of anime, and then reproducing it.

In sum, the citation of these recognizably anime models is the execution of an "anime-esque act," and what we think of as anime is performatively constituted through the enactment of a large number of those anime-esque acts in animation. This means that anime become recognizable as such through the repeated performance of anime-esque acts, and is thus constituted through this repetition. This is how anime sustains itself as a recognizable category of media, as a particular product. As such, because recognizability is so important to its success, a problematic arises: if a performance strays too far from an anime-esque model, it becomes unrecognizable as anime, but too similar a repetition implies redundancy and potential failure. Every anime-esque performance becomes a negotiation between its relation to the historical success of prior instances, and the particularity, the distinctiveness of the current iteration. In this way, anime's performances must always straddle between reiteration and variation, unity and diversity, while tending to keep towards repetition in order to maintain its recognizability, engaging "an improvisational possibility within a field of constraints."[29] Indeed, this is evident in the very practice of anime production. As Pang notes, the physical copying of characters is how (cel) animation itself operates,[30] where each image must resemble the character models they are based on yet still be distinct to produce movement.[31] Furthermore, having animators (and other producers) that can consistently (re)produce anime-esque conventions also enable a regularity of production and smoothing over of complex production processes via the reliance on the performance of those conventions.

Considering anime as a performance of a media-form has implications on the current context of anime as a creative industry across Asia, in particular in relation to China. It means that anime is no longer dependent on Japan as a defining characteristic. If anime is constituted through the repetition of anime-esque conventions, this would apply to productions made both inside and outside of Japan. Anime-esque elements become something external to all performers (animators, directors, etc.), something that must be learned, taught, practiced, enacted regardless of locale. Furthermore, anime's creativity becomes less about innovation and departure from trend, relying on the refined execution of pre-existing conventions, a mixing and matching of cited anime-esque elements. Because anime is itself sustained by recognizable repetition within a restricted field (i.e., the anime-esque models), we see an emphasis on minor variation over departure from trend.

Such a conception of creativity is very different from that of the Western modernist, artistic creativity of the individual. But this should not be understood as some appeal to a culturalist tradition in Japan (or Asia in general). Instead, as Rupert Cox reminds us, "with the ubiquity of copies through commodification and the attraction of new sensory experiences made possible through copying machines, the copy may speak much more to personal desires and feelings than to national qualities."[32] To echo Pang's words, "at a time when we can foresee no more breaks, when creativity cannot bring us any shocks of the new, I hope that we can gain a different understanding of the relationship between the established and the new by reverting to the logic of copying."[33] Informed by this approach to anime's creativity, which resembles the logic of copying in the citationality of the anime-esque, we may be able to reconsider anime's performances in China specifically, and across Asia broadly.

ANIME'S CREATIVITY IN CHINA: EXAMPLE 2

At first glance, anime's creativity might appear to fit the specific demands of the creative industries in China. Anime's creativity is about sustaining an aesthetic through recognizability, variation within the field of constraint as opposed to the valorization of disruptive difference; it does not have to privilege novelty, instead focusing on maintaining, on reiteration. This does not mean innovation completely vanishes, but that repetition is not viewed negatively as it is the very mechanism by which anime is identifiable as such. This closely resembles the logic of copying that Pang details, who explicates a "correspondence between China's piracy culture and the Japanese cartoon [anime] culture in the common affinity for mimesis."[34] In one example, Pang explores an illegally produced book that displays information and images about director Hayao Miyazaki's works, which mixes and matches images and articles from different sources but inserts minor variations and produces a distinct product in the process. This is also evident in *dōjin*[35] culture, in China and elsewhere, where fans make their own versions of anime or manga (or game) characters, carefully staying faithful to the designs and narratives, while still deviating enough to produce a distinctive work.[36] Such practices produce a sense of community between those who make and read such works, as well as other fans, often because of their mutual familiarity with the various conventions that they are repeating.[37]

This affinity with anime is not necessarily something that is new, either. Early anime works like *Astro Boy* (*Tetsuwan Atomu*, 1963) and *Kimba the White Lion* (1965–1966) were "the first batch of popular culture reaching the Chinese masses" just as China was (re)opening up to the world in 1978.[38] In the 1980s and 1990s, works like *City Hunter* (1987–1988), *Dragon Ball* (1986–1989), and *Slam Dunk* (1993–1996) were also quite popular (as they were in Japan), and anime continues to be widely consumed in China. The result of this popularity in an entire generation who are now coming of age, growing-up their entire lives with a familiarity with anime. Affinity with the anime-esque and the capacity to both recognize and perform it, then, does not have to be isolated to Japan. Indeed, as Pang notes, "animation in general has been shown to be a culture of appropriation,"[39] and it should not be surprising that anime's explosive popularity (and history of outsourced production) in China would give rise to the desire to produce anime for domestic and/or global audience.

Here the example of the promotional materials for the omnibus film titled *Shikioriori* (2018) may be illustrative. The film is a co-production by Haoliners (with their studio Emon in Tokyo) and Japanese studio CoMix Wave (also located in Tokyo). It features three short anime films depicting life in Shanghai (*Shanghai Koi*, directed by Haoling Li, president of Haoliners), Guangzhou (*Chiisana Fashion Show*, directed by Yoshitaka Takeuchi), and Hunan and Beijing (*Surprise*, directed by Xiaoxing Yi). Each work is done in the characteristic style of CoMix Wave, with detailed, painterly backgrounds and nostalgic, often bittersweet undertones[40] made famous by works directed by Makoto Shinkai (such as the 2016 hit *Your Name*, popular in both China and Japan). It is important to note that Li and Yi are both part of the generation that grew up with anime, and it appears that their nostalgia for the past of a locale in China is something they feel is best expressed through anime.

This sentiment appears most clearly on a promotional Japanese website, where all three directors provided short comments about their films.[41] Li discusses how, for those of their generation, the traditional Shanghainese architectural style were like a "family home" of closeness and warmth, but "just like eras, people disappear, and these Shanghainese buildings are little by little torn down." Takeuchi, though Japanese, espouses a similar feeling, noting a trip to Guangzhou and describing "modern, brand new buildings" juxtaposed next to various "areas that maintained the scenery of an older era," and remarked on the rapid speed of change, "as if the changing of eras was represented in an image [of the landscape]."[42] Yi notes how his shot was based on a story written when first arriving in Beijing, reminiscing about his hometown, and noted that, though he received offers to film this story in live-action cinema, when hearing of this project, he decided to give directing a try and make this in anime.[43]

These are brief paragraphs, but Li's and Takeuchi's focus is on the effect of shifts in the landscape, and Yi appears to see anime as the preferred media-form for the adaption of his work. Taken as a whole, we can see how modernity and its expression in anime are intertwined here in a manner that is (although promotional) revealed as meaningful for the Chinese and Japanese producers, published with the presumed recognition that it would resonate with readers. To draw on these statements, taken at face value, anime's creativity is appealing because it is germane to the contemporary form of modernization China is undergoing: moving toward a creative, rather than industrial, economy. Anime's creativity is decidedly late (or post) modern, engaging with the problematics of (re)combination and citationality, and due to its reliance on conventions, fits well with the regularity of output required in the competitive field of global media.

That said, we need to delve further into the transnationality at play here. As far as I can find, there are no official Chinese language versions of the above Japanese press release, but only unofficial translations on blogs and news sites. One might presume that not publicizing it in Chinese is to further "authenticate" this production as focused on the Japanese market. Put differently, the film, which is set in three different places in China, is made through a performance of anime's media-form to depict China's transitions, one which is a co-production with Chinese and Japanese producers and appears to court Chinese (as well as global audiences) *through* Japan via the comments by producers in Japanese. This degree of transnationality is difficult to place under our current frameworks, prompting us to further consider the dynamics of anime's creative industries across Asia.

JAPAN AS CENTRAL NODE IN A NETWORK

Though anime's creative industry appears as crossing borders in both directions here, there is still the very complicated issue. While on a formal level we can see anime-esque performance as a matter of textuality rather than national culture, there should be no denying of the anime-esque as heavily conditioned to be equated with Japan. The association is so strong that Chinese production of anime has partially migrated to Japan: Haoliners has a prolific studio called Emon in Tokyo, the studio involved in *Shikioriori*'s production. But this is not only an issue of "authenticity" related to locale (and nationality) of production ("real anime is Japanese"), which is often based on economics. There are long-standing tensions between China and Japan due to the history of Japan as an imperial aggressor. This makes performance of the anime media-form in China not just an issue of imitation but a disconcerting political issue. The long-term usage of Japanese studios' outsourcing of anime's animation also occurs in South Korea, the Philippines, and Vietnam, parts of Asia where Japanese management could be seen as re-inscribing a history of oppression. With such complex transnational dynamics of production, we must carefully consider the labor involved here, to explore the potential of introducing a degree of participation.

In anime's production processes, hierarchies are prevalent, with those who hold the IPR wielding significant control,[44] even over high-ranking directors, producers, and designers at the top. With sometimes hundreds of people working on a single production, there are different degrees of agency at each level of the production hierarchy, and the animators are often found at the very bottom. But this is not limited to outsourced work. In Japan, most animators are notoriously underpaid and overworked, struggling to survive on their salaries.[45] As such, this suggests a transnational hierarchy in the very structure of production, with animators at the very lowest rungs, the often unacknowledged and undervalued labor of anime's production. This is a common problem in the creative industries globally, where credit is given to those with "creative control" at the top.

Putting aside the transcultural inflections in anime's media-form,[46] one cannot ignore that Japan was the locus of many of anime's innovations, settling into the conventions of the media-form we recognize today. We cannot refute the contributions, initiatives, and innovations that happened within Japan, which are connected to the social modes and histories there. Nor should we disregard the importance of the producers who are located in Japan, the influence of the domestic media ecology on anime, or how the discourse of anime as Japanese has affected its study. It is crucial to stress the locus of creative development as Japan, as the organizational center and, for much of anime's history, the main market for the taste community that spurred on anime's production. However, this might be best thought of in terms of locale and certain practices of actors with more degrees of agency in the hierarchies of production rather than nation. Japan, or rather Tokyo, where most of the studios and IPR holders are located, functions as the central organizational and "authenticating" node in a network through which production flows. Thinking in terms of the network makes it harder to sustain notions of definitive "origins" relegated to one place and more about the centrality of a node, which controls but links multiple locales. Networks are not without their own tensions, but it also enables us to accept participation across the network as each point is connected through this node.

This would make Japan (and, more specifically, Tokyo) central to this system, but how do we account for the outsourced labor across Asia? Are they merely "copying" Japanese instructions? Such a view denies them any meaningful participation in anime's production. We must remember that not just any animator can produce anime; it is ideally done by trained people to produce this particular type of animation. Put differently, the anime-esque can only be enacted by skilled bodies that can perform it, and these skills can be imposed upon the animators, an imposition that takes on another dimension for those outside of Japan. Joon Yang Kim explains that animating is a physical type of labor, and that the hands of the outsourced animators in South Korea "became more and more coded to specific cultural-industrial types of emotional and bodily expression . . . [in the] styles demanded by the Japanese and Western animation industries."[47] Repeated performances transform the animator into one that produces the anime-esque form of animation, delimiting the animator into this particular range of expression. Indeed, as Kenta Yamamoto notes, the studios in South Korea that fill contracts for Japan fill orders *exclusively* for Japanese studios, instead of Western clients (which other studios serve).[48] As such, anime-esque animations outside of Japan are the performances of skilled practitioners that were able to successfully execute anime-esque conventions to enable a regularity of production.

These conventions, though shifting over time, were constantly repeated in anime productions, creating a feedback system that has (re)produced anime as a media-form. While this creative process of anime's development into a media-form has been occurring within Japan at the top of the hierarchy, portions of anime's production have been occurring outside of Japan, across Asia. As Kim asserts, many of the boom periods in anime's history (in the 1970s, 1980s, and 1990s) were facilitated by the reliance on this transnational labor and deserve their credit.[49] Even in the early 2000s, the global demand for anime was so great, and the volume of production increased to such a degree that sometimes entire episodes were produced outside of Japan.[50] It was during these boom periods that anime became further entrenched in its performance, the patterns repeated over and over in a large number of productions. The quantity of productions, their constant expansion, allowed for anime to appear less like the work of an "original" group of artists, and more like a series of repeated conventions, making each anime production in some way resemble other anime productions. This is how anime evolved into the media-form it is today, repetition creating the recognizable anime-esque, the outsourced labor across Asia participating in (re)producing what sustains anime as a recognizable media-form.

From this perspective, anime has always been about repetition, about similarity, and as such, anime made outside of Japan can be seen as one more performance in a long series of anime performances. These performances, when in-line with anime-esque models, even when unremarked as those done by subcontractors, are then implicitly defying the dominant narrative of "anime as Japanese," physically showing that non-Japanese can perform just as well. As Choo asserts, in the domestic works by animators that were outsourced labor, "the reappropriation was to 'overcome' rather than to 'become'. . .[the] animators' overdetermined and unapologetic appropriation of Japanese anime created a hyperbolic mode of mimicry—'not only the same, but actually Korean'—that existed for the gratification of South Koreans only."[51] While Choo emphasizes that this results in a type of nationalism, there are other potentials at play here. Because the anime-esque is so closely associated with Japan, such performances receive negative receptions as they run counter to established conceptions of creativity, ownership of culture, and cultural appropriation, implicitly challenging the norms of national ownership of a cultural product.

Such a conceptualization is an attempt to see anime beyond the national framework, to radically reinterpret anime through its transnational production system, to transform anime into something beyond exclusively Japanese culture. With the centrality of Japan firmly in mind, we must not forget that anime can only become a media-form through repetition, a repetition that is possible only from other examples. As such, the performance of anime's media-form in animation by workers across Asia can be seen as not merely a performance of following orders, but one in which those images produced were later repeated in other performances, which were themselves later repeated. Furthermore, there can only be patterns if there are enough anime produced to satisfy the quantity of repetitions to create a pattern in the first place, a quantity that was in part enabled by reliance on the cheaper labor of non-Japanese animators. The animators were molded by anime's codes and conventions imposed on them, but they produced the animation, their labor's mark (in)visible in the images we see when we watch anime, part and parcel of the final product. To see anime as only Japanese is to miss seeing these performances as anything other than subjugation, where the animators' participation is lost; anime as performative is an attempt to provide a sliver of agency, distributed across the network of production, where power still lies in the hierarchy of production, mostly located in Japan, but the performance of the animation stills stands as a visible act in the production of anime that exposes the imitable nature of anime—animators across Asia are subjected to the repeated anime-esque conventions, but also the agents of their performance. Anime as a performance returns a degree of agency to the animators outside of Japan and reveals their struggle inside Japan.

TRANSFORMING ANIME, TRANSFORMING REGION

To counteract the controlling aspects of the contemporary IPR regime, Pang calls for a different approach to contemporary (Western) conceptions of creativity. She theorizes this alternative creativity as "a result of social praxis that demands labor" and "a form of textuality that proliferates on its own."[52]

This involves a community "with people influencing, observing, and copying each other," and as textuality it "resembles how cultures and history evolve."[53] Such a conception of creativity challenges the modernist individual artist, a concept that is mapped onto the contemporary creative economy where popular cultural products are exported as emblems of a nation's culture. Examining anime as a performatively constituted media-form allows us to reveal a type of creativity that satisfies many of the requirements that Pang lays out and helps us reach beyond the framework of national culture towards a networked conception of transnationality and region.

On this view, anime sustains itself through citationality, a performance that straddles the tensions between repetition and variation. As such, on the level of media-form, the locale (and nationality) of the performer is less of an issue than the fidelity to anime-esque models. Anime focuses on minor variation, moving toward citation, a type of "strict" repetition. Chinese co-productions or anime made in China or South Korea (or elsewhere) are continuing this practice of citation. Indeed, the unremarked nature of anime's vast transnational production network attests to the imitability of anime and the skill of the performers, often going unnoticed due to the felicity of their citational performances. There is great potential to see anime's media-form as shared, unable to be fully owned by one person, company, or nation, highlighting the participatory element of the labor involved. It also offers the dim, but persistent, capacity to move beyond the individualism of artistic creativity, one which is mapped onto the nation-state in the global nation-branding of creative industries, and allows us to recognize similarities, to rely on shared conventions that can operate across borders.

Stretching this perspective further, as anime performance is citing other anime, which are not produced exclusively in Japan but transnationally across Asia, on a formal level, "inter-Asia referencing" becomes the very means of sustaining the anime-esque, of enacting it. Anime like *School Shock* simply make this blatantly visible due to its conception as an anime from China, when anime is supposedly from Japan: it references what is seen as Japanese through enacting the media-form. In this sense anime's media-form becomes a network of relations across national borders, pushing one toward interrogating where those borders of cultural production (and consumption) actually lie and how they may take on a different form. Anime performance thus incites the problematic of how to even consider an area (a space we generally take as sustaining a bounded inside and outside) as it operates *across*, as network, as inter-relations that still maintain gaps and hierarchies. Anime is not representative of all of (East) Asia, but it can be trans-Asian in the sense of forcing us to reconsider "Asia" (and beyond) as a region itself, as it traverses received boundaries, gesturing from one performance to another as it consistently references the anime-esque from other places to (re)enact another anime.

Anime and other similar products may not provide the type of politics usually valorized, often in the form of direct action and challenges to the status quo—that is, anime does not often explicitly employ the Western, modernist notion of artistic creativity. Decrying this absence forecloses the opportunity for alternatives, for opening up spaces for different approaches. Anime's creativity facilitates the potential for other modes of expression, ways of being and viewing this world that should be explored. But these are difficult to grasp through established frameworks that disregard formal analysis or relegate certain media-forms exclusively to national culture. Despite their lack of overt disruption (e.g., in producing a recognizably different media-form), anime-esque performances defy received narratives of cultural exclusivity. Here, anime-esque performance frees us from the binds of national ownership. Otherwise anime is always only Japanese, its animators performing something that will never be theirs.

Because anime is not just consumed within one nation or region, the anime-esque will differ per group, even within the same nation, yet can produce a community linked by their familiarity with the anime-esque across borders. Pang notes that the degree of affinity and popularity for anime in China is indicative of contemporary cultural industries, which actively "separate cultural expressions from their community origins for the market, access rights migrate from the social to the commercial realm."[54] She notes how "we cannot assume [the Japanese anime industry] to reflect a national culture organically, because the extremely complex marketing logic carves and recarves up the national market into various niche sectors, which both segment Japanese readers and connect them to those outside the country."[55] Furthermore, this may be different between media, and communities based on locale may not overlap with the population's media diets: anime viewers may not be watching K-dramas, despite living next to someone who avidly consumes K-dramas. This is not just isolated to East Asia (or Asia in general).

Aside from consumption, as we have seen, the influx of capital and talent includes companies from Europe and the United States, like the U.S.-based Netflix, which has set up a headquarters in Tokyo to help fund and court anime licenses (among other media) for their streaming service. As such, there is an ambivalence to established categories such as nation or supranational geographic regions (e.g., East Asia), where "internal and external" become blurred and certain areas left out, but still maintains centers of power and hierarchies. The regionality that is produced in relation to anime production, then, is a network across Asia rather than in a singular locale, with most of the linkages from the major cities of outsourced production (Shanghai, Beijing, Seoul, Manila, Ho Chi Minh) to the central node of Tokyo. Works like *Shikioriori* and the productions of studio Emon in Tokyo display a different tendency than outsourcing from Japan to "the periphery," but rather a movement into Japan of capital and talent that are contracting (and subcontracting) as well as collaborating through performing anime's media-form. There are also a number of non-Japanese workers in Japan producing anime in high-ranking positions, working on direction, key animation, as well as designs. These include animators like Cheng Xi Huang, Boya Liang, Sejoon Kim, Seong Ho Park, and Yong-Ce Tu, designers like Stanlias Brunet and Thomas Romain, as well as background artists such as Arthell S. Isom, and animation directors such as Henry Thurlow and Haoling Li. Anime, in terms of both production and consumption, is situated in a network of relations that is difficult to place in our current institutional and theoretical frameworks. Trans-Asia as method could be an experiment to develop and explore new frameworks, an opportunity to rethink methodologies and disciplinary assumptions as we encounter what occurs across Asia (and elsewhere), to build a networked type of transnational community.

However, there are confounding potentials at play here as well. As Pang notes, the global IPR regime threatens to capture the productive flows across the network, and the transnational anime business is beginning to follow the more litigious footsteps of Hollywood. Indeed, continuing the patterns of the major Japanese publishing companies, Haoliners is a company set up to control IPR for the productions they make, Emon the studio in Tokyo, which helps produce the anime works. Furthermore, while a reliance on conventionality can produce a type of community, it can also be exclusionary, as those unfamiliar with the conventions are left out—a practice at the very core of the concept of "region," with those inside the region and those outside of it.

As citation is the mode of maintaining anime's identity, there is also a type of politics of citation and enactment: What gets cited, by whom, and what authenticates such performances? This is where the issue of nation-branding comes into play, attempting to capture the transnational flows by making anime seen as exclusively Japanese. This shows how important the authentication of relation to Japan is for anime. As such, it raises the question, will Chinese produced anime become cited in the future? In some sense, they already have, as anime has been transnational for much of its history, but this is difficult to get acknowledged, especially as transnationality can easily be eschewed for the single-nation framework. If anime (or other cultural products) are to be recognized as transnational, it cannot stay as exclusively "Japanese" or we foreclose on the radical, transformative possibilities enabled by modes of creativity that follow the logic of copying across national borders. This might be the great irony of anime's creative industry across Asia: that its reliance on repetition has the capacity to invoke transformation.

NOTES

1. Chen Kuan-Hsing, "Tekuchi Yoshimi's 1960 'Asia as Method' Lecture," *Inter-Asia Cultural Studies* 13, no. 2 (2012): 317–324.

2. Chen, *Asia as Method: Toward Deimperialization* (Durnham, NC, and London: Duke University Press, 2010), 249–250.

3. Ibid., 253.

4. Ani Maitra and Rey Chow, "What's 'in'? Disaggregating Asia through New Media Actants," in *Routledge Handbook of New Media in Asia*, eds. Larissa Hjorth and Olivia Khoo (Routledge: London and New York, 2014), 17–27.

5. Thomas Lamarre, "Regional TV: Affective Media Geographies," *Asiascape: Digital Asia* (2015): 93–126.

6. Marc Steinberg and Jinying Li, "Introduction: Regional Platforms," *Asiascape: Digital Asia* 4 (2017): 179.

7. Ibid.

8. Anthony Fung and Vicky Ho, "Animation Industry in China: Managed Creativity or State Discourse?" in *Handbook of Cultural and Creative Industries in China*, ed. Michael Keane (Cheltenham: Edward Elgar Pub, 2017), 276–292; Laikwan Pang, *Creativity and Its Discontents: China's Creative Industries and Intellectual Property Rights Offenses* (Durham, NC, and London: Duke University Press, 2012).

9. Justin O'Connor and Gu Xin, "A New Modernity? The Arrival of 'Creative Industries' in China," *International Journal of Cultural Studies* 9, no. 3 (2006): 273.

10. Pang, *Creativity*, 32–33.

11. Ibid., 29.

12. Ibid., 35.

13. Ibid., 29.

14. O'Connor and Xin, "A New Modernity?" 274.

15. Ibid., 275.

16. Ibid., 274.

17. Ibid., 278.

18. Ibid.

19. Fung and Ho, "Animation Industry," 283–285.

20. Ibid., 290.

21. Ibid., 280.

22. Kukhee Choo, "Hyperbolic Nationalism: South Korea's Shadow Animation Industry," in *Mechademia 9: Origins*, ed. Frenchy Lunning (Minneapolis, MI: University of Minnesota Press, 2015), 144–162.

23. Homi K. Bhabha, *The Location of Culture* (London and New York: Routledge, 1994).

24. Rupert Cox, "Introduction," in *The Culture of Copying in Japan: Critical and Historical Perspectives*, ed. Rupert Cox (London and New York: Routledge/Taylor & Francis Group, 2008), 1–17

25. Lamarre, "Regional TV."

26. Jaqueline Berndt, "Facing the Nuclear Issue in a 'Mangaesque' Way: The Barefoot Gen Anime," *Cinergie* 2 (2012): 148–162. This is an adaptation of Berndt's

conception of the "mangaesque": "what passes as 'typically manga' (or typically anime) among regular media users . . . in the sense of manga-like or typically manga . . . draw[ing] attention to practically relevant popular discourses on the one hand and on the other to critically informed, theoretical reflections on what may, or may not, be expected from manga (and anime)."

27. Stevie Suan, "Anime's Performativity: Diversity through Conventionality in a Global Media-Form," *Animation: An Interdisciplinary Journal* 12 (2017): 62–79.

28. Hiroki Azuma, *Otaku: Japan's Database Animals*, trans. Jonathan E. Abel (Minneapolis, MI: University of Minnesota Press, 2009).

29. Judith Butler, *Undoing Gender* (New York; London: Routledge, 2004), 15.

30. Pang, *Creativity*, 172.

31. Suan, "Anime's Performativity," 71.

32. Cox, "Introduction," 9.

33. Pang, *Creativity*, 22.

34. Ibid., 172.

35. In Japanese, this is normally read as *dōjinshi*, but in China and Korea as *dōjin*. These are usually made by amateurs who self-publish small runs of works that use professionally published characters in different stories, costumes, and styles.

36. Pang, *Creativity*, 179.

37. Ibid.

38. Ibid., 174.

39. While the film is not released, it is quite clear from the previews and cited press statements released that this is the aim of the film. They even include the word "nostalgia" in the preview.

40. Pang, *Creativity*, 162.

41. Haoling Li, Yoshitaka Takeuchi, and Xiaoxing Yi, "Story, Shikioriori," promotional, 2018, https://shikioriori.jp/story.html.

42. Author's translation. See Li, Takeuchi, and Yi, "Story, Shikioriori."

43. It should be noted that the word used is *"anime,"* not "Japanese *anime."*

44. The central production studio, which is often given the majority of the credit for the production in promotional materials, does not usually get many returns from the profits of the production, nor do they generally hold the rights for the anime. They are merely contracted by the production committees (a diverse group of investors) who hold the IPR. As such, outsourcing and sub-subcontracting is not uncommon.

45. This can be extreme considering the high cost of living in Japan. The Report on the Status of Animation Producers noting the salary of lower-ranking junior animators making as little as 1.127 million yen ($10,263) per year (Association of Japanese Animations (AJA) (2015)).

46. Eiji Ōtsuka, "An Unholy Alliance of Eisenstein and Disney: The Fascist Origins of Otaku Culture," in *Mechademia 8: Tezuka's Manga Life*, ed. Frenchy Lunning (Minneapolis, MI: University of Minnesota Press, 2013), 251–277; Patrick Galbraith and Thomas Lamarre, "Otakuology: A Dialogue," in *Mechademia 5: Fanthropologies*, ed. Frenchy Lunning (Minneapolis, MI: University of Minnesota Press, 2010), 366.

47. Joon Yang Kim, "South Korea and the Sub-Empire of Anime: Kinesthetics of Subcontracted Animation Production," in *Mechademia 9: Origins*, ed. Frenchy Lunning (Minneapolis, MI: University of Minnesota Press, 2015), 99.

48. Kenta Yamamoto, *The Agglomeration of the Animation Industry in East Asia* (Tokyo, New York, London: Springer, 2014), 54.

49. Kim, "South Korea," 93.

50. Hiromichi Masuda, *Dejitaru ga kaeru anime bijinesu (Anime Business, Changed by Digitalization)* (Tokyo: NTTshuppan, 2016), 8.

51. Choo, "Hyperbolic Nationalism," 154. Choo notes how this is different from Homi Bhabha's conception of "mimicry."

52. Pang, *Creativity*, 5.

53. Ibid.

54. Ibid., 174. Here Pang is referencing Jeremy Rifkin.

55. Ibid.

BIBLIOGRAPHY

Anonymous. "The Godly Seat." *Bilibili*, October 20, 2017. https://www.bilibili.com/read/cv40369/.

The Association of Japanese Animations (AJA). *"Animēshon seisaku-sha jittai chōsa hōkoku-sho* 2015 (2015 Report on the Status of Animation Producers)." January 2016. http://aja.gr.jp/english/japan-anime-data.

Azuma, Hiroki. *Otaku: Japan's Database Animals*. Translated by Jonathan E. Abel. Minneapolis, MI: University of Minnesota Press, 2009.

Berndt, Jaqueline. "Facing the Nuclear Issue in a 'Mangaesque' Way: The Barefoot Gen Anime." *Cinergie* 2 (2012): 148–162.

Bhabha, Homi K. *The Location of Culture*. London and New York: Routledge, 1994.

Butler, Judith. *Undoing Gender*. New York; London: Routledge, 2004.

Chen, Kuan-Hsing. *Asia as Method: Toward Deimperialization*. Durham, NC, and London: Duke University Press, 2010.

———. "Tekuchi Yoshimi's 1960 'Asia as Method' Lecture." *Inter-Asia Cultural Studies* 13, no. 2 (2012): 317–324.

Choo, Kukhee. "Hyperbolic Nationalism: South Korea's Shadow Animation Industry." In *Mechademia 9: Origins*, edited by Frenchy Lunning, 144–162. Minneapolis, MI: University of Minnesota Press, 2015.

Cox, Rupert. "Introduction." In *The Culture of Copying in Japan: Critical and Historical Perspectives*, edited by Rupert Cox, 1–17. London and New York: Routledge/Taylor & Francis Group, 2008.

Fung, Anthony Y. H., and Vicky Ho. "Animation Industry in China: Managed Creativity or State Discourse?" In *Handbook of Cultural and Creative Industries in China*, edited by Michael Keane, 276–292. Cheltenham: Edward Elgar Pub, 2017.

Galbraith, Patrick, and Thomas Lamarre. "Otakuology: A Dialogue." In *Mechademia 5: Fanthropologies*, edited by Frenchy Lunning, 360–374. Minneapolis, MI: University of Minnesota Press, 2010.

Kim, Joon Yang. "South Korea and the Sub-Empire of Anime: Kinesthetics of Subcontracted Animation Production." In *Mechademia 9: Origins*, edited by Frenchy Lunning, 90–103. Minneapolis, MI: University of Minnesota Press, 2015.

Lamarre, Thomas. "Regional TV: Affective Media Geographies." *Asiascape: Digital Asia* (2015): 93–126.

Li, Haoling, Yoshitaka Takeuchi, and Xiaoxing Yi. "Story, Shikioriori." Promotional. 2018. https://shikioriori.jp/story.html.

Maitra, Ani, and Rey Chow. "What's 'in'? Disaggregating Asia through New Media Actants." In *Routledge Handbook of New Media in Asia*, edited by Larissa Hjorth and Olivia Khoo, 17–27. Routledge: London and New York, 2014.

Masuda, Hiromichi. *Dejitaru ga kaeru anime bijinesu (Anime Business, Changed by Digitalization)*. Tokyo: NTTshuppan, 2016.

O'Connor, Justin, and Gu Xin. "A New Modernity? The Arrival of 'Creative Industries' in China." *International Journal of Cultural Studies* 9, no. 3 (2006): 271–283.

Ōtsuka, Eiji. "An Unholy Alliance of Eisenstein and Disney: The Fascist Origins of Otaku Culture." In *Mechademia 8: Tezuka's Manga Life*, edited by Frenchy Lunning, 251–277. Minneapolis, MI: University of Minnesota Press, 2013.

Pang, Laikwan. *Creativity and Its Discontents: China's Creative Industries and Intellectual Property Rights Offenses*. Durnham, NC, and London: Duke University Press, 2012.

Steinberg, Marc, and Jinying Li. "Introduction: Regional Platforms." *Asiascape: Digital Asia* 4 (2017): 173–183.

Suan, Stevie. "Anime's Performativity: Diversity through Conventionality in a Global Media-Form." *Animation: An Interdisciplinary Journal* 12 (2017): 62–79.

Yamamoto, Kenta. *The Agglomeration of the Animation Industry in East Asia*. Tokyo, New York, London: Springer, 2014.

Chapter 8

Trans/Asia: A Multi-Mobilities Solution to Identity Politics?

Jiyu Zhang

TRANS: PROBLEM

On October 14, 2016, a documentary titled *Out of Place: Transgender Stories from Asia* was premiered at the Ullens Centre for Contemporary Art (UCCA) in Beijing, China. The two directors of the documentary, Han Xia and Joshua Frank, along with Mr. C, one of the transgender people whose real-life experiences were registered in the film, all showed up to participate in discussion after screening. Regarding the conceivably sensitive subject of this documentary, that is, transgender communities who have been long relegated to margins of the society, this film's premiere at China's political center should be viewed as a courageous attempt to address sexual diversity and gender equality in public. On the UCCA's official website, the introduction reads that this is a documentary which not only "presents the realities of transgender individuals in Asia," but also "provides assistance to those living with unanswered questions about their own identities, giving an inside look on the process of sex reassignment surgery, as well as the social support available to LGBTQ communities."[1]

The documentary begins with the sexual reassignment surgery of Bobbie Huthart, a white trans woman (MTF, male to female) who has been living in Hong Kong for most of her life, and finally decides to change her sex at birth in Bangkok, Thailand. Centering on Bobbie's personal transition, this documentary at the same time looks at local trans people in Hong Kong and Bangkok, as well as other trans persons in Beijing and Guiyang—two cities with a distinctive gap of economic development in Mainland China. Intersecting with various boundaries such as sex, gender, race, and ethnicity, the transgender stories in *Out of Place* seem to conjure up a trans-Asian solidarity for LGBTQ movement while giving voice to a wide range of trans people

161

located in urban spaces. In response to the collective mission set out in this volume, this chapter aims to explore the critical purchase of trans-Asia as an analytical framework, by primarily focusing on the relationship between theoretical knowledge and lived experience with regard to transgender identity in a trans-Asian context. Given the broad purview of the film's emancipatory implications, I propose to examine the ways in which its transgender embodiments have challenged normative conventions in each society and culture. Furthermore, situating these transgender embodiments into interconnected categories mentioned above, I also aim to tackle the issues that might have been overlooked under a euphoric image of trans-Asian solidarity.

TRANS: ASIA

To situate the problematic of transgender embodiments in *Out of Place*, I would like first to unpack multiple implications of "trans." As de Kloet, Chow, and Chong posit in the introduction, the prefix "trans-" points to "movement, flow, traffic, connections" in various forms of border-crossing, which "bring about changes, as in trans-gression, trans-cedence, and above all, trans-formation."[2] Specifically, one of the immediate connotations of "trans" in this chapter is that of transgender. According to Susan Stryker, the term "transgender" indicates a diverse array of corporeal and psychological phenomena. Encompassing trans-sexual, bi-gender, non-binary, and cross-dressing, to just name a few, transgender is premised on and oriented toward an amorphous understanding of gender enunciation, whereby gender as a locus of personal existence is "lived, embodied, experienced, performed, and encountered" both in bodily and psychic realms.[3] As Stryker notes, the concept of transgender "seeks not only to understand the contents and mechanisms of those linkages and assumptions about sex and gender, biology and culture; it also asks who 'we' are—we who make those assumptions and forge those links—and who 'they' are, who seem to 'us' to break them."[4] Put differently, the imperative of transgender studies lies in a dismantling of power structure that has come to govern the ways in which sex and gender are formulated and articulated as indispensable categories of social identity. In turn, it exposes how these categories have in effect regulated our sense of the self. Therefore, hand in hand with other queer identities (for instance, gay and lesbian), transgender strives to unsettle social norms that have dominated the embodiment of selfhood and inhibited alternative ways of gender configuration. Moreover, rather than simply advocating that either sex or gender can shift from one end to another over a spectrum, transgender ventures to break down sexual and gender binaries, giving rise to symbiotic, fluid, and polymorphous possibilities of selfhood.

Although some have exposed the instability or constructedness of sex and gender and their supposedly fixed correlations, so as to reveal how self-identification is stipulated by heteronormative power structures, many others, in particular those who research in or on Asia, have called for a reconceptualization of theoretical framework that aims to bridge the gap between global theories and local contexts. For instance, in *Asia as Method* (2010), Chen Kuan-Hsing cautions against the latent universalizing—if not already universal—theories and concepts that originated from the West, and the imminent danger caused by uncritical slippage of such Western vocabularies into non-Western realities. Conceding to the fact that Western knowledge has seeped into vernacular cultures in Asia due to colonization and globalization, Chen stresses the specificity of indigenous histories, cultures, and material conditions, as he asserts that "[w]e must be able to understand specificity as a fundamental working assumption of critical cultural studies. Universalism is not an epistemological given but a horizon we may be able to move forward in the remote future, provided that we first compare notes based upon *locally grounded knowledge*."[5] In other words, what Chen invokes in essence is "a process of relativization" among distinct locations and cultures with multiple points of reference.[6] Rather than gauging Asian societies by Euro-American standards, Chen ushers in inter-referencing as an underlying approach to engage in Asian contexts. In accordance with Chen's position, in a special issue of *Inter-Asia Cultural Studies*, Fran Martin and Josephine Ho foreground the heterogeneity of transgender communities in Asia with an anchor in "the specificity of place," as follows:

> Highlighting the specificities of social life *as lived* in each place, these micro-geographic contexts defy interpretation as simply inconsequential containers for some singular "transgender experience" uniform across these different locations. . . . *[P]lace matters* in producing transgender identities, experiences, and knowledges, notwithstanding the ways in which globalizing forms of both social activism and academic theory inform the broader contexts for these accounts.[7]

Juxtaposing different elements of Asia, both in terms of geography and culture, a method of trans-Asian referencing first of all enables us to challenge the hierarchical structure of knowledge that has been entrenched in the dichotomy between the West and Asia (as is anywhere else of the world). One of the critical efficacies of trans/inter-Asian referencing, in the words of Chua Beng Huat, lies in "how locations in the region are trying to learn from one another's experiences, to take lessons from ostensibly successful examples and to find so-called best practice in different aspects of social, economic and political governance."[8] In this sense, a trans-Asian referencing method provides us a deeper perspective of local transgender community and individuals, as Koichi Iwabuchi point out in this volume, "trans-Asia studies more specifically aims to investigate the advancement of globalization process that engenders cross-border flows and connections of capital, people and media culture and renders many issues transnationally linked."[9] So much so that trans-Asia as method enables us to probe into the historical trajectories of different societies across Asia, I argue that an awareness of personal lived experiences, in particular sexed and gendered experiences calibrated by and stemmed from corporeal, psychical, and affective encounters must be as well taken into account. Accordingly, trans-Asia serves to articulate marginal and marginalized individuals and communities so as to generate a translocal, transcultural, and trans-ethnic/racial dimension, where these subjects can at the same time recognize their diversity in lieu of a flattened solidarity. With regard to the documentary *Out of Place*, a trans-Asian perspective allows us to examine transgender people in Asia, a perspective that encompasses both tangible and intangible boundaries, and further shows how these boundaries realign over time and space.[10]

TRANS: BORDER

As the main thread that weaves throughout the whole film, Bobbie's narrative draws a parallel of transformation in both geographical and bodily dimensions. Whereas in the documentary Bobbie does not reveal much about her prominent lineage, in an interview with *South China Morning Post* (SCMP) following the film's public release, her family background becomes clearer as she opens up more in that news article.[11] Born in the late 1940s in Hong Kong, Bobbie was formerly known as Robert Huthart, the second son of Robert Huthart Senior, who was the managing director of the retail company Lane Crawford. Raised in a successful mercantile family, Bobbie was supposed to shoulder the responsibility to thrive the family business, in which she was engrossed for the most of her life. Alongside the paramount duty ordained by the Huthart's corporate empire, Bobbie was also expected to carry on the family line—an ineluctable burden that was later exacerbated by her brother Gordon Huthart's coming out as gay.[12] Circumscribed by entrepreneurial and familial commitments, Bobbie had to fulfill such obligations while coping with anguish and regret. In 2015, despite having become a father of two daughters and a son, Robert Huthart decided to change. Like his brother, Robert came out to his family and friends, but as a transgender woman who has called herself Bobbie ever since.

As a result, Bobbie's presence in the documentary starts with a new phase of her life in Hong Kong. Showing around her hangout places in the city, Bobbie, who has already been going through hormone therapy after coming out, is planning on a sex reassignment surgery in Bangkok, in order to realize her long-time aspiration of a female body. In the SCMP interview, Bobbie adds that the reasons for her to change sex at birth, are influenced by a romance between her (with a male body back then) and a transgender woman once there. Bobbie explains:

> About 20 years ago, I had a relationship with a transgender girl in Phuket, who had changed completely to become female. She was a wonderful person and being with her was a wonderful experience which changed how I saw my situation forever. I had always assumed that transgender people were perverts—that they were hookers and dancers or in the sex industry—and I was not aware there was a normal life for many transgender people. It was a time that preceded the internet so access to information of this nature was difficult.
>
> In Hong Kong society, I was shielded from any exposure and of course, there was my family duty. Thus, this relationship made me realize that not only was a normal life as a transgender person possible, but that I was not a freak of nature. I realized I was a derivative of gender and a human being with value.[13]

Indeed, the romantic encounter of Bobbie with the transgender woman in Thailand served as a source of motivation for her transition. Speaking with a sense of what Andrew Samuels calls "gender certainty," Bobbie rationalizes her pursuit of a transsexual/transgender identity as a means to achieve human value.[14] As the documentary goes on, after her surgery, Bobbie leaves Hong Kong and begins her whole new life in Bangkok. At this point, the story of Bobbie not only unfolds a bodily transition, but also a geographical relocation. On both levels, Bobbie's transgender journey is marked by mobility of spatiality and subjectivity, a mobility that, as Lucas Crawford suggests, facilitates her to "move from place to place and gender to gender."[15] Driven by emotional intensities and availed by physical capabilities, Bobbie's gender modification has become a transformative journey that aligns subjective feelings with bodily actions toward a finite destination of selfhood. As much as the story of Bobbie informs a geographical mobilization between Asian territories, it also evokes a comparative perspective between and within Asian communities from which Bobbie, a transgender person, learns from another transgender person who belongs to a different society. The ways in which Bobbie embraces her new identity and her life in another city amount to an interconnection of individuals and locations in a trans-Asian environment. Through a strategic relativization, Bobbie is thus able to navigate corporeal and geographical boundaries to the selfhood she desires as a trans person.

Whereas a trans-Asian mobilization in social and physical space has afforded Bobbie agency to embody her transgender identity, the process of her identification also attends to a regional politics of nation, race, and ethnicity. Born to a Chinese mother and an English father while growing up in Hong Kong, Bobbie is also a transgressive subject whose transformative trajectory stretching from her growth to emigration intersects national, racial, and ethnic borders. Specifically, Bobbie's devotion to both family business and family lineage throughout decades not only follows the essential logic of capitalist economy, but more deeply complies with the value system of the local community. Insofar as the family business is a commercial organization predicated on consanguinity, it is no exaggeration to say that Bobbie's choice of life before her coming out is a concession to the familial piety in Chinese culture that looms large in her individual circumstance.

For instance, in the SCMP interview, Bobbie speaks of the causality between her gender dysphoria and constant frustration caused by her peculiar role in the family.[16] As the former oldest son, it was the primary duty of Bobbie to produce a rightful heir, by which she was compelled to act against her will. In other words, Bobbie's gender dysphoria derives from the impasse between her primogeniture and transgender identification. The tension is much more heightened by heteronormative ethics of the native culture that dictates her family, rather than patriarchal structure that governs her family business. Precisely because Bobbie comes from an interracial and interethnic background, her gender modification is gripped by the asymmetry between indigenous/Chinese and foreign/Western values. Ironically, such asymmetry in turn only stimulates Bobbie's transnational transition through which she can circumvent sexual and gender norms of the society of Hong Kong. Even though Bobbie's postoperative integration of Bangkok still entails another process of cross-cultural negotiation, both the documentary and the newspaper interview vindicate that the local culture seems far less discriminatory than that of Hong Kong with respect to transgender people. In spite of her half-Chinese and half-English heritage, and her predominately white appearance, Bobbie finds that her transgender identity is more acceptable in this Asian city. Near the end of newspaper interview, Bobbie states that she intends to start a funding for other individuals who need financial aid to implement their transgender process, due to the financial success of her family and her personal Buddhist belief.

Eventually, Bobbie's life transition from Hong Kong to Bangkok demonstrates a trans-Asian network of transgender communities, which alludes to different constellations of national, ethnic, and racial cultures. On the one hand, a paradigm of trans/inter-Asian referencing can help us recognize the nuance and diversity of socio-cultural formations in the region; on the other hand, the theoretical framework of trans-Asia would also "envision and actualize Asia as a dialogic communicative space in which people across borders collaborate to connect diverse voices, concerns, and problems in various, unevenly intersecting public sites,"[17] such as Bobbie's transnational passage of her transgender identification.

TRANS: FORMATION

Whereas the documentary follows through Bobbie's transgender migration across national borders, in the meanwhile it also features other transitional routes of transgender people in Asia. Mr. C, a transgender man who lives in the city of Guiyang, the provincial capital of Guizhou in China, indicates another approach to embody individual transgender identity. As a native, Mr. C belongs to the emerging generation of Chinese youth who bear witness to drastic transformations of the nation. To be sure, China's integration into global economy since the late 1970s has not only led to marketization and urbanization on a vast scale, but also introduced ideas and concepts from the outside world to the rapidly developing country. Along with material changes of living condition, wealth accumulation, technological advancement, and so forth, there have been intellectual tendencies that call for more civic engagement to address issues concerning the general public, such as identity politics of gender.

The storyline of Mr. C stands in stark contrast to Bobbie's transnational itinerary for transgender transition. Guiyang, which has been often portrayed as one of the most underdeveloped provincial capitals in China, still saw a burgeoning group of LGBTQ individuals like Mr. C. a trans man, Mr. C constantly encounters social discrimination, which mostly results in dismissal or rejection in the job market. Alongside the social bias he receives in employment and workplace, Mr. C still faces challenges from his personal relationship. While it is possible to have a girlfriend who accepts him as a heterosexual trans man, there is pressure from the older generation such as his girlfriend's parents who conceive transgender people through a pathological lens. Despite all these difficulties, Mr. C is a keen member of the trans community in the city. Rather than organizing public assembly to call on the authorities to protect trans people's legal rights—which is rigidly policed in Mainland China—Mr. C regularly holds group meetings with friends, some of who are trans people as well, to discuss promotional campaigns on social media platforms such as Weibo and WeChat, to raise social awareness toward trans community. It might be added that, by the time when the documentary was released in Beijing in 2016, Mr. C had already filed a case in the local court, suing his former employer who dismissed him and claiming the dismissal a discriminative act against gender equality. Following the film's public release, in December, 2016, the district court ruled in favor of Mr. C, ordering the defendant to compensate Mr. C's financial loss.[18] Although this win counts hardly as a definitive leap of the society, let alone national policy change toward legitimatization of transgender identity, the outcome of this lawsuit confers the possibility for transgender individuals in China to ward off unlawful treatments.[19] In this sense, Mr. C's personal gain is a modest yet significant step forward for minority groups, in particular transgender community under the authoritarian rule.

Apparently, unlike Bobbie, who was born into a wealthy family with racial privilege and colonial heritage that can afford her a variety of mobilities in terms of space, society, and body, Mr. C only has limited access to societal resources and bodily modification.[20] Because of his lack of financial means and social network, Mr. C largely relies on his local experience for transgender identification and social activism. Whereas Bobbie's transgender identification involves negotiations between races, ethnicities, and nations, Mr. C's transition mostly takes place in the city. In contrast, the conciliatory space for him to maneuver through repressive conditions of his transgender identity is rather small. Deprived of the opportunity to bypass the regulatory atmosphere through translocal or transnational displacement, what Mr. C's personal struggle has revealed is a situational approach to transgender identity that points to the dynamic between global tendencies and local realities. In Stryker's words, such a situational approach that attends to individual conditions concerns with "how various forms of personhood in locations around the world imagines their own relationship to those things that transgender can be made to evoke, such as modernity, metropolitanism, Eurocentrism, whiteness, or globalization."[21]

The formation of local transgender communities calls for investigation on the ways in which transgender as a Western category is incorporated into local non-Western realities. Moreover, it speaks to scenarios whereby local traditions and practices of gender, or embodiments of masculinity and femininity, touch global concepts and tendencies. Hence, Mr. C's transgender experience reflects how younger generation in contemporary China responds to transgender movement as part of global transmission of Western knowledge, so much so that the local urban space that conditions Mr. C's lived experience also doubles as a frontier of globality vis-à-vis locality in the Chinese context. The category of transgender identity in the case of Mr. C's subject formation thus can be understood in conjunction with what Stryker postulates as "a means of resistance to local pressures," "an alternative to tradition," or "a mode of survival and translation for traditional cultural forms that are unintelligible within the conceptual double binary of man/woman and homo/hetero associated with the modern West."[22] That said, Mr. C's transgender experience constitutes a form of individual subjectivity emerging from the convergence of global knowledge and local reality, as well as a site of contention between the personal and the social in the face of state regulation. Differing from a migratory route that demands one's higher social class with commensurate social capital, Mr. C with his locally grounded countermeasures contributes to a pragmatic but also confrontational position for those trans people who live in modest conditions. Aimed to enhance public visibility of trans community within the government's jurisdiction, this position has yet to deal with potential risks when activist campaigns of sexual and gender minorities—Mr. C's lawsuit of his gender citizenship— are deemed to confront the authorities'. In this sense, the protagonist's personal reaction to social discrimination can be viewed as individual resistance against social repression amid the growing movement of LGBTQ identity politics.

Whereas trans person like Mr. C prefers a confrontational position to safeguard his gender citizenship, there are also some other trans people who opt for less radical tactic to withstand bigotry. For instance, the documentary also features Chao Xiaomi, a gender queer who runs a vintage shop in Beijing.[23] Opposing the polarization of gender binary, Chao claims herself a gender-fluid person, meaning she advocates for a fluctuating expression of masculine and feminine.[24] Still, even though born with a male biology, Chao refers herself as a "she."[25] Indicating her transgender experiences, such as switching between jobs, breaking up with a man who appreciates her feminine idiosyncrasies, and walking on streets in high heels Chao adopts a flexible conception of gender identity as the most viable way to assert her personality, as she adds:

> In the eyes of the majority, I am definitely a minority. But I don't feel like a minority . . . To me, the idea of gender isn't very important. Or you can get rid of that concept when talking about me. Just consider me a human being, not a man or woman. The first time I wore women's clothes was around 2010, I remember . . . At that moment, I just felt that my deepest desires were fulfilled. I'm different from them after all. In the end, I'm only the same as them in the gender box on my ID. Everything else is different.[26]

Advancing a fluctuating position on gender, Chao's transgender identification differentiates from those of Bobbie and Mr. C, who rely on surgery and hormone medication respectively for their transgender transition. Thus these trans people in the documentary have covered a range of trans identities over the spectrum of gender expression, but not without their mutual differences. Whereas Bobbie's transgender transition coincides with his geographical relocation, Mr. C and Chao are both inhabitants in the city, whose transgender embodiments hinge less on cross-border mobility than location-based individual resistance. However, this asymmetry between transgender mobility and immobility cannot be simply reduced to an economic determinism that merely takes into account the financial capability of these subjects, but should engage with an intersectional scrutiny of interactions and interrelations between racial and ethnic identities. That said, such a scrutiny draws attention to a broader scope of identity categories in a trans-Asian context.

TRANS: ETHICS AND ETHNICS

The disparate transgender experiences shown in the documentary, extend the current inquiry into border-crossing of identity categories. As a half-Chinese and half-English person, Bobbie grew up as a native speaker of Cantonese and English in Hong Kong. It might be true that one of the immediate racial traits that she inherits from ancestry—her white appearance—has afforded her a larger tolerability as a trans person, partly due to the fact that white demographic constitutes the largest proportion of transgender population in the West.[27] However insofar as Bobbie's transgender experience is conditioned in Asia, thus her mixture of racial and ethnic traits renders the difficulty for her to *pass* as a local either in Bangkok or in Hong Kong. To be sure, even with a womanly appearance after surgery, Bobbie still appears to be a foreigner in the locals' eyes. But as the interviews indicate, Bobbie has been well adapting to her postoperative life in Thailand, to the extent that she expresses no intention to live in Hong Kong again. Bobbie's transition from her transnational journey, not only destabilizes the distinction between sex and gender, but also opens up the possibility of a transracial identity, one that foregrounds a fluidity of racial identities. As social theorist Rogers Brubaker contends, so much so that "mixed ancestry licenses choice and facilitates change," in Bobbie's case, it meanwhile "authorizes people to selectively identify with different ancestral lines in different contexts."[28]

While navigating between racial boundaries of white and Asian in her mixed lineage, Bobbie has also negotiated ethnic differences between Chinese and Thai throughout her transition. The subjective agency that allowed Bobbie to cut through gender boundaries further allows her to switch from one racial/ethnic community to another within the Asian landscape. Therefore, this mobilization of identities prompts us to re-conceptualize racial/ethnic norms imposed on Asian—norms that subscribe to stereotypical definitions imposed by the West. In consequence, Bobbie's new life as a postoperative transsexual/gender person in a foreign country gives rise to a process that not just breaks away from racial stereotypes of Asia defined by the West, but at the same time disrupts ethnocultural borderlines of Asian communities that have been long perpetuated by each other with or without Western influences. With her transnational, transgender, and transracial/ethnic transition, Bobbie has embodied the porosity of identity categories. Moreover, this mobility of identity stems from much less theoretical speculation than everyday practices. All in all, its evocation is premised on individuals' personal venture in their lived experiences, as we have witnessed from the protagonists in the documentary.

However, as much as Bobbie's transgender experience may confer an autonomous mobility of trans subjects, which leads to an ideal image of selfhood, personal accounts as such still feed into a tautological and teleological narrative that purports an essential gender identity at core.[29] Indeed, this sort of contradicts poststructuralist stance that views gender as a repetition of bodily acts. In other words, these trans stories do not so much overcome gender binary as reinforce it with substantial ramifications. For example, in the three transgender characters we have discussed so far, Bobbie is the only one who has changed her anatomical structure with sex reassignment surgery, even though she has spent a fortune, faced surgical contingency, and endured a long period of postoperative recovery at a rather older age. The considerable cost of her transsexual procedure, which attests to her mobility of identification, is invariably compliant with the binarism of antithetical sexes. In contrast, neither of Mr. C and Chao Xiaomi has the resources to undergo the same progress, a fact that makes their transgender expressions all the more pragmatic and even inspiring. Therefore the geographical, corporeal, and identitarian mobilities that Bobbie has acquired through a material basis do not necessarily revoke those categories; on the contrary, those who are restrained by immobility have contributed to a proliferation of (trans)gender practices. The mobility of sexual and gender identity at this moment appears to be a deceptive trap, which feeds into a heteronormative primacy that sustains a closed circuit of gender identities and expressions. In this sense, the critical efficacy of trans-Asian referencing as method does not lie in mobility as a tactic to achieve a "perfect" body image, nor to dismantle boundaries of identity categories for an unrestricted flexibility, but as a point of departure to reflect on "how and why the construction of transgender bodies and the public presentation of transidentities become a factor of exclusion, violence, and forced (im)mobilities."[30]

Revolving around a politics of mobility, a trans-Asian perspective can help us better understand the ways in which Asian cultures and societies have been conceived within a hierarchy of knowledge dominated by the West, not least of which are identity categories such as gender and race. Furthermore, through a comparative approach, the individual stories in this documentary attest to the local specificity of social and cultural structures, as evinced by internal differences and dynamic connections of marginal individuals in Asia.[31] However fragmented and conflicted, these situated formations of society and culture can establish a trans-Asian network that contests pervasive frameworks of concepts and practices, to the extent that it can reveal the limits of identity politics and navigate the disparities between the historical and the contemporary, the personal and the social, the local and the global.

TRANS/ASIA: A MULTI-MOBILITIES SOLUTION?

After the public release in Beijing, the producer of *Out of Place*, the North America-based media company VICE also made the documentary available via video sharing platform YouTube for free. However, a notable difference has been made to the film's title as the company advanced its international streaming. Even though the main title remains the same, the subhead has shifted from *Transgender Stories from Asia* to *The Trans Chinese Community Fighting for Gender Equality*.[32] This change becomes rather problematic because there is another protagonist, a twenty-six-year-old street bar server named Wanna. A transgender woman herself, Wanna is a Bangkok native. Therefore, the film's new title is changed at the cost of overlooking the fact that Wanna is neither a Chinese nor lives in China. The ignorance of her presence can be at best speculated as a promotional scheme that feeds on viewers' curiosity about trans community in China, a captivating idea that directs at the country's authoritative bureaucracy and heteropatriarchal culture, which make the polity itself a formidable obstacle to human rights.

Whereas the former subhead properly encompasses the scope of trans people in the film, and circumvents a head-on confrontation with China by repackaging with a broader range, the altered title reaches out to a supposedly international audience by sharpening its focus. This narrowing down of the range, on the one hand, foregrounds the collective and individual efforts that have been made by trans people in China, which indeed needs to be addressed and incentivized by means of cultural representation. On the other hand, it compromises the multiplicity and diversity of trans identification across Asia just as demonstrated in the film, even though most of the characters have lived or are living in China. Thus the production company's marketing strategy risks the blame of clickbait, insofar as it rests on a political critique of China's repression on human rights such as gender equality and citizenship, but it might simultaneously slip into a parochial liberalism that aims at a specific target with a dismissal of the transnational activist network—a network that should be most emphasized.

Given the documentary's outspoken advocate for transgender rights, however, the stories of trans individuals are limited to those who inhabit urban space. While drawing attention to a diverse array of marginal individuals whose experiences complicate the hegemonic norms of identity categories in the West, this array overlooks indelible gaps between the urban and the rural areas in Asia, as to explore how individuals and communities in rural spaces may respond to and negotiate with normative expressions. This lack of mention risks solidifying the impression that LGBTQ activism merely concerns the urban population a move that will further intensify the hierarchy of the urban vis-a-vis the rural. In this sense, the metronormative narratives this documentary has depicted are in fact partial reflections of reality, by which the vast majority of territories and demographics in Asia are missed out at large.[33] This unbalanced way of portrayal of Asian trans people could undermine heterogeneous identifications pertaining to local configurations, since it runs the stake of assimilating personal accounts and flattening geographical differences into a global imaginary—just as it is presented by a the multinational media corporation producing this film—where individuals might differ in time, place, and particular identity categories, but the deep-rooted conformist logic of these categories is still at play. The quest to tackle hegemonic discourses in society should not stop at a translocal mobility or a mobile identification, but should mobilize between knowledges in order to cover blind spots in our perception of the world, and close the gaps of ignorance they have created.

NOTES

1. Ullens Center for Contemporary Art, "UCCA x VICE Out of Place: Transgender Stories from Asia Premiere and Discussion," screened October 14, 2016 at Ullens Center for Contemporary Art, Beijing, China, accessed March 9, 2018, http://ucca.org.cn/en/program/out-of-place-transgender-stories-from-asia-screening-and-discussion-2/.

2. See Gladys Pak Lei Chong, Yiu Fai Chow, and Jeroen de Kloet's introduction to this volume.

3. Susan Stryker, "(De)Subjugated Knowledges: An Introduction to Transgender Studies," in *The Transgender Studies Reader*, eds. Susan Stryker and Stephen Whittle (New York, NY: Routledge, 2005), 3.

4. Ibid.

5. Chen Kuan-Hsing, *Asia as Method* (Durham, NC: Duke University Press, 2010), 245. Emphasis added.

6. Ibid., 254.

7. Fran Martin and Josephine Ho, "Editorial Introduction: Trans/Asia, Trans/Gender," *Inter-Asia Cultural Studies* 7, no. 2 (2006): 186. Emphasis in the original.

8. Chua Beng Huat, "Inter-Asia Referencing and Shifting Frames of Comparison," in *The Social Sciences in the Asian Century*, eds. Carol Johnson, Vera Mackie, and Tessa Morris-Suzuki (Canberra: Australian National University Press, 2015), 73.

9. See Koichi Iwabuchi's chapter in this volume (chapter 1).

10. Helen Hok-Sze Leung, "Trans on Screen," in *Transgender China*, ed. H. Chiang (New York: Palgrave MacMillan, 2012), 185.

11. Rachel Blundy, "How a 'Ruthless Playboy Businessman' in Hong Kong Became a Transgender Woman," *South China Morning Post*, August 26, 2017, http://www.scmp.com/news/hong-kong/education-community/article/2108317/how-ruthless-playboy-businessman-hong-kong-became.

12. Robert's late brother Gordon was the founder of Disco Disco, one of the earliest gay clubs in Hong Kong. After Disco Disco was sold by Gordon Huthart

in 1986, the building in which it was located later turned into Lan Kwai Fong (蘭桂坊), Hong Kong's most popular night club nowadays. For details, see: Kenneth Howe, "Pink Power," *South China Morning Post*, September 1, 2000, http://www.scmp.com/article/325266/pink-power. Isobel Yeung, "Funky Town: How Disco Fever in the Late '70s Changed Hong Kong's Nightlife Forever," *Post Magazine*, June 15, 2014, http://www.scmp.com/magazines/post-magazine/article/1529999/funky-town-hong-kongs-disco-heyday.

13. Blundy, "How."

14. Andrew Samuels, *The Plural Psyche: Personality, Morality and the Father* (New York: Routledge, 2016), 72.

15. Lucas Cassidy Crawford, "Transgender without Organs?: Mobilizing a Geo-Affective Theory of Gender Modification," *WSQ: Women's Studies Quarterly* 36, no. 3&4 (2008): 129.

16. Blundy, "How."

17. See Iwabuchi's chapter in this volume (chapter 1).

18. Lindsay Maizland, "Transgender Activists in China Just Scored a Historic Victory," *Vox*, July 27, 2017, https://www.vox.com/world/2017/7/27/16049820/china-transgender-discrimination-lawsuit-mr-c.

19. Emily Rauhala, "Transgender Chinese Man Wins First-of-Its-Kind Labor Discrimination Case," *The Washington Post*, July 27, 2017, https://www.washingtonpost.com/news/worldviews/wp/2017/07/27/transgender-chinese-man-wins-first-of-its-kind-labor-discrimination-case/?utm_term=.1c753ebc87b1.

20. In the documentary it remains unclear whether or not the protagonist has undergone a sex reassignment surgery, but Mr. C's physical and vocal appearances are shown with effects of hormone medication.

21. Susan Stryker, "De/Colonizing Transgender Studies of China," in *Transgender China*, ed. Howard Chiang (New York, NY: Routledge, 2012), 291.

22. Ibid.

23. Chao Xiaomi (超小米) is a moniker given by the protagonist herself, which means "super little grain of rice." On the social media platform Weibo, Chao Xiaomi has also an active account under the same name.

24. Jamie Fullerton, "Chao Xiaomi: We Have the Right to Use the Bathroom," *Timeout Beijing*, July 26, 2016. http://www.timeoutbeijing.com/features/LGBT/151516/Chao-Xiaomi-We-have-the-right-to-use-the-bathroom.html.

25. Nanlin Fang and Chieu Luu, "Chao Xiaomi Leads China's Fight for Transgender Rights," CNN, June 1, 2017. https://edition.cnn.com/style/article/china-transgender-activist/index.html.

26. Transcribed and excerpted from English subtitles of this documentary.

27. The report points out that among the general transgender population of the United States, white demographic takes up the percentage. However, among the general adult population of the United States, demographics of racial and ethnic minorities have higher ratios in regard to transgender population. For details, see Andrew R. Flores et al., *Race and Ethnicity of Adults Who Identify as Transgender in the United States*, The Williams Institute, UCLA School of Law, October 2016.

28. Rogers Brubaker, *Trans: Gender and Race in an Age of Unsettled Identities* (Princeton and Oxford: Princeton University Press, 2016), 5.

29. Crawford, "Transgender without Organs?" 131.

30. Amy E. Ritterbusch, "Mobilities at Gunpoint: The Geographies of (Im)mobility of Transgender Sex Workers in Colombia," *Annals of the American Association of Geographers* 106, no. 2 (2016): 424.

31. Fran Martin, "Transnational Queer Sinophone Cultures," in *Routledge Handbook of Sexuality Studies in East Asia*, eds. Mark McLellan and Vera Mackie (Abingdon: Routledge, 2014), 40.

32. *VICE*, "Out of Place: The Trans Chinese Community Fighting for Gender Equality," YouTube video, posted on July 19, 2007, https://www.youtube.com/watch?v=tuuXJ3ghxZw.

33. Miriam J. Abelson, "You Aren't from around Here: Race, Masculinity, and Rural Transgender Men," *Gender, Place & Culture* 23, no. 11 (2016): 1537.

BIBLIOGRAPHY

Abelson, Miriam J. "You Aren't from around Here: Race, Masculinity, and Rural Transgender Men." *Gender, Place & Culture* 23, no. 11 (2016): 1535–1546.

Blundy, Rachel. "How a 'Ruthless Playboy Businessman' in Hong Kong Became a Transgender Woman." *South China Morning Post*, August 26, 2017. http://www.scmp.com/news/hong-kong/education-community/article/2108317/how-ruthless-playboy-businessman-hong-kong-became.

Brubaker, Rogers. *Trans: Gender and Race in an Age of Unsettled Identities*. Princeton, NJ, and Oxford: Princeton University Press, 2016.

Chen, Kuan-Hsing. *Asia as Method: Toward Deimperialization*. Durham, NC: Duke University Press, 2010.

Chua, Beng Huat. "Inter-Asia Referencing and Shifting Frames of Comparison." In *The Social Sciences in the Asian Century*, edited by Carol Johnson, Vera Mackie, and Tessa Morris-Suzuki, 67–80. Canberra: Australian National University Press, 2015. DOI: 10.22459/SSAC.09.2015.

Crawford, Lucas Cassidy. "Transgender without Organs?: Mobilizing a Geo-Affective Theory of Gender Modification." *WSQ: Women's Studies Quarterly* 36, no. 3&4 (2008): 127–143.

Fang, Nanlin, and Chieu Luu. "Chao Xiaomi Leads China's Fight for Transgender Rights." CNN, June 1, 2017. https://edition.cnn.com/style/article/china-transgender-activist/index.html.

Flores, Andrew R., Taylor N. T. Brown, and Jody L. Herman, The Williams Institute, UCLA School of Law. *Race and Ethnicity of Adults Who Identify as Transgender in the United States*. October 2016. https://williamsinstitute.law.ucla.edu/wp-content/uploads/Race-and-Ethnicity-of-Transgender-Identified-Adults-in-the-US.pdf.

Fullerton, Jamie. "Chao Xiaomi We Have the Right to Use the Bathroom." *Timeout Beijing*, July 26, 2016. http://www.timeoutbeijing.com/features/LGBT/151516/Chao-Xiaomi-We-have-the-right-to-use-the-bathroom.html.

Howe, Kenneth. "Pink Power." *South China Morning Post*, September 1, 2000. http://www.scmp.com/article/325265/pink-power.

Leung, Helen Hok-Sze. "Trans on Screen." In *Transgender China*, edited by Howard Chiang, 183–198. New York, NY: Palgrave Macmillan, 2012.
Maizland, Lindsay. "Transgender Activists in China Just Scored a Historic Victory." *Vox*, July 27, 2017. https://www.vox.com/world/2017/7/27/16049820/china-transgender-discrimination-lawsuit-mr-c.
Martin, Fran. "Transnational Queer Sinophone Cultures." In *Routledge Handbook of Sexuality Studies in East Asia*, edited by Mark McLellan and Vera Mackie. Abingdon: Routledge, 2014. DOI: 10.4324/9781315774879.
Martin, Fran, and Josephine Ho. "Editorial Introduction: Trans/Asia, Trans/Gender." *Inter-Asia Cultural Studies* 7, no. 2 (2006):185–187.
Rauhala, Emily. "Transgender Chinese Man Wins First-of-Its-Kind Labor Discrimination Case." *The Washington Post*, July 27, 2017. https://www.washingtonpost.com/news/worldviews/wp/2017/07/27/transgender-chinese-man-wins-first-of-its-kind-labor-discrimination-case/?utm_term=.1c753ebc87b1.
Ritterbusch, Amy E. "Mobilities at Gunpoint: The Geographies of (Im)mobility of Transgender Sex Workers in Colombia." *Annals of the American Association of Geographers* 106, no. 2 (2016): 422–433. DOI: 10.1080/00045608.2015.1113112.
Samuels, Andrew. *The Plural Psyche: Personality, Morality and the Father*. New York: Routledge, 2016.
Stryker, Susan. "(De)Subjugated Knowledges: An Introduction to Transgender Studies." In *The Transgender Studies Reader*, edited by Susan Stryker and Stephen Whittle, 1–17. New York: Routledge, 2006.
Stryker, Susan. "De/Colonizing Transgender Studies of China." In *Transgender China*, edited by Howard Chiang, 287–292. New York: Palgrave Macmillan, 2012.
Ullens Center for Contemporary Art. "UCCA x VICE Out of Place: Transgender Stories from Asia Premiere and Discussion." Screened October 14, 2016 at Ullens Center for Contemporary Art, Beijing, China. Accessed March 9, 2018. http://ucca.org.cn/en/program/out-of-place-transgender-stories-from-asia-screening-and-discussion-2/.
VICE. "Out of Place: The Trans Chinese Community Fighting for Gender Equality." YouTube video. Posted on July 19, 2007. https://www.youtube.com/watch?v=tuuXJ3ghxZw.
Yeung, Isobel. "Funky Town: How Disco Fever in the Late '70s Changed Hong Kong's Nightlife Forever." *Post Magazine*, June 15, 2014. http://www.scmp.com/magazines/post-magazine/article/1529999/funky-town-hong-kongs-disco-heyday.

Chapter 9

Dwelling, Aspirations, and the Good Life: Inter-Referencing Young People in Beijing and Hong Kong

Gladys Pak Lei Chong

IN SEARCH OF THE GOOD LIFE

Global culture that promotes tasteful living has grown exponentially popular among urban young people. These aspirations for better quality of life have also resonated with the governing practices of the People's Republic of China (PRC), which encourage citizens to search for the good life as articulated in the discourse of *xiaokang* ("building a moderately prosperous society") and the Chinese Dream. The discursive emphases on the good life are reflected and materialized in everyday life regarding where and how one lives, such as the kind of apartment or house one lives in, the furniture, electrical appliances, and decor within it, and the spatial organization of the physical dwelling. Across the border, Hong Kong, a Special Administrative Region under the sovereignty of China since 1997, became a developed economy under British colonial rule. The PRC's call for a *xiaokang* society and the Chinese Dream are read (in)differently in Hong Kong. This diverging path of historical development begs the questions of how these aspirations for the good life are shaped, guided, and regulated in the specific context of the two top-tier Chinese cities of Hong Kong and Beijing, how their dwellings reveal these aspirations, and the political and cultural implications of the good life.

Home, in the form of a physical dwelling, reveals the very conditions that enable as much as confine the ways one experiences the social world. Home is also a crucial space that shapes subjectivities but, curiously, this has been significantly understudied in cultural studies and China studies.[1] The few existing home studies were written predominantly from Anglo-Saxon perspectives,[2] and very often their concept of home conflated family with the physical dwelling or house. In a journal article that aimed to present an overview of home studies, while Mallett acknowledged the importance of

177

cross-cultural perspectives in understanding the concept of home, the author claimed that, "although important, these perspectives fall beyond the scope of [the] paper."[4] This exclusive focus on Anglo-Saxon experiences has rarely been subjected to interrogation because other cultural experiences are usually considered exceptions that are too diverse and that lack the universality and authority represented by the West. Similarly, in the psychological study of home, such as Cooper's "The House as Symbol of Self,"[5] Jung's concept of the collective unconscious in interpreting home as a symbol of the self has been widely adapted as universally applicable without paying attention to social and cultural contexts.[6] In the sociology of home, scholars[7] have indicated that the idea of home is "culturally bounded,"[8] but few beyond Euro-American experiences have been included in home studies. Words such as "social" and "cultural contexts" are buzzwords researchers have used to pay lip service to diversity and internationalism. This epistemological marginalization of other social and cultural contexts has led to the necessity of intervention, some tactics of which can be found in Koichi Iwabuchi's "trans-Asia" research trajectories discussed in this volume, Chen Kuan-Hsing's *Asia as Method*, and in Inter-Asia Cultural Studies.

In addressing this research lacuna, this chapter will put inter-Asia referencing into practice by examining how a set of converging but also diverging historical, socioeconomic, and political contexts bearing the cultural and spatial heritage of being "Chinese"—despite sharing an elusive set of Chineseness—have shaped young people's subjectivities. This research interest in home and epistemological production was driven by my personal enquiry, reflection, and engagement in "how" to conduct research and develop theoretical works without reproducing the epistemological hierarchy. This empirical study explored the merits, challenges, and limitations of the aforementioned epistemological tactics, and the findings provide an argument for an inclusive approach that embodies the potentials of "trans"—transcendence, transgression, and transformative—in trans-Asia as method.

In what follows, I will first give a brief account of the methodological notes, and then discuss the three epistemological methods—Asia as method, inter-Asia referencing, and trans-Asia as method. This will be followed by an examination of how the concepts of home and housing are intertwined in a specific set of governmental practices in Beijing and Hong Kong. Finally, the analysis of three aspects—beds, electrical appliances, and furnishings and personal items—will be presented to explore how the "realities" of a dwelling reflect young people's aspirations for the good life and their subjectivities. The chapter will end with a reflection of the epistemological tactics of "trans"-Asia as method, which takes into account the non-sharedness and the dangers of methodological nationalism and is a crucial step toward global knowledge production.

METHODOLOGICAL NOTES

The subject of China's young people has been politicized as can be seen in existing literature, which has tended to approach it through a political lens.[9] What these studies have gravely overlooked is that the seemingly apolitical, mundane, and even hedonistic everyday aspects in which government intervention seems to be minimal are important venues that shed light on the intertwining relationship between governing practices, global culture, and young people.

Beijing and Hong Kong were selected for their shared historical background on "forced modernization," similarities in ethno-cultural practices, and their strategic and symbolic significance in China today. As the historical, political, and cultural capital, Beijing has witnessed the country's upheavals, from the invasion of Western imperial powers and the fall of imperial rule to its transition to the PRC. Beijing today represents China to the world. With the country's best universities located there, young people in Beijing are considered the finest. While Hong Kong has been discursively described as a fishing village with barely any history until the arrival of the British government in the nineteenth century, the city is now presented as a leading financial center with ample opportunities and China's gateway to the world. Both cities' converging yet diverging paths of modernization have created divergences, and at times conflicts and tensions, in their socioeconomic and political practices.

Combining ethnographic observations that included in-depth interviews and visits to informants' dwellings in both cities from 2015 to 2017, the analysis focused on eight informants' dwellings in Beijing (table 9.1) and seven in Hong Kong (table 9.2).[10] All of the informants, whose names have been changed in this chapter to maintain their anonymity, were between the ages of twenty-three and thirty during the research period. This age category was chosen for two reasons. First, in the context of Mainland China, these young people were born after the economic reforms introduced by the Open Door Policy (1978), which was followed by the one-child policy (1979), two significant policies that marked a dividing line in the development of contemporary China.[11] How growing up in a modernizing and more prosperous society that has gradually opened up to global culture has shaped young people's subjectivities of important academic and socio-political interest in China and across the world. Second, how young people transit from school to work is central in examining the process of subjectification—how individuals become self-directed subjects of their own while negotiating and engaging with the social relations surrounding them in their transition to "adulthood"[12]—and therefore crucial in revealing the well-being of a society.

All of the Beijing informants, except one, had attended a tertiary education institution in the city, and their monthly income ranged from RMB 4,000
($580) to RMB 8,000 ($1,160). The majority of these informants, except
the one from rural Beijing, were internal migrants. In Hong Kong, all of the
informants had at least a bachelor's degree. Three of them were born in Hong
Kong and the rest had migrated to Hong Kong when they were children. Their
monthly income ranged from HKD 10,000 ($1,280) to HKD 20,000 ($2,560).[13]

FROM ASIA AND INTER-ASIA TO TRANS-ASIA: BEIJING AND HONG KONG

Chen's *Asia as Method*[14] is considered a political intervention that sought to
break away from the Western-dominated epistemological paradigm. Building
on earlier works, such as Takeuchi Yoshimi's lecture in 1960 and Mizoguchi
Yuzo's (1996 [1989]) work, Chen proposed using Asia as the anchoring point
and as an emotional signifier to unify the region and challenge Western domination. As discussed in the introduction, this approach ran the risk of reproducing reductive categories. By foregrounding solidarity within an imagined
Asia, it unfortunately masked the divergence, dominance, and violence
within this entity. Nonetheless, the domination of the West remains a daunt-
ing reality, and much of Chen's critique about the uneven power relations and
Asian academics caught in this desperate spiral of catching up with the West
while being reduced to empirical data for universal theories is still evident.
    Beijing and Hong Kong share similar historical trajectories of forced
modernization. By inter-referencing them, this study was exempt from the
burden of "local informants" providing empirical data in the original universalist Western context. Nonetheless, Beijing and Hong Kong have gone
through different trajectories of socio-political developments; the latter was
under British colonial rule until its retrocession in 1997, while the former
went from being a socialist regime to implementing post-socialist economic
reforms at the end of the 1970s. China's rise in politico-economic power and
Hong Kong's subsumption into the Chinese Communist Party's (CCP) rule
reveal some very complicated historical and social developments. Similarly,
many of the existing studies on Chinese young people have not included
young people in Hong Kong, failing to notice the importance of this population in the overall development of China and Sino-Hong Kong relations. The
Umbrella Movement in Hong Kong in 2014 and the recent rise of localist
discourses in the media[15] have revealed the growing tension between the territory and China.[16] This contextual complexity has exposed the blind spot of
Asia as method and inter-referencing that often looks at a nation-state as a

point of referencing and assumes homogeneity within a state. A case study by Iwabuchi investigated the issues of marginalization, non-sharedness, and the danger of methodological nationalism, claiming that

[a] nation-centred analysis of iteration and East Asian sensibilities might lose sight of the ways in which highlighting "national-territorial" similarities, differences and interactions works to dampen our attention to sociocultural marginalization within and across the nation.[17]

Denationalization is urgent and should be a priority. Beijing and Hong Kong, as subjects of dialogue, have shifted their focus from a nation-based comparison to that of their local populations. Through an analysis of the empirical data collected on young people's dwellings, this inter-referencing study revealed not only the diverse processes of subjectification within a nation-state; more significantly, through the process of relativization,[18] the analysis also revealed critical reflections of the informants both empirically and theoretically. Echoing Chong, Chow, and de Kloet's chapter in this volume, trans-Asia as method embodies the capacity to *de*-nationalize and to locate the complexities and differences within a nation, and in listening, conversing, and transgressing boundaries, transformation is made possible. The following section will present a brief account elaborating the centrality of "home" in relation to both localities' practices of government.

HOME, HOUSING, AND GOVERNMENTAL PRACTICES

News about cash-rich Chinese buying up properties have made international headlines.[19] The first buying spree was by Hong Kong migrants in mainly North America and Australia around the time of the 1997 handover, and the second wave was by Mainland Chinese—including speculators and migrants—across top-tier Chinese cities as well as those overseas. This real estate boom was not essentially Chinese per se. Rather, it unveiled a set of governmental practices in relation to China's and Hong Kong's path to modernization. These governmental practices refer to a multifarious form of "government," including not only the administration of the state. As Foucault elucidated, on the concept of governmentality, government also "concerns many kinds of people: the head of a family, the superior of a convent, the teacher or tutor of a child or pupil."[20] Governmental practices are therefore about how the state manages, guides, and shapes possible actions by guiding people to govern themselves and others.[21]

BEIJING IN CONTEXT

In the PRC, the frenetic drive to catch up with the superior West resulted in economic disasters and material deprivation for nearly three decades after the CCP took power in 1949. The economic reforms implemented by the Open Door Policy changed socialist collectivism in economic planning. Social life that was once centralized and organized around the work unit (*danwei*) in urban China has gradually been replaced by a more individualistic and family-oriented society.[22]

Xiaokang society, an irresistible discourse, was strengthened and supported by the sensory experiences of mundane everyday life. Individuals were inspired to desire the material comforts associated with modern electrical appliances, such as television sets, refrigerators, and rice cookers. This state-directed logic of economic growth encouraged wealth accumulation and consumption. Ngai Pun's study on female workers (*dagongmei*) showed how China's new economy turned the masses (i.e., labor force) into "both a desired producer but also a desiring consumer."[23] Consumption is a powerful seductive force that has convinced people to embrace progress and a better quality of living.[24] The state-orchestrated Chinese Dream has furthered this desire by encouraging young people growing up in an affluent China to contribute to the country.

Young people from less developed areas with a sluggish economy have explored opportunities in top-tier cities such as Beijing. After leaving their homeland (*lao jia*), they acquired a certain degree of freedom and learned to become autonomous. The informants in this study consistently said that they would have been married and had children if they were in their *lao jia*. Moving away was therefore a suspension of a regulated life trajectory, a suspension that was often conditional and calculated as the family evaluated it as an investment for the whole family.

China's household registration system (*hukou*) regulates citizens' mobility, manages population growth, and motivates self-discipline. A Beijing *hukou* gives citizens access to numerous social benefits, such as public schooling and health care services. Young people often prioritize jobs that promise a Beijing *hukou*, while the less qualified young migrants either endure the inconvenience and uncertainties of living in Beijing or save enough money to return to their *lao jia*.

China, as a single-party authoritarian state with the authority to intervene and regulate economic activities, from the stock exchange to mortgage rates, has pushed wealth accumulation in the form of property ownership as essential for both social and economic security. The property price growth rate of 13.1 percent in top-tier cities between 2003 and 2013 has further stimulated this mass interest in real estate.[25] Home ownership is a key indicator in how citizens are evaluated regarding their achievement, success, and upward social mobility.

HONG KONG IN CONTEXT

Local authorities offer minimal social welfare to Hong Kong residents. The earlier generations were mostly refugees fleeing wars and political turmoil in Mainland China. Hong Kong was intended to be a (temporary) shelter in which to rebuild their lives, and the survival and well-being of the family were prioritized. The British colonial government did not start providing public housing until after the 1953 Shek Kip Mei fire, which resulted in more than 50,000 people losing their homes. According to Rooney, the relatively inexpensive public housing units in the 1950s were designed and built below the United Nations standards of requiring "a space allowance of 24 square feet per adult."[26] The space allowance has since increased: the average living space per person is 13.2 square meters (142 square feet) in Hong Kong Housing Authority (HKHA) flats (there are no records for private housing). The majority of refugees tolerated their cramped living conditions because living in Hong Kong was better than living in the war-ridden mainland. Living conditions and housing quality have improved as the city has progressed over the years, as have citizens' expectations of what constitutes the good life.

The prevailing sense of discontentment in today's Hong Kong has, to a large extent, been triggered by an influx of mainland investment in real estate, which is considered China's economic encroachment. The city has ranked at the top of the list of the least affordable housing markets across the world.[27] The difference between median housing prices and median incomes is so enormous that owning a home—one of the common indicators of having a good life—has become a distant dream, especially among young people.[28] Absurdly small apartments called nano flats, typically less than 200 square feet and with a price tag of approximately HKD 4 million (roughly $511,000) per unit, are the only realistic option for the majority of citizens. Nano flats are not entirely new, but their price tags are. Anxiety about deteriorating quality of life and the city's fading political autonomy has created mushrooming resentment, especially among young people.

While young people in Mainland China are marked by their mobility, their counterparts in Hong Kong are comparatively stationary. The latter have seldom experienced separation and independence from their family home.[29] As a territorially small metropolis with a well-developed economy, Hong Kong provides sufficient schooling and job opportunities. Daily commuting between school, work, and dwellings is plausible, making it neither urgent nor necessary to live outside the familial home. This relatively self-sufficient spatial setting has conditioned familial expectations and young people's ambitions toward their surroundings. Moreover, high property prices have further deterred many from experiencing autonomy away from parental care and control. Home ownership remains a yardstick with which to measure one's achievement and marriageability, and better-off parents often offer financial help to their children. While young people are looked after, they are also locked into a not-the-best-not-the-worst situation.

THE DWELLINGS: YOUNG PEOPLE'S SUBJECTIVITIES AND ASPIRATIONS FOR THE GOOD LIFE

Despite sharing ethno-cultural similarities, young people in Beijing and Hong Kong have different aspirations for their future. What appears to be paradoxical is that competitive and harsher social and living environments, away from the care and protection of the family home, have allowed young people in Beijing to be relatively more autonomous. Discontent with their native home—a lack of growth opportunities and sluggishness associated with their *lao jia*—have led them to a persistent search for better living in the future. In Hong Kong, while young people live in a relatively secure and prosperous society, they cannot exercise much freedom as they are often cared for as well as controlled by the more collective family-based living environment.

The analysis in this study examined three aspects of the dwellings: (1) beds; (2) electrical appliances; and (3) furnishings and personal items. From the essential, the optional, and the personal, these three areas open up the possibilities in which to understand the processes whereby individuals engage with their social surroundings to become self-directed. Beds are an essential piece of furniture for resting, electrical appliances are selectively added to elevate the quality of living, and furnishings and personal items are traces of the inhabitants, indicating how they (want to) live. The very spatial organization of a dwelling—how the domestic space is used—not only reflects but also transforms the kind of subjectivity produced in a particular historical, socio-cultural context. The informants' dwellings indicated three interconnected levels of temporality: where they were from, how they are living at the present, and where they are going in the future.

The very notion of comfort, privacy, security, domesticity, and intimacy attached to the socio-cultural idea of home in Euro-American houses[30] needs to be contextualized. Rooney, in her analysis of interior design in Hong Kong Public Housing, claimed that "the high cost of property and the lack of land for development cause Hong Kong people's expectations for a comfortable home to be quite different from those in many societies in the West."[31] Building on Rooney's analysis, this study showed that the informants' intersectional differences[32] in education, professions, and sexuality, as well as diverging historical and socio-political contexts affected how these young people experienced and constructed their dwellings.

BEDS

The dwellings I visited ranged from a staff dormitory provided by a work unit, an apartment in a gated residential community (*xiaoqu*), and units on narrow streets or alleys (*hutong*) to a nuclear bunker bed/room underground. All of these dwellings were very basic, and in each the bed was one of the few essential pieces of furniture that could not be discarded. The bed space, including the "things" found around it, was where the young people imagined and negotiated their subjectivit(ies) with the social world.

The level of tidiness in the dwellings reflected the temporality of the young people's daily lives and their daily practices. The bunk bed in figure 9.1 was shared by Xiao Mao (a high-school graduate originally from a village in Shandong) and his cousin. They were both couriers for China's booming e-commerce industry. Their income depended on the number of packages they picked up and dropped off. The more packages they delivered, the more they earned. On an average day, Xiao Mao made between 100 and 120 deliveries. Time and speed were essential for this job. Xiao Mao was among the army of young migrant workers who ensured the city dwellers' good life by picking up goods from sellers and delivering them to shoppers swiftly and effortlessly at a low cost. Xiao Mao mentioned that Beijing was a temporary stop, as he intended to accumulate enough savings to build a house, start a business, find a wife, and start a family in his *lao jia*. His move to Beijing assisted his transition to manhood as the wealth he made would qualify him as an eligible husband and father. The posters of erotic foreign female models on the wall next to his bed spoke of an imagination that motivated him to work harder to fulfill his manly desires.

Xiao Xun and his roommate (see figure 9.2) had master's degrees from universities in Beijing and were working toward a conventional family-based aspiration for the good life—owning an apartment in Beijing, getting married, and starting a family in a few years time. They shared a dormitory with four bunk beds provided by their work unit (a university in Beijing). They were unhappy with the room's condition but said, self-comfortingly, "It's in bad shape but we paid very little rent, so we can't be demanding. It's also close to work so it's okay." They chose their beds for sleeping and the unused ones became storage space. Their only other pieces of furniture were budget (i.e., small) cabinets to store some personal belongings. Their reluctance in making their room a "home" was an investment for a better life in the future.

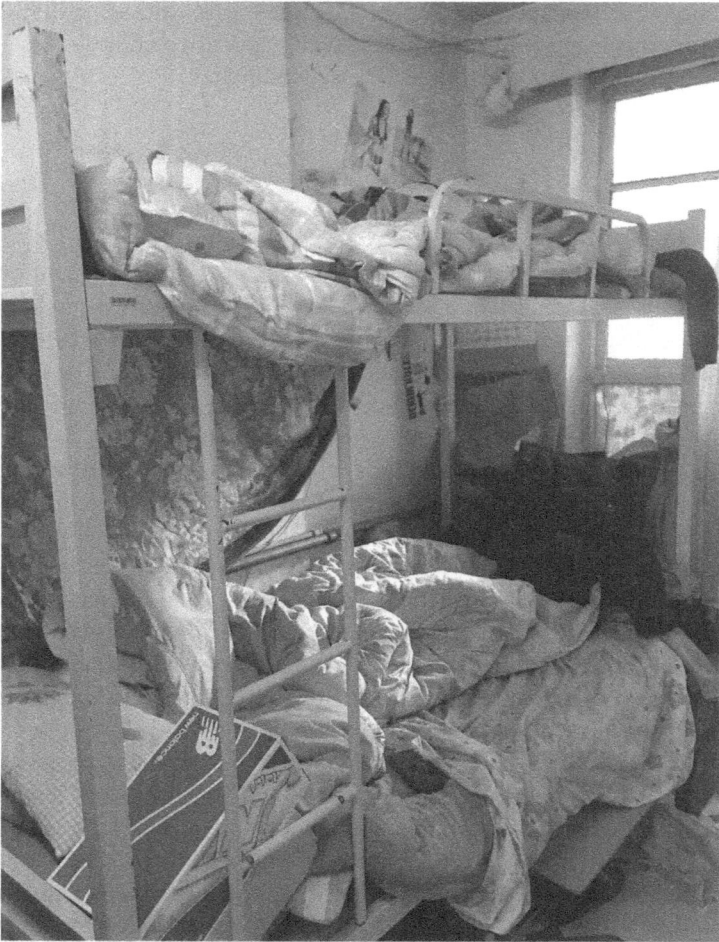

Figure 9.1.   Xiao Mao's bunkbed with erotic posters on the wall.

Many, especially those originally from rural China, are willing to sacrifice instant gratification and comfort in exchange for deferred gratification. When wealth accumulation and home ownership are bundled, rent is considered money wasted, given away without return. The pressure to own a home and to provide material comfort for the family often falls harder on (rural) males because they are perceived as the future patriarch responsible for the whole family's well-being. Most minimized their expenses on rentals by sharing an apartment, a bedroom with relations or friends, or renting a subdivided unit. Their dwellings were often a temporary residence, a shelter, or a sleeping place at night or between shifts.

Figure 9.2. Xiao Xun's dwelling.

The informants who had a good income, future career prospects, or familial financial support could afford to pay more, approximately RMB 4,500
($650) to RMB 8,500 ($1,230), for dwellings in better condition. These
informants had at least queen-size or even king-size beds of better quality
and with trendy bedding, such as those from IKEA. Many of them worked
extremely long hours. Moreover, financial and personal freedom enabled

them to pursue an active social life after work, and they had more leisure time and travelled during the holidays. The tidiness and the condition of the informants' beds represented both youth transition in progress and the city's temporal development.

While the Beijing informants, such as Xiao Mao and Xiao Xun, shared a unit with their relations,[33] their dwellings were considerably more spacious than those in Hong Kong, where home, family, and the physical dwelling are often linked together. Acute land shortage and high property and rental prices make having one's own bedroom a luxury. The chronic lack of space in Hong Kong's small apartments also makes it hard to find privacy as there is literally no place to hide, and it is not uncommon for brothers and sisters to share the same room. Similar to the city's vertical development, a bunk bed with storage space is the usual and logical choice. The informants in Hong Kong often had to share their bedroom with siblings, family members, or foreign domestic helpers. This packed living condition challenged the very oppositional division of the private/public usually associated with a bedroom. Revealingly, a few female informants identified the toilet as their favorite private space.

The small dwellings conditioned the Hong Kong informants' daily practices. They rarely needed to make their bed or clean the dwelling because their mother or a domestic helper performed these household duties. The stuffed toys and cute collectable items around their bed space suggested a kind of continuity from their childhood to the present day. There were no drastic breaks, moves, or abrupt changes that required them to get rid of these childhood items. In brief, they were provided for and allowed to remain a child at heart. A small home can bring intimacy and care but can also easily slide into control and parental pressure (and expectations). While some informants found that their need for private space was urgent, they all found ways to navigate watchful eyes and create their own space by developing different daily routines (e.g., going out when their parents were home) and staying up late at night when the family was asleep.

ELECTRICAL APPLIANCES

In the eyes of many of the informants, the urban population—especially in top-tier cities—has lived in moderate prosperity, as promoted in the *xiaokang* discourse. Tian Tian, who was born in 1988 and was from rural Beijing, talked about *xiaokang* society as a remote past linked to his parents' generation: "*Xiaokang* is not a concern now, because we are already quite well-off. My parents' generation wanted to live comfortably like having the fridge, the television set; nowadays, we don't even watch television anymore. We have plenty now, not in lack of anything. China is rich."

Electrical appliances (e.g. televisions, refrigerators, and washing machines) were once markers of the good life. Today, mobile smartphones have rendered most of the once sought-after electrical appliances obsolete and even redundant. The television has lost its centrality in many dwellings. Similarly, the desktop computer, once a luxury and symbol of advanced technology, has lost its value and desirability. The thick layer of dust on Xiao Mao's desktop (see figure 9.3) suggested that it was left idle, yet the difficulty in discarding it prompted him to resurrect it as a karaoke screen with a microphone attached to it.

Social network sites such as WeChat, Internet platforms such as Taobao (a Chinese online shopping website), and food-delivery platforms such as Ele. me have facilitated the younger population to live in (im)mobility, rendering the material constraints related to their dwellings less confining. Long working hours, coupled with high rental prices and rental conditions, make home cooking a rare and irregular activity. The refrigerator, an appliance often placed next to the television (in the living room), has also become redundant.

Contrary to the popular belief that Chinese Internet censorship (the Great Firewall) is restrictive and limiting, the informants linked this recent technology development to convenience, autonomy, and empowerment. They often illustrated pride and wonder in the possibilities opened up by their smartphone. They felt that the world was within arm's reach, here and there

Figure 9.3. Xiao Mao's computer.

at the same time, or, as Harvey called it, "time-space compression."[34] While this everyday technology has released the tension and urgency for a place-anchored good life, at least temporarily, it has unfortunately heightened the demand for speed and efficiency that normalize long working hours. The informants lamented the loss of a work–life balance because technology made them accessible whenever and wherever they were.

In Hong Kong, most young people (including the majority of the informants) live with their family, and electrical appliances are bundled with familial needs, which makes it neither urgent nor necessary to live differently. In the often-dense living room, the television remains stubbornly at the center, right next to the dining table (see figure 9.4). This spatial arrangement

Figure 9.4.   TV at the center of living, with the refrigerator and the dining table next to it.

has organized and regularized young people's relationship with their family and visual media. Television programs provide conversation topics but also distract and divert discussions to less personal subjects to avoid conflicts and arguments. Even familial intimacy is mediated through this appliance; as one informant said, "[I watch television] very little now, but sometimes still do, when spending time with my mother." By the same token, withdrawal from the familial activity of television-watching, despite physical proximity within the same space, is a gesture to acquire autonomous space through different activities. The continuous presence of household appliances reveals familial care, comfort, and stability, but also, to a certain degree, it confines and limits young people's choices and actions. The chronic lack of space limits the kinds of autonomous activities one can engage in, while laptops and smart devices offer an alternative space as a means for instant gratification and escape.

FURNISHINGS AND PERSONAL ITEMS

Furnishings and personal items make a dwelling one's own, and what is personal is always intertwined with the socio-cultural and political. The SF Express courier motor helmet in Xiao Mao's dwelling (see figure 9.5)

Figure 9.5.   Xiao Mao's SF Express helmet.

revealed both discontent with his *lao jia* and a desire to realize the good life elsewhere. The helmet symbolized not only physical mobility, leaving his hometown in Shandong to drive in Beijing for a living, but also social mobility, as the money and experiences he gained in Beijing would convey recognition in his rural community. The dust and its position high above the wardrobe, however, suggested that the helmet had been idle for a prolonged period. China's fast-growing platform economy has generated an explosive demand for courier services. Work safety regulations require couriers to wear a helmet. Xiao Mao explained that the helmet was bulky and took too much time and effort to put on and take off in a job that demanded speed. Despite its peripheral position, the helmet represented a hopeful yet unknown and unrealized search for the good life.

The emerging young middle class, which is highly educated, with good job prospects, better income, and more global exposure and travel experiences, often pays more attention to and puts more effort into personalizing their dwelling in an attempt to portray that they make a good living. Wang, a university employee in his late twenties originally from Guangzhou, embodied the ideal prototype of a young man with a bright future and unlimited potential. His work unit had already applied for a Beijing *hukou* for him, which would give him the opportunity to get a PhD and the housing benefit of buying an apartment at a huge discount in Beijing. At the time of the interview, he was sharing a two-bedroom staff dormitory with a former professor and a new colleague for a monthly rent of RMB 300. He found the dilapidated condition of his temporary dwelling unbearable: "Home is not just about having a wife and a kid; the environment is also important to make one feel anchored." He gave his dorm room a facelift, for around RMB 4,000–5,000, the amount he would have paid for a private rental per month (see figure 9.6).

This facelift was a home-making experiment for the apartment he would eventually purchase. Wang talked specifically about not having fluorescent tube lighting and white walls, identifying them as the style of an "ordinary" home. He added that the ordinary (or the usual practices) emphasized functionality rather than the sensual and visual aesthetics of making a comfortable living environment. He used wallpaper to cover the poor wall condition, changed his steel-framed bunk bed to a king-size bed, replaced the fluorescent tube lighting and incandescent lamps with different light fixtures, added a new desk and an Eames-style chair, and furnished the room with decorations, such as (plastic) plants, better curtains, and Union Jack bedding.

Wang had placed a laptop, a water kettle, and a sculpture that resembled Rodin's "The Thinker" on his small tidy desk (see figure 9.7). In this twenty-square-meter room, he spent most of his time at his desk (apart from sleeping). "The Thinker," a Western cultural symbol of intellect, occupied an unusually significant space. Not only did the sculpture show his distinctive

Figure 9.6. Wang's bedroom image.

taste, it also served as a reminder of and a model for self-improvement. Wang was not alone, as the other young, ambitious informants looked eagerly and broadly outward, with a strong curiosity of the West, for inspirations of self-realization. Ah Lei, an informant in his late twenties originally from Shaanxi, worked at a public relations company and was one of the very few from his hometown who had managed to attend university and earn a decent income in Beijing. His rental was a bedroom in a gated community. It was spacious, with a queen-size bed and a desk, on top of which was a double-layer book-shelf filled with self-help books, such as the *New York Times* bestseller *Rich Dad Poor Dad* (1997), which discusses financial literacy and responsibility.

As shown in the figures above, Wang's refurnished dwelling was aes-thetically very "Western." The informants frequently identified IKEA, with its minimalistic styles and smart storage spaces, and the Muji style (often linked to discussions of keeping spaces neat and tidy, with less clutter)[35] as examples of good living that constituted an essential part of the good life. The e-commerce platform Taobao and IKEA make this idea of good living imaginable, accessible, and affordable. The informants' curiosity, shown in the ways they tried to acquire a higher quality of living in their dwellings, was related to their personal capability of making a decent living in a competitive environment, and their aspirations for the good life, in turn, endowed them with hope in realizing their own imagined good life.

Figure 9.7. "The Thinker" on Wang's desk.

Home is often linked to family-building, and a dwelling is a physical home that embodies the very quality of grounding an individual. For a homosexual person, home is a heteronormative space that forces one to conform to patriarchal and social orders, as well as worldly views and responsibilities, controlling and confining one's desires. Ah Xuan, a gay activist and renowned documentary filmmaker, said, "I don't feel safe at home, [and] this is especially the case when I am at [my] *lao jia*." He added, "If I have a home, meaning that you will be confined, forced to settle down, I am a little scared by this thought; honestly, I am scared of home." Ah Xuan has resisted the governmental practices of the social heterosexual norms of family-building and the growing social norms of home ownership as evidence of success. On his business card, he descr bed himself as "No Job. No Home" (for a free-lancer, everywhere is home).

Ah Xuan shared a two-bedroom apartment with a friend and was one of the privileged few who was able to travel around the world. He had glued postcards, film posters, boarding passes, film tickets, city maps, and maps showing hotspots for LGBT (lesbian, gay, bisexual, and transgender) people all around his bedroom (see figure 9.8). He said, "I like intensity, dense meanings, also in this work, how to materialize what I am doing. I [have] demonstrated traces of *wandering* [expressed in English] around the globe. Although I am in this particular space now, there are many things on the walls that helped me connect with the world."

In this fairly basic bedroom, these traces were vital as they asserted the contributions and significance of what he has contributed to LGBT commu-nities in China and beyond amidst the fear and anxiety of living in a hostile anti-homosexual environment. These traces expressed his yearning for the good life—based in Beijing but not succumbing to the heteronormative social pressure of owning a home as a sign of success.

Figure 9.8. Ah Xuan's furnishings (e.g., photos, boarding passes).

Like the majority of young people in Hong Kong, Edward, who was born in 1987, did not believe he could ever afford to buy an apartment. He had lived with his mother in a 300 square foot flat in a public housing estate since he was eight. Despite the limited space, he had his own room. After getting his master's degree, he started working for a local newspaper. With his newly acquired financial freedom and free time, he was able to renovate the apartment. He painted the walls white, replaced the old beds, and bought a new bookshelf and new chairs.

The bookshelf and his loft bed with a desk underneath were the center of his refurbishment. An IKEA bookshelf occupied more than half of the wall in the living room (see figure 9.9). Its centrality in the apartment spoke of the intimate connection between books and Edward's aspirations for the good life: a constant search for self-improvement through reading and learning. On his loft bed, he created a bedtime reading corner with a reading lamp, a wall shelf for his book, and a poster. The desk underneath the loft bed was his work desk, on top of which he had placed decorative items—candle holders, a skincare bottle, an ashtray, and other accessories, such as a pencil holder. On the wall near the desk was a corkboard full of posters and images, mostly fashion and cultural events, in English and Japanese (see figure 9.10).

This renovation project was enriching but also confronting, as it involved rethinking and reflecting on the very practices of his past self, the present, and his future. Catalogues from the Japanese household retail company Muji and European brands of great design and good quality were his sources of references in constructing a good living environment. In his reflection, Edward shared why he valued his appearance more than his dwelling condition in his teens: "I had low self-esteem. When socializing with people of my age, they won't see your home, then how you left them an impression, it must be from your appearance, so I pretended. I spent a lot of effort to create this image, I ignored things at home, I only needed a space to study, the rest I did not care [about]." While his physical home was not a space for self-exploration and social interaction, Edward (like many others in his age group) had to look outside his home for social assertion and self-realization. It was this spatial relation that gave birth to his interest in fashion and, in turn, his expert knowledge and his profession today.

His love of Japanese culture was shown by the large quantities of magazines and books in his home and his recent visits to Japan. While admiring Japanese sophistication, he posited that China was the exact opposite. Given China's increasing control over Hong Kong, Edward was critical of China and Chineseness. To Edward, his relations, who were originally from Mainland China, exemplified the unpleasant Chineseness in the practices of everyday life. He questioned their thrifty habit of collecting things, which made their dwelling messy: "I don't understand why Chinese don't have any living

Figure 9.9.   Edward's bookshelves.

concepts, how to change that?! They always said it's good enough to have a roof over your head . . . I did not like covering the chair with this cloth . . . you know Chinese, they wanted to cover this and that."

Despite this confronting generational and cultural struggle, IKEA seemed to provide magical living references for the home renovation. Edward's relations initially found it unnecessary to renovate their dwelling, but IKEA had trans-formative power: "[IKEA] has this inspirational power. . . . [IKEA] was very effective in educating people [about] living concepts, it was like brain-washing her, a thorough 'cleansing' [of her old habits]."

Figure 9.10.   Edward's desk under the loft bed.

Other informants in Hong Kong also favored Japan and Europe as their sources of aspirations for a modern and progressive lifestyle. This subjective belief is largely a remnant of the city's colonial history and the forced modernization mentioned above, which has produced a cultural hierarchy that ranks the West above the local. For these informants, the West, the English, and Japan (Hong Kong's advanced Asian counterpart) were considered modernized models that provided ideas and the means for self-enrichment. David and his sister, both born in the 1990s, lived in a 400-square-foot two-bedroom private apartment and had collected manga dolls and figures since high school. The family bought new shelves for their collections. Around the TV area was familial space, and Japanese dolls in kimonos were placed next to family photos. The family had started going on holiday together two years ago, but David's parents found Taiwan too similar to Mainland China—chaotic—so Japan was chosen as their destination. Their fond experiences there linked Japaneseness to quality time that was treasured and remembered.

The bunk beds, the (foldable) dining table, and the wall-size multilayer living room cabinets were specifically tailored for the limited space in Hong Kong. The furniture represented spatial challenges, but its spatial relationship also guided aspirations for the good life—upward social mobility by working hard—in the past. With the fading autonomy of Hong Kong, this furniture was looked upon nostalgically. However, in the context of current housing conditions, this material Hongkongness is treated ambivalently as it symbolizes the survival need of compromise. Extremely high property prices have dashed young people's hope for a better future. Many are disenchanted and have started re-imagining an alternative understanding of success and the good life. The cultural references to the West and neighboring countries such as Japan, Taiwan, and Thailand have offered sources of imagination as well as sites of escape. The informants used, for example, world maps, Western paintings (e.g., Van Gogh's "The Starry Night"), cultural events posters, and photos, to transform their living spaces, which transcended their spatial constraints into aspirations—elsewhere—away from pressing reality and to an imaginable space. Chineseness in the form of material objects was not valued in this transformative capacity.

Iwabuchi and Chua have noted that Taiwanese TV consumers now look to Japan and its products for their modern appeal.[36] Young people in both Hong Kong and Beijing are following a similar practice by looking for modern aspirations beyond their immediate socio-cultural environment. Ambitious young people in Beijing have aspired to attain neat and tidier living conditions, a condition that is identified in their modern developed counterparts. The unpleasant living environment in Hong Kong has urged many to look beyond Hong Kong and China for aspirations, imaginations, and hope. Japanese and Western furnishings and decorative items are considered aesthetically pleasing and psychologically comforting in making their dwelling a home.

TRANS-ASIA AS INTERVENTION: IMAGINING AN ALTERNATIVE WORLD

In *Asia as Method*, Chen pinpointed the West's domination as affecting "our bodies and minds" and our desires and pains.[37] Inter-Asia referencing is meant to empower Asia as a whole. I put this Asian inter-referencing into practice and explored and critically assessed not only what this method offers but also, equally important, what is at stake if one looks *only* at "Asia" for reference. By inter-referencing the two top-tier Chinese cities of Hong Kong and Beijing, I explored in what ways the physical dwellings revealed diverging historical, socioeconomic, and political contexts yet shared a varying set of socio-cultural "Chineseness" that shaped the subjectivities of young adults. In this case study, it was *trans*-Asia (Asia and beyond) and the coevalness of culture—a globalizing discourse of the good life—that motivated the young Chinese/Asian informants to explore a range of possibilities for a better living environment.

Theoretically, Asia as method departs from this non-sharedness with the West, and the non-West is burdened by an irresistible drive to catch up to the superior West. Chen has advocated a quasi-exclusionary retreat to the local and the regional because he does not believe that dialogues on Western theories are helpful in the Asian context: "[T]he real problem is that Euro-American theory is simply not all that helpful in our attempts to understand our own conditions and practices."[38] This method takes Western-centrism as its central problem. From the many homes I visited, the furnishings and the decorative accessories showed that the West was not necessarily imposing or oppressive. Quite the opposite, the West and often Japan (especially in the Hong Kong context) symbolized the sources of aspiration for the good life as reflected in the minimalistic furnishings and more advanced and better-quality materials found in the informants' dwellings. In both localities, the young informants were looking outward beyond China for sources of aspirations. Edward's case vividly demonstrated how Japan and the West offered him aspirations of the good life in renovating his once-depressing and overcrowded living conditions. The logic of "catching up" in daily life also functioned as a productive force for self-improvement, offering alternative perspectives about living well, in decency and with integrity.

By categorizing the West as a collective and a point of opposition for Asians, Asia as method retreats to the very dualistic mode of operation that Chen sought to break away from.[39] Even with good intentions, this boundary-drawing is problematic. In de Kloet's analysis of European Baroque styles in China, he argued that Europe represents "the hope for slowness, a reduction of speed."[40] Europe-as-façade represents the process of cultural translation that problematizes the notion of purity and originality, pinpointing the troubling fact of the dichotomy of East versus West.[41] Chen's approach blocked plausible communication and dialogue that could have generated productive discussions and epistemological reflections. In "Inter-Asia Banality and Education," Meaghan Morris[42] re-emphasized that dialogue with the West is important.

This research was motivated by a personal quest to explore the problems and challenges of using Western theory to understand China and Hong Kong in particular and Asia in general. I engaged Michel Foucault in my analysis of China, and this often triggered a recurrent set of questions—for many China studies scholars and advocates of Foucauldian studies—about why one would use Western theories to study conditions in China and whether Foucault is applicable in an authoritarian society. The former often see my position as "selling out to the West," while the latter have simply accused me of being wrong about or ignorant of Foucault's works. Even though their viewpoints diverge, these two parties converge in the argument that China and the West have diverged significantly in historical, socio-cultural, and political aspects and therefore the two are not compatible. Cultural theorists, such as Rey Chow and Kwai-Cheung Lo,[43] have warned against this reductive and conservative approach, which is only meant to preserve the interests of very few in the field, blocking communication and dialogue.

Having said this, the use of academic celebrities such as Michel Foucault cannot go unquestioned. In "Communitarian, or, How to Build East Asian Theory," Margaret Hillenbrand asked, what does it mean "to think 'theoretically' in contemporary East Asian studies?"[44] Hillenbrand critically and self-reflectively addressed the issue of academics working in and on East Asia's regular use of Western theory, explaining that this was not only about the "institutional histories of East Asianists" that endowed Western theory, "the cruel academic capital," with publishability and tenurability,[45] but also how Western theories were considered "naturalized backdrops that succeeds via everyone's complicity with the illusion."[46] This explains why the West is considered the equivalent of the global and why (East) Asia remains at the margins. Hillenbrand also pointed out the huge inequality that exists in the global intellectual landscape: very few Western writings refer to East Asia.[47] It is this significant gap that has drawn many postcolonial scholars (working in Asian Cultural/Postcolonial Studies) to actively search for alternative approaches to alter this domination. Hillenbrand's idea was to make East Asian intellectual development visible, heard, and gradually normalized in academia.

Even though I may not agree with the quasi-exclusionary ideas behind Asia as method, I am in alignment with Chen's critique on the West's domination in the existing knowledge structure. This acute non-presence of non-Euro-American Studies in home studies is astonishing, and the academic practices that have rendered the West as universal and the non-West as empirical data/reality, where "eventually our writings [will] become a footnote that either validates or invalidates Western theoretical propositions,"[48] require academic communities to strategize and bring attention to locally produced knowledge.

As such, in addition to putting Asian inter-referencing into practice, this study also explored Hillenbrand's idea of developing "East Asian theory" by drawing on works produced by Asian intellectuals such as Takeuchi Yoshimi, Chen Kuan-Hsing, Kochi Iwabuchi, Ien Ang, Rey Chow, Shu-mei Shih, Jeroen de Kloet, Sun Ge, Ge Zhaoguang, and Naoki Sakai. These "practical, small-scale, workday strategies—such as reading, teaching, citation, and curriculum designs" are crucial to the emergence of East Asian theory.[49] In doing so, I am engaging with what Hillenbrand has suggested: discourse-building.[50] As Hillenbrand has stated, the suggestion that "good ideas need well-read, industrious intermediaries if they are to achieve critical mass is very salutary."[51] By citing and discussing (Asian) theorists' ideas, scholars are cultivating "new forms of intellectual dialogue" and forming an "Asia Knowledge

Community."[52] In sum, Asian mutual referencing exposes the challenges of a consuming focus and a reactionary Asian centrism, urging (Asian) theorists to engage in a more open trans-Asia method and dialogue.

ACKNOWLEDGMENTS

I would like to thank all the informants for sharing their engaging and thoughtful reflections; their openness made this project possible. I would also like to thank Professor Koichi Iwabuchi and Monash University Prato Centre for organizing the conference "Trans-Asia as Method," held in the Summer of 2017. I am indebted to the reviewers' generous comments as well. This project was supported by the Hong Kong Research Grants Council (project number 22609415 and project number 12610118).

NOTES

1. Exceptions are the three books on space and gender, space and imagination, and space and power written by Bi Heng-da. Two of the editors here have written a co-authored article about the idea of home that takes into consideration home-making, belonging, and citizenship in their discussion (Chow, van Wichelen, and de Kloet, 2016).

2. Alexa Griffith Winton, "Inhabited Space: Critical Theories and the Domestic Interior," in *The Handbook of Interior Architecture and Design*, eds. Lois Weinthal and Graeme Brooker (London and New York: Bloomsbury Press, 2013), 50–59; Peter King, *Private Dwelling: Contemplating the Use of Housing* (London: Routledge, 2005); Peter Saunders and Peter Williams, "The Constitution of the Home: Towards a Research Agenda," *Housing Studies* 3, no. 2 (1988): 81–93.

3. Witold Rybczynski, *Home: A Short History of an Idea* (New York: Penguin Books, 1986); Shelley Mallett, "Understanding Home: A Critical Review of the Literature," *The Sociological Review* 52, no. 1 (2004): 62–89.

4. Mallett, "Understanding Home," 65.

5. Clare Cooper, "The House as Symbol of Self," in *Designing for Human Behaviour: Architecture and the Behavioural Sciences*, eds. Jon Lang, C. Burnette, W. Moleski, and D. Vachon (Stroudsburg, PA: Dowden, Hutchinson and Ross, 1995), 130–146.

6. Jeanne Moore, "Placing Home in Context," *Journal of Environmental Psychology* 20, no. 3 (2000): 212.

7. See Duncan Case, "Contributions of Journeys away to the Definition of Home: An Empirical Study of a Dialectical Process," *Journal of Environmental Psychology* 16, no. 1 (1996): 1–15.

8. Moore, "Placing Home," 213.

9. See James R. Townsend, *The Revolutionization of Chinese Youth* (Berkeley, CA: University of California, 1967); Ngai Pun, Chau-Kiu Cheung, and Chi-Kei Li,

"China's Youth Policy Formulation and Youth Participation," *Children and Youth Services Review* 23, no. 8 (2001): 651–669; Terry Woronov, "Class Consciousness, Service Work: Youth and Class in Nanjing Vocational Secondary Schools," *Journal of Contemporary China* 21, no 77 (2012): 779–791.

10. In Beijing, I interviewed more than eighty young people and visited thirty-eight dwellings, as I expanded this research into another research project funded by the Hong Kong Research Grants Council (project number 12610118) in 2015.

11. As Jones and Wallace (1992) have argued, the concept of youth varies from place to place and is often determined by numerous factors, such as socio-political and cultural contexts.

12. Pak Lei Gladys Chong, *Chinese Subjectivities & the Beijing Olympics* (London: Rowman & Littlefield, 2017).

13. It is beyond the scope of this chapter to discuss the gender dimensions of their dwelling.

14. Kuan-Hsing Chen, *Asia as Method: Towards Deimperialization* (Durham, NC, and London: Duke University Press, 2010).

15. See Stephen Ching-Kiu Chan, "Delay No More: Struggles to Re-imagine Hong Kong (for the Next 30 Years)," *Inter-Asia Cultural Studies* 16, no. 3 (2015): 327–347; Iam-Chong Ip, "Politics of Belonging: A Study of the Campaign against Mainland Visitors in Hong Kong," *Inter-Asia Cultural Studies* 16, no. 3 (2015): 410–421; Yun-Chung Chen and Mirana M. Szeto, "The Forgotten Road of Progressive Localism: New Preservation Movement in Hong Kong," *Inter-Asia Cultural Studies* 16, no. 3 (2015): 436–453.

16. According to Veg, these localist discourses attracted media attention in early 2016. Despite being "a confusing galaxy of ideas," these discourses are based "to varying degrees on prioritising local over national identification" (Veg, 2017, 325). See Sebastian Veg, "The Rise of 'Localism' and Civic Identity in Post-handover Hong Kong: Questioning the Chinese Nation-state," *The China Quarterly* 230 (2017): 323–347.

17. Koichi Iwabuchi, *Recentering Globalization: Popular Culture and Japanese Transnationalism* (Durham, NC: Duke University Press, 2002), 54.

18. Chen, *Asia as Method*, 254.

19. "China's Property Bubble Represents a Social Risk: Renowned Chinese Economist," CNBC, accessed May 1, 2017, http://www.cnbc.com/2017/03/24/boao-forum-chinese-property-bubble-a-social-risk-economist-says.html.

20. Michel Foucault, "Governmentality," in *The Foucault Effect: Studies in Governmentality*, eds. Graham Burchell, Colin Gordon, and Peter Miller (Chicago, IL: University of Chicago Press, 1991), 91.

21. Ibid.

22. *Danwei*, according to E. M. Bjorklund (1986), was the first territorial work unit to organize the urban population after Communist China embarked on its modernization project.

23. Ngai Pun, "Subsumption or Consumption? The Phantom of Consumer Revolution in 'Globalizing' China," *Cultural Anthropology* 18, no. 4 (2003): 470.

24. Lisa Rofel, *Desiring China: Experiments in Neoliberalism, Sexuality, and Public Culture* (Durham, NC: Duke University Press, 2007).

25. Hanming Fang, Quanlin Gu, Wei Xiong, and Li-An Zhou, "Demystifying the Chinese Housing Boom," in *NBER Macroeconomics Annual 2015* (Vol. 30), eds. Martin Eichenbaum and Jonathan Parker (Chicago, IL: University of Chicago Press, 2015). A decade ago, the state discontinued its practice of providing homes. According to Glaser et al. (2017, 103), the state built only 13 percent of total floor space in the PRC in 2013, compared to 70 percent in 2000. Growth and construction go hand in hand, but the state curbed speculation, restricted second and third home purchases, and limited the resale of homes in less than five years (Glaser et al., 2017, 104).

26. Nuala Rooney, "Making House into Home: Interior Design in Hong Kong Public Housing," in *Consuming Hong Kong*, eds. Gordon Mathews and Tai-Lok Lui (Hong Kong: Hong Kong University Press, 2001), 55.

27. "Hong Kong the World's Priciest Home Market for the Seventh Year," *South China Morning Post*, accessed May 31, 2017, http://www.scmp.com/business/article/2064554/hong-kong-named-most-expensive-housing-market-world-seventh-straight-year.

28. According to the HKHA, more than 44.8 percent of the population lived in HKHA flats, whereas 54.6 percent lived in private housing, in 2016. The average monthly rent for HKHA flats was between HKD 54 to HKD 61 per square metre (around $6.88 to $7.8) in 2017, whereas the average monthly rent for private flats with less than 70 square metres was around HKD 249 to HKD 408 per square metre (around $31.7 to $52) in 2017. Given the strict requirements for HKHA flats, the majority of the population must resort to the private housing market. Monthly rent for a private apartment with 70 square metres is between HKD 17,430 to HKD 28,560 (around $2,220 to $3,700). See Hong Kong Housing Authority, "Housing in Figures 2017," accessed August 24, 2018, https://www.thb.gov.hk/eng/psp/publications/housing/HIF2017.pdf.

29. Exceptions are those studying abroad or those going abroad for working holidays, but upon their return, they stay with their parents.

30. Rybczynski, *Home*, 66.

31. Rooney, "Making House into Home," 48.

32. Kimberlé Crenshaw, "Mapping the Margins: Intersectionality, Identity Politics, and Violence against Women of Color," *Stanford Law Review* 43 (1991): 1241–1279.

33. I use relations here to include not only family relatives but also friends and people the informants knew from the same village or hometown.

34. David Harvey, *The Condition of Postmodernity* (Oxford: Basil Blackwell, 1989).

35. Muji is a Japanese company that sells a great variety of household and consumer goods. It is known for its minimalistic design and "no-logo" policy, as its Japanese name "Mujirushi Ryohin"—No Brand Quality Goods—suggests. Its simple design style has gained huge popularity across the world. It has expanded into the hotel business, and two of its three hotels are in Shenzhen and Beijing.

36. Iwabuchi, *Recentering Globalization*; and Beng Huat Chua, "Conceptualizing an East Asian Popular Culture," *Inter-Asia Cultural Studies* 5, no. 2 (2004): 200–221.

37. Chen, *Asia as Method*, xi.

38. Chen, *Asia as Method*, 226.

39. Ibid., 216.

40. Jeroen de Kloet, "Europe as Façade," *European Journal of Cultural Studies* 17, no. 1 (2013): 15.

41. Rey Chow, *Primitive Passions: Visuality, Sexuality, Ethnography and Contemporary Chinese Cinema. Film and Culture* (New York: Columbia University Press, 1995); de Kloet, "Europe as Façade," 15.

42. Megan Morris, "Inter-Asian Banality and Education," *Inter-Asia Cultural Studies* 11, no. 2 (2010): 157–164.

43. Chow, *Primitive Passions*; Kwai-Cheung Lo, "Rethinking Asianism and Method," *European Journal of Cultural Studies* 17, no. 1 (2013): 31–43.

44. Margaret Hillenbrand, "Communitarianism, or, How to Build East Asian Theory," *Postcolonial Studies* 13, no. 4 (2010): 317–334.

45. Ibid., 322.

46. Ibid.

47. Ibid., 317.

48. Chen, *Asia as Method*, 226.

49. Hillenbrand, "Communitarianism," 323.

50. Ibid., 324.

51. Ibid., 325.

52. Ibid., 329.

BIBLIOGRAPHY

Ang, Ien. "Can One Say No to Chineseness? Pushing the Limits of the Diasporic Paradigm." *Boundary 2* 25, no. 3 (1998): 223–242.

———. *On Not Speaking Chinese: Living between Asia and the West*. London: Routledge, 2001.

Bi, Heng-da. *Space Is Gender*. Taipei: Psygarden, 2004.

Bjorklund, E. M. "The Danwei: Socio-Spatial Characteristics of Work Units in China's Urban Society." *Economic Geography* 62, no. 1 (1986): 19–29.

Case, Duncan. "Contributions of Journeys away to the Definition of Home: An Empirical Study of a Dialectical Process." *Journal of Environmental Psychology* 16, no. 1 (1996): 1–15.

Chan, Stephen Ching-Kiu. "Delay No More: Struggles to Re-imagine Hong Kong (for the Next 30 Years)." *Inter-Asia Cultural Studies* 16, no. 3 (2015): 327–347.

Chen, Kuan-Hsing. *Asia as Method: Toward Deimperialization*. Durham, NC, and London: Duke University Press, 2010.

———. "Takeuchi Yoshimi's 1960 'Asia as Method' Lecture." *Inter-Asia Cultural Studies* 13, no. 2 (2012): 317–324.

Chen, Yun-Chung, and Mirana M. Szeto. "The Forgotten Road of Progressive Localism: New Preservation Movement in Hong Kong." *Inter-Asia Cultural Studies* 16, no. 3 (2015): 436–453.

Chong, Gladys Pak Lei. *Chinese Subjectivities and the Beijing Olympics*. London: Rowman & Littlefield, 2017.

Chow, Rey. *Primitive Passions: Visuality, Sexuality, Ethnography and Contemporary Chinese Cinema. Film and Culture*. New York: Columbia University Press, 1995.

Chapter 9

———. "Can One Say No to China?" *New Literary History* 28, no. 1 (1997): 147–151.

Chow, Yiu Fai, Sonja van Wichelen, and Jeroen de Kloet. "Introduction: At Home in Asia? Place-making, Belonging and Citizenship in the Asian Century." *International Journal of Cultural Studies* 19, no. 3 (2016): 243–256.

Chua, Beng Huat. "Conceptualizing an East Asian Popular Culture." *Inter-Asia Cultural Studies* 5, no. 2 (2004): 200–221.

Cooper, Clare. "The House as Symbol of Self." In *Designing for Human Behaviour: Architecture and the Behavioural Sciences*, edited by Jon Lang, C. Burnette, W. Moleski, and D. Vachon, 130–146. Stroudsberg, PA: Dowden, Hutchinson and Ross, 1995.

Crenshaw, Kimberlé. "Mapping the Margins: Intersectionality, Identity Politics, and Violence against Women of Color." *Stanford Law Review* 43 (1991): 1241–1279.

Fang, Hanming, Quanlin Gu, Wei Xiong, and Li-An Zhou. "Demystifying the Chinese Housing Boom." In *NBER Macroeconomics Annual 2015*, vol. 30, edited by Martin Eichenbaum and Jonathan Parker, 105–166. Chicago, IL: University of Chicago Press, 2015.

Foucault, Michel. "Governmentality." In *The Foucault Effect: Studies in Governmentality*, edited by Graham Burchell, Colin Gordon, and Peter Miller, 87–104. Chicago, IL: University of Chicago Press, 1991.

Glaeser, Edward, Wei Huang, Yueran Ma, and Andrei Shleifer. "A Real Estate Boom with Chinese Characteristics." *The Journal of Economic Perspectives* 31, no. 1 (2017): 93–116.

Harrison, Mark. "How to Speak about Oneself: Theory and Identity in Taiwan." In *Cultural Studies and Cultural Industries in Northeast Asia: What a Difference a Region Makes*, edited by Chris Berry, Nicola Liscutin, and Jonathan D. Mackintosh, 51–70. Hong Kong: Hong Kong University Press, 2009.

Harvey, David. *The Condition of Postmodernity*. Oxford: Basil Blackwell, 1989.

Hooks, Bell. *Yearning: Race, Gender and Cultural Politics*. London: Turnaround, 1991.

Hillenbrand, Margaret. "Communitarianism, or, How to Build East Asian Theory." *Postcolonial Studies* 13, no. 4 (2010): 317–334.

Ip, Iam-Chong. "Politics of Belonging: A Study of the Campaign against Mainland Visitors in Hong Kong." *Inter-Asia Cultural Studies* 16, no. 3 (2015): 410–421.

Iwabuchi, Koichi. *Recentering Globalization: Popular Culture and Japanese Transnationalism*. Durham, NC: Duke University Press, 2002.

———. "De-Westernization, Inter-Asian Referencing and Beyond." *European Journal of Cultural Studies* 17, no. 1 (2013): 44–57.

Jones, Gill, and Claire Wallace. *Youth, Family and Citizenship*. Milton Keynes: Open University Press, 1992.

King, Peter. *Private Dwelling: Contemplating the Use of Housing*. London: Routledge, 2005.

de Kloet, Jeroen. "Europe as Façade." *European Journal of Cultural Studies* 17, no. 1 (2013): 58–74.

Law, Wing Sang. *Collaborative Colonial Power*. Hong Kong: Hong Kong University Press, 2009.

Lin, Angel M. Y. "Towards Transformation of Knowledge and Subjectivity in Curriculum Inquiry: Insights from Chen Kuan-Hsing's 'Asia as Method.'" *Curriculum Inquiry* 42, no. 1 (2012): 153–178.

Lo, Kwai-Cheung. "Rethinking Asianism and Method." *European Journal of Cultural Studies* 17, no. 1 (2013): 31–43.

Mallett, Shelley. "Understanding Home: A Critical Review of the Literature." *The Sociological Review* 52, no. 1 (2004): 62–89.

Mizoguchi, Yuzo. *China as Method*. Trans. Li Suping, Gong Ying and Xu Tao. Beijing: China Renmin University Press, 1996.

Moore, Jeanne. "Placing *Home* in Context." *Journal of Environmental Psychology* 20, no. 3 (2000): 207–217.

Morris, Meaghan. "Inter-Asian Banality and Education." *Inter-Asia Cultural Studies* 11, no. 2 (2010): 157–164.

Pun, Ngai. "Subsumption or Consumption? The Phantom of Consumer Revolution in 'Globalizing' China." *Cultural Anthropology* 18, no. 4 (2003): 469–492.

Pun, Ngai, Chau-Kiu Cheung, and Chi-Kei Li. "China's Youth Policy Formulation and Youth Participation." *Children and Youth Services Review* 23, no. 8 (2001): 651–669.

Rofel, Lisa. *Desiring China: Experiments in Neoliberalism, Sexuality, and Public Culture*. Durham, NC: Duke University Press, 2007.

Rooney, Nuala. "Making House into Home: Interior Design in Hong Kong Public Housing." In *Consuming Hong Kong*, edited by Gordon Mathews and Tai-Lok Lui, 47–79. Hong Kong: Hong Kong University Press, 2001.

Rybczynski, Witold. *Home: A Short History of an Idea*. New York: Penguin Books, 1986.

Saunders, Peter, and Peter Williams. "The Constitution of the Home: Towards a Research Agenda." *Housing Studies* 3, no. 2 (1988): 81–93.

Shih, Shu-mei. "Theory, Asia and the Sinophone." *Postcolonial Studies* 13, no. 4 (2010): 465–484.

Townsend, James R. *The Revolutionization of Chinese Youth*. Berkeley: University of California, 1967.

Veg, Sebastian. "The Rise of 'Localism' and Civic Identity in Post-handover Hong Kong: Questioning the Chinese Nation-state." *The China Quarterly* 230 (2017): 323–347.

Wagner, David. *Checkerboard Square: Culture and Resistance in a Homeless Community*. Boulder, CO: West Press, 1993.

Wardhaugh, Julia. "The Unaccommodated Woman: Home, Homelessness and Identity." *The Sociological Review* 47, no. 1 (1999): 91–109.

Winton, Alexa Griffth. "Inhabited Space: Critical Theories and the Domestic Interior." In *The Handbook of Interior Architecture and Design*, edited by Lois Weinthal and Graeme Brooker, 50–59. London and New York: Bloomsbury Press, 2013.

Woronov, Terry. "Class Consciousness, Service Work: Youth and Class in Nanjing Vocational Secondary Schools." *Journal of Contemporary China* 21, no. 77 (2012): 779–791.

Appendix on Informants

Table 9.1. Beijing Informants

Name	Year of Birth	Gender	Hometown	Education Level	Occupation	Beijing Hukou
Xiao Mao	1989	M	Shandong	High school	Couriers	No
Xiao Xun	1988	M	Sichuan	Master's degree	Admin staff (counselling) at a university in Beijing	Yes
Ah Lei	1990	M	Shaanxi	Master's degree	Public relations	Yes
Wang	1889	M	Guangdong	Master's degree	Admin staff for a university in Beijing	Yes
Ah Xuan	1985	M	Jiangsu	Bachelor's degree	Film industry	No
Xiao Hong	1991	F	Sichuan	Bachelor's degree	Advertising	No
Xiao Mei	1992	F	Sichuan	Bachelor's degree	Marketing	No
Tian Tian	1988	F	Beijing Suburb	Bachelor's degree	Market research	Yes

Table 9.2. Hong Kong Informants

Name	Year of Birth	Gender	Place of Birth	Education Level	Occupation
Venus	1991	F	Hong Kong	Bachelor's degree	Banking
Edward	1987	M	China	Master's degree	Journalist
David	1993	M	China	Master's degree	Journalist
John	1988	M	China	Bachelor's degree	Administrative Work
Cindy	1992	F	Hong Kong	Master's degree	Freelancer
Elizabeth	1991	F	China	Bachelor's degree	Media Practitioner
Zoe	1993	F	Hong Kong	Master's degree	Media Practitioner

Coda

Rolling Back toward a Trans-Asia Future?

Yiu Fai Chow, Gladys Pak Lei Chong, and Jeroen de Kloet

When socio-cultural and political tensions—Brexit, U.S.–China trade war, and a powerful resurgence of populism across the world—are intensifying locally, nationally, regionally, and globally, it is urgent and important to pursue an inclusive epistemological paradigm that probes critical self-reflection and that aspires *trans*-formation. The continuous struggle and debate surrounding the Brexit is a case in point. This ever-expanding protectionist sentiment justifies exclusion by emphasizing boundaries and unbridgeable divergences, as we vividly recall from Samuel P. Huntington's infamous thesis on the "clash of civilizations,"[1] and the forceful rebuttal by Edward Said, who titles his text "clash of ignorance." There, Said categorizes Huntington as an ideologist, "who wants to make 'civilizations' and 'identities' into what they are not." By making them into "shut-down, sealed-off entities," Huntington conveniently ignores humankind's "far less visible history," one of "exchange, cross-fertilization and sharing."[2] Unfortunately, it remains tempting to ignore, and history tends to foreground the more spectacular— conflicts, warfare, and myriad acts of so-called self-defense and protectionism. The planned building of a wall on the border between the United States and Mexico presents another example: boundaries have returned with a vengeance. Amid this increased fortification of the world, the call for transnational knowledge production, with envisioned moments of transgression and transformation, may seem both naïve and utopian. In our view, however, it is precisely this context of fortification that propels the need for us to recuperate Said's attention to exchange, cross-fertilization and sharing, for us to reinstigate trans-Asia as method.

Trans-Asia as method is aligned with Asia as method and the Inter-Asia Cultural Studies movement in their political and epistemological missions. We diverge in our theoretical, conceptual, and methodological approaches.

But, as we have shown, we diverge only to a certain extent, as the fields of inter-Asia and trans-Asia studies conflate and are above all profoundly messy. The prefix "trans" accentuates an inclusive approach that traces cultural flows within Asia and beyond. The situation in Hong Kong, where two of the editors are based, offers a complex and critical prompt. With the perceived encroachment of the powerful "motherland" China, many Hong Kong young people resist by rejecting and refusing to be identified with China. They look *trans*-border, regionally and even intercontinentally for alternative socio-cultural imaginations. Trans-Asia—that is, inter-referencing to the neighboring Asian localities such as Japan, Korea, Taiwan, and the West—provides sources of imagination, hope, and escape from the oppressing force associated with the economic and political China that limits and confines. In this instance, the West cannot be easily reduced to be an oppressive force that dominates and controls us, the Asians, epistemologically and ontologically. The West can also be the source of inspiration that brings change. Trans-Asia—beyond Hong Kong and China—is thus a method, a strategy, and a daily tactic to tackle the ever-growing presence of Chineseness at home.

Unwittingly, this example also lays bare a complex issue we are wrestling with: we claim to aspire an inclusive paradigm, but how inclusive are we? The Hong Kong example abovementioned Mainland China, Korea, Japan, and Taiwan, precisely the localities that dominate the very book you are reading. If these localities can be grouped as East Asia, where is Southeast Asia, South Asia, Central Asia, West Asia, and so forth? We also flagged this issue in the introduction. We may rally support from scholars like Sun Ge who argues to take East Asia not as a geographical imaginary, but as a knowledge domain[3]; we will still be confronted with the issue of why we call our approach here trans-*Asia* instead of trans-*East Asia*. To add that the same issue has also been nagging similar efforts—such as Inter-Asia Cultural Studies whose conferences and journals have received far more contributions from and/or on East Asia—is not to mitigate the situation, but precisely to put in sharp relief the power involved in processes of knowledge production and the practical challenge any theoretical claim to inclusivity has to reckon with. And sometimes, *even* theoretically speaking, things are often far more complex. For instance, to revert to our Introduction, when we cited Meaghan Morris' reflection on herself as an "outsider," do we also consider her, then an Australian female academic not specializing in China studies but teaching in a Hong Kong university, an outsider or from the West? Is she them? Who are us? Jeroen de Kloet, one of the authors of this coda, experiences the ambiguity sometimes cheerfully, sometimes with reluctance. While Gladys Chong and Yiu Fai Chow, the other two authors, with their Asian sounding names and faces, are readily included in the imaginary of Asia, de Kloet cannot assume the same. As a Dutch and Amsterdam-based scholar whose research has always been on China and who spends a substantial amount of his time in China, de Kloet would feel part of the academic community when he mingles smoothly at "Asian" occasions; he would, however, feel intensely estranged when, again occasionally, he or merely his name would disqualify him as an Asian scholar.[4] Is he then a Western scholar? When the three of us use the pronoun "us" here, who are we including, and thus excluding? When we wrote "the West cannot be easily reduced to be an oppressive force that dominates and controls us, the Asians, epistemologically and ontologically," who are *us*, who are the Asians, what is the West?

We need to linger longer with the West. Trans-Asia as method does not want to bypass the West. Rather, we acknowledge that Asian societies share a coevalness with the West. Similar to what Gavin Walker and Naoki Sakai argue in their introduction to a special issue provocatively titled "The End of Area," we hold up trans-Asia as another method to call "into question the binary of the West and the Rest"—without resorting to the "indigenous" position of rejecting "Western knowledge" and privileging "local tradition." For Walker and Sakai, their inquiry is to "dislodge both the West and the Rest from the identity politics of civilizational transference and from the logic of anthropological difference" and their target is the American tradition of area studies.[5] For our purposes here, we also want to imbricate the politics and discussions in this collection of texts to another tradition: postcolonial studies. More specifically, we want to situate our project in the long series of efforts to rethink the relationship between Europe and the Other(s), especially Asia, and vice versa.

We are reminded of the pioneering conference "Europe and Its Others" hosted by the University of Essex in 1984. Six years after Said published his seminal work *Orientalism*, the conference marked a milestone in an emerging field of postcolonial studies, dedicating itself to reflect on Europe's convoluted relations with Asia and the Third World. More than twenty years later, in 2006 and on the other side of the world, the National Taiwan Normal University responded with another international conference on "Asia and Its Other."[6] Three decades after the Essex conference, in 2014, two of the authors of this coda and editors of this volume, published a special issue stemming from a conference titled "Looking after Europe"—in both senses of being concerned with what Europe or Western theory has to offer, and "looking at a world after Europe, and seek what trajectories outside of Europe are possible, desirable and feasible."[7] Speaking primarily to practitioners in cultural studies, their postcolonial take is not only to unsettle Eurocentrism in knowledge production; they call for stronger engagements between cultural studies and area studies. According to Chow and de Kloet, "[t]he former needs the latter's sensibility to spatial and cultural context as much as the latter needs the former's theorizations."[8] In their final analysis, what the authors call the specter of Eurocentricism is as palpable and elusive as the emerging Asiancentricism.[9] As one way to take up this postcolonial challenge, we want to borrow Kwame Anthony Appiah's discussion on a "neotraditional" Yoruba sculpture *Man with a Bicycle*, when he contends: "it matters little whom the work was made *for*; what we should learn from is the imagination that produced it."[10]

We should learn. In the same special issue edited by Chow and de Kloet, Kwai-Cheung Lo examines Yoshimi Takeuchi's Asia as method. According to Lo, Takeuchi's contribution lies in his confronting acknowledgment of the influence of Europe—be it the constructive or the destructive aspect— in Asian cultures in the modern era. Expanding on his earlier provocative assertion that there is no such thing as Asia,[11] he goes against the tide of an expanding yet inward-looking Asian cultural studies and introduces Takeu-chi's concept of "rollback" to urge academics to reference with the West. As Lo argues, "By re-embracing western values, that is to say, the 'rollback,' Asia is not necessarily a passive and inferior imitator or follower, since it is a willing act of 're-embracing' rather than a simple embrace of western values that historically refers to the way in which Asian countries were coerced to adopt western culture for their own survival."[12]

One then recognizes the alleged qualities of an epistemological European tradition that claims to encourage criticism, reflection, and transformation. "The 'rollback' or re-embracement suggests neither hostility nor alliance, but their simultaneity materialized in a virtual presence together, without clear distinction or borderline. Different from revolt against the West, the act of rolling back treats the European other (as oneself) as though they were friend and enemy at the same time."[13] In his rereading of Takeuchi, Lo rescues Euro-pean thought and its problematic universalist claims from mere oblivion. The rollback method is what also inspires trans-Asia as method, referring not just to the to-and-fro movement between Asian and European knowledge produc-tion, a movement that involves borrowing, stealing, appropriation, copying, and translation, but also between East Asia and South Asia, or between Asia and Latin America. *Ad infinitum.*

The idea of "rollback" urges us to recognize and make use of the alleged qualities of the epistemological European tradition. And our use of the word "alleged" here points to a certain discomfort, as we want to avoid equating Europe with universalist ideas of critique and reflexivity. But the articulation of Europe with such ideas can be productive when using the rollback method. And in our view, this method can as well be read in a more empirical, practi-cal way. To conclude, our emphasis on trans-Asia is not about a return to the origin (as the discourse of searching for the roots) but a political strategy in that by coining this conceptual framework "Trans-Asia as method" we form a discursive realm: enabling the formation of objects of inquiry, establishing networks and relations between researchers and their objects of inquiry, and in doing so, scholars, researchers, and observers in this field can enunciate themselves in relation to this discursive realm. This discursive realm of trans-Asia as method should acknowledge the centrality of coevalness between Asia and the rest of the world, and it is this unstoppable movement of rolling back and forth that directs us to critical trans-formation.

NOTES

1. Samuel P. Huntington, "The Clash of Civilizations?" *Foreign Affairs* 72, no. 3 (1993): 22–49.

2. Edward Said, "The Clash of Ignorance," *The Nation*, October 4, 2001, http://www.michelecometa.it/Said_The%20Clash%20of%20Ignorance.pdf.

3. Sun Ge, 我们为什么要谈东亚：状况中的政治与历史 (*Why Do We Have to Discuss East Asia: Politics and History at Present*) (Hong Kong: Joint Publishing, 2012).

4. Jeroen de Kloet submitted a book proposal, together with two friends and academics from Mainland China, for the book series "Made in . . ." on popular music. The proposal was turned down. According to the series' rules, all editors have to come from the country the volume focuses on. Such strange belief in speaking positions—only when you are from, and based in the country the volume focuses on, are you eligible to speak about that place, strikes us as a reductive form of geographical essentialism, despite its good intentions.

5. Gavin Walker and Naoki Sakai, "A Genealogy of Area Studies," *positions* 27, no. 1 (2019): 17.

6. Jung Su, "Thinking Otherwise: Asia Revisited," *Concentric: Literary and Cultural Studies* 34, no. 2 (2008): 3–12.

7. Yiu Fai Chow and Jeroen de Kloet, "The Spectre of Europe: Knowledge, Cultural Studies and the 'Rise of Asia,'" *European Journal of Cultural Studies* 17, no. 1 (2014): 4.

8. Ibid., 4.

9. Ibid., 14.

10. Kwame Anthony Appiah, 'Is the Post- in Postmodernism the Post- in Postcolonial?" *Critical Inquiry* 17, no. 2 (1991): 357. Emphasis in original.

11. Kwai-Cheung Lo, "There Is No Such Thing as Asia: Racial Particularities in the 'Asian' Films of Hong Kong and Japan," *Modern Chinese Literature and Culture* 17, no. 1 (2005): 133–158.

12. Lo, "Rethinking Asianism and Method," *European Journal of Cultural Studies* 17, no. 1 (2013): 37.

13. Ibid.

BIBLIOGRAPHY

Appiah, Kwame Anthony. "Is the Post- in Postmodernism the Post- in Postcolonial?" *Critical Inquiry* 17, no. 2 (1991): 336–357.

Chow, Yiu Fai, and Jeroen de Kloet. "The Spectre of Europe: Knowledge, Cultural Studies and the 'Rise of Asia.'" *European Journal of Cultural Studies* 17, no. 1 (2014): 3–15.

Huntington, Samuel P. "The Clash of Civilizations?" *Foreign Affairs* 72, no. 3 (1993): 22–49.

Lo, Kwai-Cheung. "There Is No Such Thing as Asia: Racial Particularities in the 'Asian' Films of Hong Kong and Japan." *Modern Chinese Literature and Culture* 17, no. 1 (2005): 133–158.

———. "Rethinking Asianism and Method." *European Journal of Cultural Studies* 17, no. 1 (2013): 31–43.

Said, Edward W. "The Clash of Ignorance." *The Nation*, October 4, 2001. http://www.michelecometa.it/Said_The%20Clash%20of%20Ignorance.pdf.

Su, Jung. "Thinking Otherwise: Asia Revisited." *Concentric: Literary and Cultural Studies* 34, no. 2 (2008): 3–12.

Sun, Ge. 我们为什么要谈东亚：状况中的政治与历史 *(Why do we have to discuss East Asia: Politics and History at Present)*. Hong Kong: Joint Publishing, 2012.

Walker, Gavin, and Naoki Sakai. "A Genealogy of Area Studies." *Positions* 27, no. 1 (2019): 1–30.

Index

List of Contributors

Ien Ang is Distinguished Professor of Cultural Studies at Western Sydney University (Australia), where she was the founding director of the Institute for Culture and Society until 2014. Her books include *Watching Dallas: Soap Opera and the Melodramatic Imagination* (1985), *Desperately Seeking the Audience* (1991), *On Not Speaking Chinese: Living Between Asia and the West* (2001) and, most recently, the co-authored *Chinatown Unbound: Trans-Asian Urbanism in the Age of China* (2019). She has collaborated extensively with others on strategic research reports including, for the Australian Council of Learned Academies, the report *Smart Engagement with Asia: Leveraging Language, Research and Culture* (2015).

Gladys Pak Lei Chong is Associate Professor of the Department of Humanities and Creative Writing at Hong Kong Baptist University. Her research interests include Chinese governmentality, cultural governance, power-relations, discourse analysis, gender, place making, social credit, security, surveillance and technology. She is the author of *Chinese Subjectivities and the Beijing Olympics* (in the series of Critical Perspectives on Theory, Culture, and Politics, Rowman & Littlefield International 2017). Her two researches on 1) youth aspirations and 2) technology, security and risk are funded by the Hong Kong Research Grant Council.

Yiu Fai Chow is Associate Professor at the Department of Humanities and Creative Writing, Hong Kong Baptist University. His publications cover gender politics and creative practices, including *Caring in the Time of Precarity: A Study of Single Women Doing Creative Work in Shanghai* (2019) and *Sonic Multiplicities: Hong Kong Pop and the Global Circulation of Sound and*

Image (2013, co-authored). Chow is also an award-winning writer in lyrics and prose. He has penned more than 1,000 lyrics for a variety of artists in Hong Kong, Taiwan and Mainland China.

Rossella Ferrari is Reader in Chinese and Theatre Studies in the Department of East Asian Languages and Cultures at SOAS University of London. She specializes in Chinese-language theatres, focusing particularly on avant-garde and intercultural production, collaborations within the Sinophone region, and interactions between Sinophone and other Asian performance cultures. Her publications have appeared in *positions*: *asia* critique, *TDR*: *The Drama Review*, *New Theatre Quarterly*, *Postcolonial Studies*, and elsewhere. She is the author of three monographs, including *Pop Goes the Avant-Garde*: *Experimental Theatre in Contemporary China* (2012) and *Transnational Chinese Theatres: Intercultural Performance Networks in East Asia* (forthcoming).

Koichi Iwabuchi is Professor of Media and Cultural Studies of School of Media, Film and Journalism at Monash University, Melbourne. From April 2020, Iwabuchi will take up a new post of Professor of Media and Cultural Studies at the School of Sociology of Kwansei Gakuin University in Japan. His main research interests are media and cultural globalization, trans-Asian cultural flows and connections (including Australia), and diversity, multicultural questions and cultural citizenship in the Japanese and East Asian contexts. His recent English publications include *Resilient Borders and Cultural Diversity: Internationalism, Brand Nationalism and Multiculturalism in Japan* (2015); "Globalization, Culture, and Communication: Renationalization in a Globalized World" (*Oxford Research Encyclopedia of Communication*, 2018); "Media and communications" (co-authored with Nick Couldry et.al., International Panel on Social Progress (IPSP) (ED.), *Rethinking Society for the 21st Century: Report of the International Panel on Social Progress Vol.2* (2018).

Soyoung Kim is Professor of Cinema Studies, Korea National University of Arts, the Director of Trans:Asia Screen Culture and the President of the Association of Korean Cultural Studies (2018–present). She is the author of numerous books on colonial modernity, gender and cinema, including *Cartography of Catastrophe: States of Emergency and Fantasy* (Korean, 2014) and co-editor of *Electronic Elsewheres: Media, Technology, and the Experience of Social Space* (2010). She is also the editor of the 10 Volumes of the Compendium of the history of Korean cinema (Korean, 2018); and an independent filmmaker of *Women's History Trilogy* (2000–2004) and *Exile*

Trilogy (2014–2019) and *Viewfinder* (2010), distributed by Alexander Street and Cinema Dal.

Jeroen de Kloet is Professor of Globalization Studies and Director of the Amsterdam Centre for Globalisation Studies (ACGS) at the University of Amsterdam. He is also affiliated to the Communication University of China. He is the principal investigator of a project funded by the European Grant Council (ERC), titled "From Made in China to Created in China. A Comparative Study of Creative Practice and Production in Contemporary China." See also http://jeroendekloet.nl and http://chinacreative.humanities.uva.nl

Stevie Suan is an Assistant Professor at the Department of Global and Interdisciplinary Studies at Hosei University in Tokyo, Japan. He holds a doctorate in Manga Studies from the Graduate School of Manga Studies at Kyoto Seika University, and a Masters in Asian Studies from the University of Hawai'i at Mānoa. His main area of expertise is in anime aesthetics through which he explores various modes of existence. In his recent research he has been developing an approach that uses performance theory and media theory to approach issues of area studies (Japan studies and Asian studies), using anime as a prime example of the shifting currents of cultural production and consumption in our moment of globalization.

Chih-Ming Wang works at the Institute of European and American Studies, Academia Sinica, Taipei, Taiwan. He is the author of *Transpacific Articulations: Student Migration and the Remaking of Asian America* (2013) and the guest-editor of the "Asian American Studies in Asia" special issue of *Inter-Asia Cultural Studies* (June 2012). He also co-edited (with Daniel PS Goh) *Precarious Belongings: Affect and Nationalism in Asia* (2017) and (with Yu-Fang Cho) the *American Quarterly* special issue entitled "The Chinese Factor: Reorienting Global Imaginaries in American Studies" (June 2017). His research focuses on Asian American literature and cultural studies in transpacific and inter-Asian contexts. He is currently working on the institutional history of foreign literature studies in Taiwan.

Jiyu Zhang is a PhD candidate in the Department of Film and Literary Studies at Leiden University, the Netherlands. His research interest mainly includes film and literature, gender and sexuality, race and ethnicity, modern and contemporary China. His dissertation, "Sinoscope: Nation, Modernity, and Chinese Cinema," situates the emergence of Chinese cinema—an increasingly contested notion in and of itself—into modern China's nation-building process over the past century. In a bid to foreground the cultural mechanisms through which the idea of nation casts a long shadow over Chinese cinema, his current project further demonstrates how individuals assert their own subjectivities against the grain of collective formation through the apparatus, technique, and aesthetics of cinema. Bringing together a wide array of Sinophone films into a vigorous dialogue, his dissertation aims to unfold both the limits and potentials of Chinese cinema with recourse to its vernacular genealogies, and epistemic paradoxes thereof.

www.ingramcontent.com/pod-product-compliance
Lightning Source LLC
Chambersburg PA
CBHW030647270326
41929CB00007B/249